CHRISTINA M HARRIS

THE ONE HOUR THOUGHT

The Curious Life of Harry Lawton

First published in paperback by
Michael Terence Publishing in 2022
www.mtp.agency

Copyright © 2022 Christina M Harris

Christina M Harris has asserted the right to be identified as
the author of this work in accordance with the
Copyright, Designs and Patents Act 1988

ISBN 9781800944626

No part of this publication may be reproduced, stored
in a retrieval system, or transmitted, in any form or
by any means, electronic, mechanical, photocopying,
recording or otherwise, without the prior
permission of the publisher

Cover design
Copyright © 2022 Michael Terence Publishing

Michael Terence
Publishing

For Harry
Wish you were here.

This story is based on Harry's own recollections but as these were, at times, incomplete, my imagination has had to fill the gaps and I apologise for any details which may not be entirely accurate.

Some names and locales have also been changed in order to maintain privacy.

PART ONE

Just Another Day

The Journey Home

Up the Stairs

Just Another Day

I just knew it was going to be a nice day. For one thing the sun was shining and for another I'd managed to get a really good night's sleep. Some nights I just couldn't get off for my left leg aching. But today it wasn't aching as much as usual and to top it all it was Tuesday. I knew it was Tuesday 'cos my niece had been last night and stocked up the fridge for me. She always comes on a Monday night on her way home from work. Also, I could see my best tweed jacket hung over the back of the big purple leather chair the Social Services had sent me. I don't ever use the chair as it's uncomfortable. The seat cushion is too hard but it's useful for hanging my coat on and I put all the newspapers there, too, before I put them in the outside bin. I have lots of tweed jackets. All good quality although some are now a bit worse for wear. The man who owned the posh menswear shop in the village gave me one every year for years. But now I don't clean windows anymore I don't need new jackets.

Anyhow, there was my jacket, so I knew it was Tuesday. I hang it there as it gets some of the creases out by leaving it overnight. Otherwise, it's in one of my wardrobes crushed up with all the others. I go to a Day Centre near Ilkley on Tuesdays and Thursdays and I like to be as smart as possible. It's only right when everyone else seems to put on their Sunday best. Some of the ladies even wear pearls and posh earrings. It's nice to have a reason to get dressed up. I like going out but I like getting back, too, and tonight I'd promised myself a fish and chip supper. Always good and tasty and something else to look forward to.

I knew the sun was shining 'cos as I lay on my bed, I could see a little spot of sunlight on the wall at the side of my bed. I wondered how the budgie had managed to peck yet another hole in the curtains large enough to let the light in. I let it fly round every day so it must have done it yesterday when I wasn't looking. I'd two budgies until last Monday when the blue one disappeared. Anyway, the curtains are dark red velvet and are just the job to keep the light out, providing I fasten the sides to the wall with drawing pins. My niece, Christina, bought them for me. The curtains, not the drawing pins. She's not my actual niece but the wife of my nephew who is the son of my sister, Annie. I always say niece, though, as it's simpler when people ask who she is. She calls in a lot and helps me out with shopping and housework. We always have a good natter as well when she's here. Anyway, she bought the curtains and, as well as keeping the light out they keep the draughts out, too. The window frames are old metal ones and let in the cold. Some of the flats have got nice new windows with double glazing and I keep hoping I'm next. My windows all face east and when the wind blows from that direction, I can see the curtains moving. I live in sheltered housing on the first floor. I call it my Flower Apartment 'cos it's on Heather Road.

So, I'd seen the budgie on the curtains a few times pecking away but always managed to knock it off with the fishing rod I've got from the village pet shop. It's useful for catching the little tinker when it's time for it to go back into its cage. But on some occasions it has other uses as well such as picking things up off the floor like a pen, if I drop one. I keep it stood next to my bed just under the window. The budgie likes pecking all sorts of things 'cos before it went for the curtains, he seemed to have an obsession with the wallpaper above the curtain rail. In fact, they both did. They flew onto the rail and then hopped together along the top pecking as they went. My niece eventually had to put up a piece of border to cover up all the damage and it was then that they started on the curtains. I don't think they liked the taste of the new border.

My budgie is called Monty 'cos I got him, and the one that disappeared, the same year as the D-Day landings. I don't mean in 1945, of course, otherwise Monty would be well over 80 years old and I don't think budgies live that long. Mind you, if they did and their life span was the same as, say a dog, that's seven years for each real one, then Monty would have been 560 years old. I wonder if his feathers would have gone grey. No, I got him in 1994 when we celebrated fifty years since the D-Day landings in Normandy. My niece thought it would be a bit of company for me. It is, I suppose, but it's also a lot of hard work cleaning the cage and putting in the food and water. Sometimes I forget and my niece tells me off. She does this in a nice way and I think she's probably right. She says it gives me something to do but sometimes I wish I didn't have to.

The budgie that disappeared was called D-Day and I think it flew into the bathroom and fell into the toilet. I knew I'd only caught one and put it back in the cage and just thought D-Day had gone under my bed looking for something else to peck. So, I went to bed thinking it would be up there on the curtains in the morning. I couldn't look under the bed myself as I can't bend down that far and if I did, I don't think I'd ever get up again. Anyhow, just before I turned the light off nature called and it was one where I'd to flush the toilet. The next morning there was no blue budgie on the curtains but there was a scattering of little blue feathers floating in the water in the toilet. I spent all day wondering where it had gone to. I hoped the little fellow had made it through the pipe and popped out in the sewage works in one piece. If he had, maybe he'd fly back like a homing pigeon. The sewage works is only a couple of miles away. I can smell it sometimes if the wind's in a certain direction. It wasn't that far to fly. I left a window open for a few days but it never came back. So, as I was saying, there it was, another hole in the curtain, letting in the light of day. I made a mental note to fasten the hole up with a safety pin.

I must have nodded off a bit after all that 'cos when I eventually looked at the clock it was half past six. I actually have seven clocks but they all manage to keep different times and I have to made an educated guess as to which one is going to be right. Sometimes I reset them all when the six o'clock news comes on but a day or two later they're all different again. They all seem to have minds of their own. In any case, by the time I've reset the last one the news has finished and I don't know what the real time is anyway. I've had two of the clocks for years. I can't remember where they came from. Then, I've bought three from the Rington's man who comes every week in his little green and yellow van and sells me tea and biscuits and other fancy stuff. Then I've won another two clocks at the Day Centre. I'm very lucky with the bingo and generally win something every week. So, today I used the green and blue Westclox. This is my favourite clock and was the nearest in any case as I couldn't see any of the others. That wasn't 'cos I didn't have my glasses on, which I did, but 'cos all the others were on the mantelpiece which is on the far wall at the other end of my bed. Anyway, I knew it was half past six 'cos both hands were pointing downwards. At any other time it was a bit difficult to tell the real time as the big hand has the end missing and is just about the same length as the little hand. But, as they were both hanging there together, I reckoned it was time to get up. Another day was about to begin.

The One Hour Thought

Now, I can't move as fast as I used to and getting out of bed is a major achievement some days. I've already told you that sometimes I don't sleep very well and that's caused sometimes, apart from my aching leg, by the sheets getting wrapped round my legs so that I'm trapped in a sort of shroud. Only last week I fell out of bed wrapped up like that and was saved from serious injury by the duvet thing slipping onto the floor a moment or two before I did. This is another innovation from my niece who says that a duvet is more hygienic than woolly blankets and that, by having a sheet under the cover, it saves washing. I liked my blankets. Anyway, that morning I'd a right job getting myself unwrapped, not to mention having to remake the bed afterwards, though I must say it's a lot easier with the duvet thing than with blankets. In the end it took me nearly half an hour to ease myself up again from the floor onto the bed.

Then, other nights, I can't sleep 'cos I'm too hot and seem to be throwing the duvet thing off all the time, only to have to pull it back up again as I get cold. Then I have nights when I'm really thirsty and can't be bothered to go and get more water when I've drunk all I've put out the night before. I put my night time water in a Yorkshire Tyke pint pot. It's one of those that has the motto 'See all, hear all, say nowt. And if tha ever does owt for nowt allus do it for thissen'. I've got four of these pots now, all won at the Day Centre. I don't want any more but if the next win is a clock then I'll keep it. I'm just thankful that I'm not troubled by having to go to the toilet in the night. Catheters are just the job for solving that one. But, having said that, catheters are both a hindrance and a blessing. It's a blessing 'cos without one I'd be forever getting up in the night, as I've just said, and I'd also be forever leaving wet patches wherever I went, not to mention the constant washing of trousers and underwear. I've been like this for nearly four years and have got used to it but it was a big shock at first, to say the least, especially when the District Nurse started coming to change it every week. I was more embarrassed than her as I expect she does this sort of thing every day but I certainly don't have women looking or touching my twiddly bits and I found it very awkward.

Now, though, she's left me some spares and shown me how to change it myself although it takes me ages to get it right. I've now got eight boxes of catheters and there's six in each box. I keep them on top of my mahogany chest of drawers. It's like the Meals on Wheels all over again. I get them delivered as well, whether I want them or not. I'm on the list, I suppose. I don't eat the puddings very often so now I've got at least ten apple crumbles in my freezer. I've told them I don't want any more but they still insist on bringing them. I didn't want a freezer, either, but my old fridge conked out so my niece bought me a new tall fridge with a freezer underneath it. It's useful for the apple crumbles, I suppose, but there was a bit of trouble when the Coke tins I'd put in exploded. And my niece says I mustn't freeze lettuces any more either. The catheter boxes I was telling you about, are next to the boxes of dressings the District Nurse uses when she comes to see to my leg ulcers. She asked if she could leave a few spares so she didn't have to remember to bring them with her but I think she forgets that I have some and brings more every time she comes. I keep meaning to tell her but she's so nice I don't want to upset her. I have nine boxes of these now.

Going back to the catheter problem, the hindrance side, so to speak, is that the bag soon seems to fill up. This is 'cos my doctor says I have to drink a lot to help my health and I also needs lots of tea to get all my pills down. I used to drink beer and had a pint in The Bull up in the village most nights before I came home, but it's quite a walk up there and it's too far for me these days. I could probably walk there but getting back would be a right problem. The fish and chip shop is as far as I go these days. So, the bag filling up all the time can be a proper nuisance when I'm outside. My trips to the fish and chip shop seem to take longer every time I go and there's been a couple of times I've had to empty the bag into the gutter to avoid it bursting. I don't know what I'd do if it burst whilst I was in the fish shop queue. I suppose I'd just have to stand there and hope no one noticed.

Anyhow, when I use the gutter, I just pretend to be fastening my shoe lace but actually pull up my trouser leg, let the valve down and release it. I can do this 'cos I strap the bag to my calf. I keep it there 'cos experience has taught me that that's the best and quickest way to get at it. It's also the furthest place I can bend over to reach. Sometimes I get my sock wet. All this, of course, is best done in the dark. It's not easy when it's light. On a morning I just sit on the toilet seat, lift my leg over the side of the bath and let the contents drain into the bath. It's the quickest way and there's not much risk of it spilling out all over the floor. It's a special low bath for old people. I can do all this 'cos I wear trousers but I don't know what a woman would do. She couldn't wear a dress and strap the bag to her leg like I do as everyone would see it. I suppose she'd have to wear trousers all the time.

So, I needed to empty the catheter bag and this morning my legs appeared to have a life of their own. I fair hopped out of bed like a youngster. Well, it seemed like that to me in comparison to all the other times when it's taken me over ten minutes just to move my left leg which swells up during the night. So, I pulled myself up, thankful I wasn't tangled in the sheets, pushed the duvet thing to one side and, feeling very pleased with myself, swung my legs to the floor. My left foot went straight into the plate on the floor at the side of my bed. The remains of last night's dinner. A Meals on Wheels special of liver and onions. I'd made some more mashed potato as well, with loads of butter. And some more fried onions. I like fried onions a lot. I'd eaten the liver 'cos it's good for me and all the onions but most of the mashed potato was still on the plate. I wasn't bothered too much, though, as it had come out of a packet and it's not like the real thing. I'd made too much. Now it was all over my foot but, in particular, between my toes.

I looked at the Westclox. The hands had moved and the broken one was now at 11. So, I reckoned it must be about 7 o'clock. Having thought I'd got a lot of time to get ready, I now had to rush around as there was hardly any time left at all. The taxi for the Day Centre comes for me at half past eight prompt and I'd such a lot to do before then. The mashed potato would have to wait. I made a mental note to deal with the plate when I got home. In any case I was going to the chiropodist on Friday and she'd be able to clean my toes for me. The potato would probably have dried up by then and rubbed off into my sock. I could wash the socks. That was providing I could put my socks on. Sometimes I go without them as I can't reach over if my leg is having a bad day. I'm well over six feet tall and now and then I can't reach over far enough to get to the other end of my legs. However, as my catheter bag wasn't full to bursting, I decided to go to the bathroom later to empty it and have all my pills now. I live in a first-floor council bed sit which has a large living room cum bedroom with a separate kitchen and bathroom at each end. I don't mean I've got two kitchens and two bathrooms, I'm not that posh. I mean that the kitchen is at one end and the bathroom is at the other and me, my bed, budgies and tv are in the middle near the kitchen. It suits me very well, 'cept it's taking me longer and longer to get down the stairs to get out, never mind getting back up home again.

The lady from Social Services who got me the uncomfortable purple leather chair also got me a zimmer frame to help me walk about better, especially outside. But she never gave a thought as to how I'd get up and down the stairs with it. It's the same all the time. People want to help and they think of a solution to a problem but don't think of the problem the solution causes. My niece did this when she got me the duvet thing. Maybe I should just get rid of the sheet. Then it would only be the duvet thing which wrapped itself around my legs. Anyway, it's hard enough taking my walking stick out with me, never mind the zimmer frame. I only take the walking stick to the Day Centre 'cos they have their own zimmer frames there. So, going down the stairs, I have to put the stick through my belt like a sword so I can have my hands free to hold onto the hand rail. Sometimes the stick catches on a step and I have to cling on and steady myself before I can keep going down. I go down one step at a time. Climbing back up isn't quite as hard but then I often have shopping bags to carry as well. At the Day Centre they have a little stall where they sell tins of baked beans and other food stuffs. They make a bit of money from it and it's convenient for me so I buy what I think I need and, by the time I leave, my carrier bag is often full. My niece says I mustn't buy so much, especially as she generally does some shopping for me every Monday. And I must say the tins in my pantry are mounting up. I think there's four if not five layers of tins stocked on the shelves right now. That's why I began to put them in the freezer.

Going back to the zimmer frame, though, my solution has been to hoist it onto my chest and put my arms through the sides. It's a bit awkward but if I go slowly, I can manage. There's a cupboard at the bottom of the stairs and I keep meaning to ask the warden if I could pop it in there. Anyway, I've found that by going down one step at a time, I can manage quite nicely as my hands are free to hold on to the rail. I can also hang the shopping bag on it so it's quite useful from that point of view. I've only encountered one problem whilst doing this and that was one evening when I was setting off for my fish and chips. Just as I got to the bottom of the stairs the paper boy barged straight through the front door, which is right opposite the stairs, and knocked me over. His newspaper bag gave my leg a real whack. Fortunately, Beryl, the lady who lives opposite me on the same landing, heard the commotion and came out to see what was going on. She lifted the zimmer frame off me and she and the paper boy helped me to my feet. It's a good job I was at the bottom or I would have slid down the stairs like a human sledge with the zimmer frame bouncing along as we went. As it happens, it was only my leg which was injured. I say only my leg but if one of the ulcers gets a knock then it hurts for a long time. I didn't feel like going to the fish and chip shop after that so Beryl helped me back up to my flat and she made the paper boy go and get my fish and chips for me. I was going to ring the newsagent and tell him what had happened but in the end I decided not to as I didn't want to get the lad into trouble.

I've been asking for a ground floor flat for a long time now. Well, my niece has I should say. Someone came to see me a few weeks back but I haven't heard anything since. Last year I was offered another flat down the road but it was still on the first floor so I said no thank you. Two ground floor flats have come empty recently on the opposite side of the road to me but I've not been offered either one, even though my niece rang the council up. Anyway, they've both gone now. I've decided to take my pills and made a mental note to wash my socks tonight.

I take nine different sort of pills. They're all in various bottles and packets and it's a bit fiddly getting them out. I've got big hands which go with my big feet. My niece says we could cross the Atlantic in my boots. Some of the bottle tops are very small and need squeezing to get them open. I'm forever using the fishing rod to pick up pills or dropped bottles. Sometimes my hands are a bit shaky too, which doesn't help. This morning was no better and, even though I'd put my glasses on, before I knew it, I'd lost another two pills as they fell to the floor. This time they rolled under the bed. There must be loads of them under there by now. Vacuuming under the bed must be coming up the list of jobs my niece does. It hasn't been done for ages 'cos I keep coming up with excuses for her not to do it. But I think the time has come to see to it. The budgies go under there sometimes and if they did manage to peck a pill, if they had any ulcers or a heart condition there would be, hopefully, an improvement. That's what they call a positive thought, although we'll never know if they did D-Day any good.

So, I carefully lined up all the pills on the blue Formica table which is just next to my bed and is, as they say, the centre of my universe. I got it from the charity shop in the village just after I moved into my little flat. It was standing outside with a lot of books on it. At that time, I was still working as a window cleaner in the village so, after I'd done the shop windows, I asked John, the shop man, how much the table was. Not only did he give it to me for nothing he even brought it to my flat himself that same day. That was a few years ago before my legs got bad. The shop is opposite The Bull and, as I've already told you, I can't get up that far anymore. So, as I was saying, I lined my pills up on the table.

Anything which is important is on the table. Near the edge is a thick black line which I drew with one of those marker pens. This makes sure I don't put the pills too near the edge and lose even more by knocking them off. I got the idea from the lines on stairs to show you where the edges are so you don't fall. Maybe you're wondering why I don't have one of those containers which is divided into little compartments where you put your pills for a whole week. Well, I tried one a few weeks ago. I bought it at the Day Centre. But, it was really difficult to open with my big fingers. Then one day when I did manage to open it the top came off with such a jerk that all the pills fell out. That accounts for why there are so many under the bed at the moment. I tried to pick them up with the fishing rod but not only did they come back up covered in fluff, I couldn't get them back in the right bottles. It was all too fiddly for me. You have to match them to the right bottle 'cos otherwise you'd get the wrong pills. In the end I just put the dirty pills in a brown paper bag and found a place for it under the kitchen sink. Just in case I needed them in the future.

I don't like those pills in the silver foil wrappers, either. I get them for my wind and keep them in an old marmalade jar in the fridge just in case I have an emergency but, as I make a point of never eating cabbage or sprouts, I'm hoping that's where they'll stay. I always have a pint of water on the table, too, as I told you earlier, in my Yorkshire mug, just in case I'm thirsty in the night. What's left does for my pills if I don't feel like getting up and making a pot of tea. Today there was enough water left and not enough time to make tea, so I picked the mug up to start taking my pills. What the heck is that? I wondered. I looked a bit closer and saw that it was a spider. Not the small sort of house spider which comes down from the ceiling on a string when you're laid in bed but one of those with the body the size of a football and legs made of wire to match. The sort you can hear walking up and down walls and across the carpet. It must have died of exhaustion swimming around in there all night. Now I can't stand spiders even though someone once told me that spiders are clean but, none the less, I was glad I hadn't needed a drink in the dark. I would have had an early breakfast. So, I fished the thing out with the spoon I'd used for last night's dinner and threw it on the floor, making a mental note to pick it up when I got the potato plate. I'd a sip of water and it tasted alright so I started taking my pills. I've to take some before a meal, some with a meal and some after a meal. I can't always read the labels, either, and as I can't remember which are which, I reckon that as long as I take them all within an hour, with a meal somewhere in the middle, it'll be alright. It's worked so far, anyway.

It was time I saw to the catheter bag, so I heaved myself off the bed and made my way across my flat to the bathroom. I'd been sat on the edge of the bed for ages. I don't know where time goes. It was now about half past seven 'cos when I looked at the Westclox one hand was straight down and the other was roughly near seven. All the other clocks were showing a time between quarter past seven and eight o'clock. Seven thirty was about right, I thought. Sometimes an hour seems like a minute and time just disappears. I think it's true that time goes faster and faster as you get older, though sometimes it goes slowly if I haven't seen anyone all day. It isn't that far to the bathroom from my bed but some days it takes me ages to get there. I've arranged all the furniture so that I have something to get hold of if I feel a bit unsteady. Once in the bathroom, I rolled up the right leg of my pyjamas, sat on the lid of the toilet which is next to the bath and slowly lifted my leg up and over the side of the bath. I've already told you it's a special low bath for old people which is very useful. The bag quickly emptied and a quick rinse from the cold tap was all that was needed to send the contents on their way. Having seen to that I gave my neck and face a quick swipe with a new pink flannel I'd been given by one of the ladies at the Day Centre. It had come with a piece of soap wrapped in a picture of a ship. I hadn't got round to using that just yet.

There was no time for a shave, so I went back as fast as I could to get my breakfast. On the way back it seemed like a good idea to get dressed. I'd left my things, as usual, on the back of my little green armchair, the purple leather one being draped with my tweed jacket. So, I picked them all up and carried them over to my bed. I sat down to put them on. The thing was, though, when I got to the bed, I couldn't find my shirt. I've got loads of shirts. Some are hung up in my wardrobes and then there's more in the big mahogany chest of drawers. I'm never short of clothes 'cos, like the Meals on Wheels and the catheters, people are always giving me stuff. Only last week someone I know in the village, Florence she's called, came round with two black bin liners full of her husband's clothes. I knew her husband had died 'cos I'd read about it in the paper and she came to give me some of his things as he, obviously, wouldn't need them anymore. She said that most of them were quite new and, as she thought we were a similar size, she'd rather I got them than throw them away. She could have taken them to John's charity shop, I suppose, but I didn't say anything.

I also didn't like to go through them whilst she was there so made an excuse and opened the bin liners later that evening to see what I'd got. From the first one I pulled out a Sainsbury carrier bag filled with ties, which I don't wear. Then another carrier bag came out this time filled with fancy bow ties which I definitely don't wear. Next, I pulled out a bright blue dressing gown with what looked like white dots all over it. However, as I looked closely, they turned out to be little footballs. It looked expensive but I wasn't too keen on it and it also looked like it could be a Leeds United souvenir, a team I've never liked. The dressing gown was followed by some matching blue pyjamas with more little footballs on them. I held them up to make sure they weren't meant for kiddies but they seemed large enough for a grown up. Another carrier bag was filled with loose socks. I emptied them all onto the bed and tried sorting them but couldn't make up a proper matching pair. I pushed them all back to where they had come from.

In the other bin-liner I found some shorts. There were five pairs, all brightly coloured with palm trees on them. Then there were seven shirts. Three of them were those fancy white shirts with ruffles down the front which men wear when they're going to posh dinners. I didn't really have any use for these except they did go with the bow ties I'd already found. All the other shirts had short sleeves and were as brightly coloured as the shorts. They were what I'd call holiday wear. Some had pictures of palm trees on which matched the shorts. Others had pictures of beaches and one had pictures of rockets on with the words 'I lurve Florida' all over it. I didn't care for these, either. After that I found a pair of white cotton trousers and a dark green boiler suit, like Churchill used to wear. Next, I pulled out a brown and white checked sports jacket with a torn pocket and the last item turned out to be a black suit. It was lovely material with shiny lapels but as I've never been to a fancy dinner dance in my life and never likely to, either, it went back into the bin-liner with all the other things. I pushed the bags into the bottom of one of my wardrobes. After all, the clothes were good quality and, although completely useless to me at the moment, might come in handy one day.

But, that was last week and now I'd to get up again and go to find a shirt and get my breakfast. I found a blue shirt in a drawer of the old chest and went back to sit on the bed to put it on, only to find I already had one on. I'd never taken it off the night before and had put my pyjama jacket over the top. No wonder I'd been overheating during the night. Anyhow, it was good news to me, as I only had my trousers and socks to see to. I usually keep my underpants on in case of mishaps in the night and it's less to struggle with each day. I also had my vest on which was another layer to keep me hot. Anyway, after undoing the pyjama cord and letting the bottoms fall down, I managed my trousers one leg at a time and stood up to pull them up, giving the plate of mash a nudge with my foot to push it under the bed. I picked up the pyjama bottoms with the fishing rod and put them on my bed along with the pyjama jacket.

As I said, I don't wear a tie these days, not that I ever did, so that's a time saver, too. My socks are another thing altogether, though. Today I seemed to have one dark blue sock and one brown and red striped sock. How that happened is a mystery but at least I'd two. As I've told you before, I've got long legs so I leaned over and just about managed to pull the blue sock over my left foot. Luck was with me 'cos then I did the right foot quickly, too, by hooking the brown sock on my toes the first time of trying. They were more or less on and the potato between my toes had started to dry out, too, leaving bits on the carpet. The budgie could have a go at cleaning that up.

After all this exertion I began to feel rather warm and realised the central heating was on and the room was getting quite hot. There's a dial on the wall near the bathroom where you can change the settings for the time it comes on and goes off and another for the temperature but they don't seem to work properly. I've told the warden but I'm still waiting for someone to come. She says she's reported it and that I'm on the list like everyone else. My niece says that two weeks is too long to have to wait but I know how busy everyone is these days and I don't like to bother the warden any more than I have to. She's lots of others to see besides me. Anyhow, that's also why I'm sometimes too hot in the night 'cos it doesn't go off and at other times I'm cold 'cos it doesn't come on. Sometimes when I get back from the Day Centre my flat is really chilly and I have to put the gas fire on at full blast for ages before the place has warmed up. The old metal windows don't help either, I suppose. The easiest way, when it's working, is to put the timer on the 'on all the time' setting and have done with it. But I forget about it and anyway, it costs too much, so I don't bother with that too often. Sometimes my niece changes it all for me but I don't think she understands it either. It uses that 24-hour clock. My niece says that 2 o'clock in the afternoon is fourteen hundred but I know its two thousand so I have to fiddle with it when she's gone. I don't tell her what I've done.

So, where was I – ah – yes- after the socks I'd to get my shoes on. I used to wear a pair of black Doc Martens boots which are very strong and don't let water in but even though they are comfy they're really heavy so they're under the table gathering dust like all the other spare shoes I have. I usually wear some special trainers my niece got for me from a place which sells things for big people like me. My feet are size 14. She got me some slippers at the same time. When I say big, I mean my hands and feet. I'm not wide like some people are. I just have long legs and long arms and big feet and big hands to go with them. We looked them up in a catalogue – the trainers, not my feet and hands – then we filled in a form, and they came three days later in a big green box through the post. I like getting things through the post. Sometimes my sister, Alice, sends me a surprise package. Well, it's not really a surprise 'cos its always the same sort of thing. She keeps sending me those padded workmen's shirts. The thing is, they're all bright red or blue checks and the sleeves are never long enough. The packets show pictures of lumberjacks in Canada wearing them. I think I've got five now, all in the bottom of a wardrobe and all in the packets they came in. They'll come in handy one day.

The trainers I was telling you about are very good for my feet 'cos the leather is really soft and there's plenty of room in them. The slippers are made of a sort of felt. They're red and fasten with those sticky bits. Anyhow, I managed to get my feet into the trainers. I push my feet in and then lift each foot onto a little footstool I keep under my table, so I can reach the laces. But, today, I didn't pull the laces as tight as usual, 'cos sometimes my feet and ankles swell up so I left them a bit on the loose side, just in case.

Another look at the Westclox showed the big hand had moved to 2. Another fifteen minutes gone. There was no time for a fry up, although the frying pan is always ready. I like eating. Sometimes there's nothing else to do. My cooking skills are, to say the least, limited but I do know how to use a frying pan. I've had my frying pan a long time now so it's nicely run in. I keep it in the oven with the fat always left in so it's quick and easy to use. I made last night's fried onions in it. Saves on washing up, too. So, not having enough time for a fry up I put some margarine on two slices of bread and slapped two cold sausages I found in the fridge between them. A good dollop of brown sauce was just the finishing touch needed. I made a cup of tea in another Yorkshire mug and, making two journeys to my bed one with the sausage sandwich and the other with the tea, sat down as I'd another set of pills to take. These were the ones to be taken with a meal. I put the plate and the mug on the table. I enjoyed the sandwich more than the pills and wondered if I could put the pills in the sausage sandwich next time. That would be even quicker if I ever needed to make up time.

As far as washing up is concerned, I have to be a bit careful as my sink gets blocked up really fast. A few months ago, the plumber had to come and it turned out to be a load of fat in the u-band. That's another reason why I don't wash the frying pan. I don't want all that grease going down the plug hole. A few weeks ago, it got blocked again and, although I told the warden, nothing was done. It was like that for over a week. I'd to be very careful what I did at the sink. I tried to do all the washing up last thing at night 'cos it took over four hours for the water to go down. Sometimes, though, if I washed up during the day, I used an old pink bucket I keep in my pantry and poured the dirty water down the toilet. It wasn't easy, either, carrying the bucket to the bathroom but it's surprising what you can do when you have to. My niece bought blocked drain clearing stuff and goodness knows what else but nothing worked. I was forever pouring something down the plug hole. The plunger thing wasn't any good either. Anyhow, the plumber eventually turned up when I was at the Day Centre. He pushed a note through my letter box, so it all had to be arranged again which caused another delay. When I finally got to see the whites of his eyes, he was here five minutes and the job was done. It was nothing to do with me sending fat down the plug hole. He produced a blue sock which had lodged itself in the u-bend. My sink has never had a little grille thing over the plug hole and it must have happened when I washed my socks there. I think it belonged to the one I put on this morning.

I've also got a microwave which my niece bought for me so I can heat up the Meals on Wheels which now come five times a week. That's every day including Tuesdays and Thursdays when I go to the Day Centre. That's ten a week as they bring a main course and a pudding. It gives me enough for the weekend, though. 'Cos I don't eat them up as they arrive this causes what they call a glut and sometimes I've got ten or twelve of them stored up waiting to be eaten. I've told the ladies who deliver them about this but they still leave them with my neighbour if I'm out. They come frozen and are quite nice but one or two are on the small side so sometimes I eat two at a time. I don't mean the ladies are frozen, just the dinners. I stick them all in the freezer. Sometimes the puddings are really small, too, so I have to have three of these at a time. I'm not too keen on the apple crumbles, though, so they're often left for another day. I like the ladies who deliver these meals and it's nice to have someone calling even if they don't have much time for a chat. I'd rather have a fry up or fish and chips than the frozen Meals on Wheels.

When I go down to the village for my fish and chips, I always take my shopping bag with me to put them in. I line it with newspaper for a bit of insulation to keep them as hot as possible, although if they're a bit cold when I get them home, I just stick them in the microwave for a minute or two. I hang the bag from the frame with an old leather belt. I used to have one of those shoulder bags but I can't find it. I must look through my wardrobes one day. As I've said, I do like fish and chips. I don't want to give them up so keeping the walking going is important. Having them a few times a week is also another reason I don't get round to the Meals on Wheels. Sometimes, though, when I've walked down for my fish and chips at the end of the day, I've been too tired when I got back to be bothered with them so I've stored them in the oven with the frying pan and warmed them up in the microwave the next day for breakfast.

So, this morning I looked at the Westclox again and it was at two. I was sure it had been that the last time I'd looked, so I turned round to see what the other clocks were showing on the mantelpiece. I have a

Rington's picture clock I particularly like and which seems to keep reasonable time. As I've said, the Rington's man calls every week and I usually buy something from him. He sells lots of different things as well as tea which is why Rington's was set up in the first place. He's got models of cars which I've started collecting and different types of clocks which I've started to collect as well. Then there's fancy picture frames and tea towels and a good variety of biscuits, too. As with the Meals on Wheels, I don't always eat what I get but he's such a nice man and I like him calling in to see me. It breaks up the afternoon. I put the biscuits on the chest of drawers next to the catheter and ulcer dressings boxes. Sometimes the budgies find the biscuits and peck through the wrapping paper. I don't mind, though, 'cos it gives them something to think about.

The picture clock is in three parts. There are two flaps on the side which fold over the bit in the middle. When you open it up there's a picture of an old fashioned Rington's tea cart on the middle bit and the sides make up the rest of the picture. I can remember when the Rington's man came round with his horse and cart when I was a nipper and that's why I like the clock so much. The clock face is in the middle bit and it keeps better time than the others as long as I change the battery every now and then. I keep a box of batteries under the kitchen sink. I can't remember when I've last adjusted this one but now it was showing twenty minutes past eight. The taxi comes bang on time at half past eight so I quickly put on my tweed jacket, picked up my wallet from the fruit bowl and hastily managed to take the remaining pills with the last of the water. I'd make the bed and do everything else when I got back. It's a good job I don't have false teeth to mess about with or I'd be even longer getting ready. I still have my own, though they're not looking too good these days. It's years since I've been to a dentist but I've managed. They hurt from time to time but nothing that bothers me too much. I like to think I can bite into an apple whenever I want without my teeth falling out.

On the way to the door, I passed the budgie cage and, pulling the night cover off, said hello to the little fellow. I was pleased to see there was some millet seed left. I hadn't enough time to give it any more to eat so that would have to wait until I got home. I made a mental note to change the water, too. So, I closed the green door to my flat, locked it and put the key in my pocket. With my walking stick stuck down my belt I went down the stairs one at a time to wait on the pavement outside. I'd no sooner got onto the pavement when I realised I hadn't put my raincoat on. Never mind, I'd be home again before the rain came.

The Journey Home

It had begun raining. The sort of gentle rain which doesn't seem to be doing much but which soaks you through anyway. I'd got myself under an old lilac tree, near the blue wooden gate, trying to keep out of the rain whilst I waited for my taxi. I'd forgotten to put my raincoat on this morning. I've been at the Day Centre all day. I like going there 'cos I get to talk to others my own age who remember the things I do, as well as getting a really good home cooked dinner. I'd stay for tea as well if they did one but it closes at 4 o'clock so that was why I was stood under the tree waiting for the taxi.

The food is great. Those women know how to cook a proper man's dinner. Sometimes I get fed up of fry ups and meals on wheels, although I do like fish and chips. I was thinking of having them tonight but maybe I'll just have a tin of rice pudding, which I've got from the shop here today. The Meals on Wheels have all started to taste the same. My niece got me into the Day Centre and I'm glad she did. I didn't want to come at first but she said that I should go once and if I didn't like it then I'd no need to go again. Anyway, I did like it, especially as I won on the bingo that day and brought home a nice little clock. It looks like a Swiss chalet. That was about four years ago and I've been coming twice a week ever since.

Anyway, here I am waiting for my taxi. I've filled two carrier bags today and I've kicked them a bit further under the tree to try and keep them dry. The rain seems to be getting heavier. I've got lots of things in those bags. The Day Centre runs a little shop and today I got two tins of peaches, three tins of peas, two tins of macaroni cheese, a tin of sweetcorn and the last tin of rice pudding. Then I got a box of tea bags, some nice red serviettes, a can of coca cola, two pink toilet rolls and a cuttle fish for the budgie. I don't know where all these things come from. They must be donated by well-wishers. I tell myself every week to stop buying all this stuff but I know it helps them out. I think they buy the bingo prizes with the money they make, so as I win something at the bingo nearly every week, I'm getting my money back, so to speak. I know the pantry is getting a bit full but I like having plenty in stock. I've started putting spare tins in the chest of drawers. They seem to be ok in there. Some of the smaller tins also fit in my boots and shoes under the table. They help to keep them in shape. Sometimes I put the tins in the freezer.

I wish the taxi would come soon. My left leg is starting to ache. I'm glad I didn't fasten my laces too tightly as, when I've had my shoes on all day, like I have to do when I come to the Day Centre, my feet swell up. Sometimes they swell up so much it takes me ages to get my shoes off. If they're really stuck on then I've had to sleep in them and take them off in the morning. I've called them shoes but I suppose they're what are called trainers these days. They're made of black leather with some red stripes down the sides. I'm not too keen on the red stripes. They can't be repaired, either. Once they're worn out I'll have to get another pair. I think that's called the throw-away society. It was much better when things could be repaired and lasted for years.

Anyway, as I said, the Day Centre generally closes at 4 o'clock and, although they don't mind if you stay a bit longer, today they all seemed in a great big rush to get off and the manager locked up promptly. She's called Janette Parker and is very suited to her role. She looks a bit like Hattie Jacques and makes sure everyone does what they are supposed to be doing. It's a bit like an army camp sometimes but I think she's a lot of responsibility and she makes sure we all have a good time. So, that's why I'm under this tree. I can understand why they wanted to dash off. Two of the helpers hadn't turned up this morning and the rest of them had been rushed off their feet, working non-stop all day. I don't blame them for wanting to get home. There seemed to be a lot of us today, as well. I sat with Billy, as usual. He was in the war, same as me, and we like to swap tales. There's only three men who go to the Day Centre. The other one is Alf but he didn't come today. It didn't matter, though. There must have been twenty of us as all the chairs were used up. I won the bingo again. Another clock. It's in one of the carrier bags.

The rain is definitely getting heavier. I've moved as far under this tree as I can but I don't know if it was a good idea 'cos some big drops of water have fallen down the back of my neck. I've pulled my collar up. I wish I'd gone back for my raincoat. My jacket's going to take days to dry out. I'm wondering what I'll do if the taxi doesn't come. I'll have to go to one of those houses over the road and ask them to get me one. The trouble is I don't know what I'd do with my carrier bags. I suppose I could leave them here. Those are big houses and they have long paths up to the doors. I'd have to hope the bags weren't stolen whilst I was gone. I don't mind the tins going but I wouldn't want to lose the clock. I'd have to put it in my pocket to keep it safe. I've got enough money to pay for any phone calls they might have to make.

Oh! He's here! Hallelujah!

I've been doing a bit of day dreaming to pass the time. I've been dreaming about the fish and chips I'm going to have tonight instead of rice pudding. Maybe I'll have the rice pudding afterwards. It doesn't look like the usual driver who comes. He's stopped the car just near the kerb. I've had a quick look at him and I think he's in a bit of a temper 'cos he's just shouted at me to ask if I'm going to Baildon. He wasn't very polite. Better get my carrier bags and walking stick and get in the car. I don't like walking over wet grass. I wish he'd get out of the car and help me like the other driver does. This door is difficult to open. There, I've done it and managed to put the bags on the back seat. I've managed to get the walking stick in and now, if I turn round and get in back side first, I should be ok. There, right leg in. I'll just lean over and get hold of the door and get my left leg in, too. I could do with a bit of help but I daren't ask this fellow. Nearly there. Ah! I've caught my left foot on the car edge and my trainer's fallen off. It's gone into the road and I've closed my door. How did that happen? And now he's moving off. Stop! But he doesn't listen. He's going up the road and turning round. I've asked him to stop again but he's ignoring me. Now we're going down the road past the Day Centre and I can see my trainer in the gutter where it fell. I wish I'd fastened the laces.

He must be running very late. I think he's forgotten he has me in the back. The usual driver goes the main road way but this one's going over the moors. He's all brakes and accelerator, as they say. This seat's a bit slippery. I'm sliding from side to side along with my carrier bags. It's a very winding road with lots of bumps along the way. He didn't give me a chance to put my seat belt on. My carrier bags have fallen over. My tins are rolling on to the floor. There goes the tin of sweetcorn. It's been joined by the tin of peas. Now the rice pudding has gone too. That's the one I fancied for my tea. I'm trying to stop any more falling out but he's going so fast round these bends I can't keep hold of anything. I've already bashed my left leg against the front seat. I'm just going to close my eyes 'til we get there. It's no use calling out to him to slow down.

I think we've stopped. Yes! I'm home. I don't think he's going to bother helping me out, either. I'll just have to open the door myself. Look! It's never been fastened properly. I could have fallen out and he wouldn't have noticed, I bet. I'll pull the bags nearer the door. Now, if I shuffle to the edge of the seat, I can get my left leg out. He's gone and parked over a puddle and my foot is going to get wet 'cos I've lost the trainer. There, soaked right through. Now, all I need to do is swing my right leg out as well. Good, I'm out. Now for the carrier bags. I can use the walking stick to pull them near the door. They're a lot lighter now 'cos so many things have fallen out. I'll just have to leave everything on the floor. The driver can take them home for his family. I'll just give the door a push to close it. Now he's moving off again. I'd shout a thank you but I don't suppose he'd hear it.

Up The Stairs

The taxi moved off and left him standing in the rain with a wet sock and his carrier bags. He put his walking stick down the belt of his trousers, like a sword, picked up the bags and went through the front door of the flats. His legs were aching and he could feel a trickle of something wet going down his left leg. He was sure one of the ulcers had opened up. He would deal with it later. So, taking a deep breath he grabbed hold of the hand rail with his right hand and, with the bags in his left, managed to get himself onto the first step. The sock was very wet and he'd made footprints in the entrance.

Slowly he lifted each foot onto the next step and gradually went up the stairs. The wet footprints became fainter on each one. He made several stops so he could catch his breath. Near the top, the hand rail wobbled. He made a mental note to tell the warden about it. At the top, he turned left to the green door to his flat and felt in his pocket for the key. It wasn't there. It had fallen down a hole in the lining but, after fumbling around, he managed to retrieve it and opened the door. He was home. He made a mental note to sew up the pocket lining.

He closed the door and headed left across the room to his bed, taking care not to trip over the old yellow rug in front of the gas fire. The budgie chirped as he went past the cage. When he reached his bed, he pulled the walking stick out of his belt, sat down wearily on the bed, the carrier bags slipping slowly from his big hands to come to rest on the floor. Then, he laid back across the bed and rested his head against the pale magnolia painted wall. Well, it was magnolia under the dark greasy spot created by many head restings. The cold wetness of his shirt pressed against his neck and his damp jacket flopped open. He knew his left foot was encased in a wet sock and wondered idly what had happened to the mashed potato between his toes. His right leg was aching too but he just wanted to stay as he was for five minutes. Five minutes was all he needed to recover and then he'd get ready and go down to the fish and chip shop for his supper. He closed his eyes. It was nearly ten minutes to five.

He awoke with a start. For a moment he didn't know where he was. The curtains were open and he could see that it was nearly dark. The room felt cold. Reaching over, he managed to switch on the bedside light and get hold of the Westclox. He could just about make out that it was nearly half past five. He'd only meant to have a nap for five minutes. He needed to put on some dry socks and another shirt although the one he had on didn't seem to be as wet as it had been. Maybe he'd keep it on. Now sitting on the side of the bed, his damp jacket creased and crumpled, he leaned forward to see to his sock.

Slowly he bent down and slowly he removed the left sock. The mashed potato oozed out as he rolled it. His foot had swollen up and was the colour of a sunset which heralded a glorious day ahead. But this sunset heralded only pain. When the wet sock was finally removed, he tossed it onto the end of the bed, ready to dry it off on a radiator. He made a mental note to move the thermostat so the central heating would come on again. He didn't know why it wasn't already on. He'd do that before he set off.

He took off the remaining trainer and put it under the blue formica table. He'd decide what to do with it tomorrow. The sock on his right foot seemed to be quite dry so it could stay where it was. Then he eased his jacket off, pushed himself off the bed and hobbled slowly across the room to find another sock. On the way there he draped the wet jacket over the back of the purple leather chair. The chest of drawers had two drawers at the top and then four very deep ones underneath. It was in the top two that he kept his socks, along with all the Christmas cards received over the years as well as the envelopes they had come in. Packs of unused Christmas cards he'd bought at the Day Centre were also in there plus the cards he'd written and addressed himself but never sent out. He could always send them next year. Also in the drawers were a dozen packets of gent's handkerchiefs, all unused bingo wins, several very old worn, knitted hats and nine assorted scarves. These had all been very useful when he was a window cleaner. Nowadays he didn't wear a hat.

He pulled open the top right-hand drawer and chose a black sock with a bright green stripe round the top. There were over forty socks in the drawer, many without partners but as no one ever saw his socks except the District Nurse and the chiropodist, it didn't really matter. He pushed hard to shut the drawer as the contents needed to be flattened for the drawer to close properly. Having done this, he shuffled off to find another jacket. Opening the door of the single beech coloured wardrobe, he chose a well cut, dark green jacket. This was one of the better gifts from another widow. His best Harris tweed jackets, which he had been given every year from the village men's shop, were in there as well. Everything was squashed up. Then he went to the other dark brown wardrobe and got a raincoat out. He wasn't going to get wet a second time. He hung it over the zimmer frame as he passed it on the way back to his bed.

Having got his dry sock and jacket he sat down on the bed again. He gingerly put the sock over his left foot. Getting it over the swollen part was the hardest bit but he persevered and eventually it was on. He was thankful he'd decided to keep the other sock on. Plus, he'd also kept the shirt on. Now he'd to find a pair of boots, as his trainers would now only be of use if he lost his left foot. So, using his walking stick, he knocked a black Doc Marten boot from out of the pile. The other one was just nearby and this got the same treatment. Although these were quite heavy, they were good for his feet because they came well above his ankles and didn't catch the top of his foot. They were also a size 15 so he'd a lot of room in them. There was a thick layer of dust on them, as they hadn't been worn for a long time. He decided he'd leave the laces undone and just tuck them into the boots. His right foot slipped in easily but something was stopping his left foot from going down into the boot. So, he picked up the boot and put his hand in to find out exactly what it was. He pulled out a blue budgie. It was dead. He couldn't believe his eyes. He thought it had drowned in the toilet but instead must have fallen into the boot, and simply suffocated in there. He put the stiff little body gently on the end of his bed.

So, now he stood up, put on the jacket and picked up a five-pound note from a dish on the table. He shuffled towards the door to get his zimmer frame. It was useful for carrying his brown plastic shopping bag for the fish and chips. Then he put his raincoat on. His last task was to move the central heating dial and he thought he'd light the gas fire as well so things would be cosy for him when he got back. He picked up the match box on the top of the fireplace, turned the gas knob and when he could hear the hissing, lit a match and the gas fire came to life. He left it on at high. He wasn't going to be very long.

Now prepared for the journey, he unlocked the door and walked out onto the landing.

He left the dead budgie lying on his bed. It was nearly six o'clock.

HARRY LAWTON...
...in Pictures

...with Norma at Napier Street

...*Caroline – Harry's mother*

...in Egypt

...at Baildon carnival

PART TWO

18:00:00 – 19:00:00

18:00:00 – 18:07:21

He closed the green door to his flat and, after locking it, carefully put the key in a pocket of the raincoat which he knew didn't have a hole in the lining. He smiled to himself as he felt the five-pound note in there as well. Sometimes he'd forgotten to take any money out with him.

He turned to his right, took a couple of steps to the top of the stairs, lifted the zimmer frame up and moved the brown plastic shopping bag to the front. He balanced himself whilst he looked down the stairs and, with a deep breath, lowered his right foot down onto the first step, holding tight to the hand rail on the wall to his left. The rail wobbled as he got hold of it. His right hand was holding onto the zimmer frame. And so, down the stairs he went, one at a time. Very slowly.

About half way down, his foot seemed to be stuck on the step so he gripped the rail even tighter and looked down. The laces had come loose and when he'd put his left foot down, he'd trapped the lace from the right foot. He wished he'd made the effort and tied them properly. By lifting the sole of his left boot a little and moving the other one, the lace came free and dangled over the edge of the step.

Now he'd to be even more careful and not tread on them again. To make matters worse his left leg was beginning to hurt. It would be a lot better when he was on the level again, he told himself. So, gradually he descended to the bottom and, on reaching the little hallway, he lowered the zimmer and opened the front door. The wet foot-prints he'd made earlier had gone.

Now there was only one more step to go down. He breathed a sigh of relief as both feet reached the pavement and he closed the door behind him. He turned right and leaned against the wall wondering what to do about the laces. He knew he couldn't bend down long enough to fasten them properly. However, just at that moment, someone he knew came by and kindly did the laces up for him. A piece of good luck there, he thought, and turned to continue his journey to the fish and chip shop. It had stopped raining.

Cultivated at Home

I'd a good start in life, looking back, and can't say there were too many hardships, at least not compared say, to that poor family down our street. The one mother was always asking me to take food to. We always had enough to eat which was a minor miracle considering father's social habits and the fact I'd four sisters and a brother. My sister, Annie, was the oldest of us all. She was born in 1918 which made her six years older than me. She was what you'd call attractive these days. Not a raving beauty but she'd a lovely smile and enjoyed going dancing as she got older. Next came Alice who had arrived in 1919. Now, she was the motherly one of them all and if I was in trouble or needed to tell someone something and mother wasn't there, well, it was Alice I went looking for. She wasn't quite as pretty as mother but had that same elegance about her. She didn't mind spending a Sunday morning doing the vegetables.

After Alice came Norma, born in 1920. Norma was only four years older than me but never wanted anything to do with me or Jack. She wanted to do everything with Annie or Alice, so Jack and me just left her to it as we got older. I suppose you could say that we never really got on. My last sister had arrived in 1923 and was called Helen. I can't remember playing out with her very much but then, again, I can't remember falling out with her much, either. Both these sisters inherited the elegance of mother but, unlike Annie or Alice, didn't seem to have that extra bit in the looks department. They all inherited father's liking of a good social life, though and later on I think they probably kept the dance halls going.

I arrived on 4th June 1924 and then, just as I was getting used to being spoilt as the baby of the family with all these sisters, my little brother Jack came into the world at the end of 1925. As far as I can remember, after Jack was walking and talking and definitely by the time he was five, him and me were inseparable. Today you'd say that we were joined at the hip. We were a happy family even though we were a bit crowded but we didn't think anything of that.

Mother didn't have a job outside the home. Not many women did unless they were shopkeepers or librarians, like Auntie Lucy, or school teachers. It wasn't until the Second World War that women started to work in other places. Anyway, mother was at home all the time. She was tall and elegant and I think well liked 'cos there always seemed to be someone sat at our kitchen table chatting to her. She'd a weekly routine and got upset if it was changed for any reason. Monday was washing day. And it wasn't a matter of throwing the dirty linen into a washing machine and pressing a switch, either. We'd a very large tub which we kept in the back yard and father would bring it in on a Monday morning before he set off to work. Hot water from the boiler was ladled in and the things which needed washing put in, together with some sort of soap. I don't know what. Then the posser came out. This was a metal cone with holes in it fastened to a long wooden handle. The posser was pushed up and down to move the clothes about and get the soapy water through them. After this was done the water was emptied by the tap at the bottom of the tub into a bucket and then the tub was filled again for the clothes to be rinsed, again using the posser.

Eventually the clothes were washed and taken out carefully before being wrung out as much as possible. We'd a clothes wringer which was kept at Grandma Coble's 'cos we didn't have enough room, so clothes were often carried over there in the big tin tub. Then they were put through the wringer and brought home and dried, hopefully outside in the back yard. We also had a clothes maid which was a rack made up of five pieces of wood and fastened to the ceiling. It could be pulled up or let down by a rope. This was always used if it was raining and was useful for drying anything else overnight. We also had a large wooden clothes horse which could be stood round the range like a screen. The kitchen was very damp on wash days.

Tuesday was baking day. I think it was Tuesday so that if the clothes were still wet the extra warmth dried them that bit faster. Anyhow, once a week mother would make pies and scones and flat cakes as big as dustbin lids. The scones often went to the poor neighbours. By poor I mean those who had even less than we did. Wednesday was ironing day which meant that the clothes disappeared unless they needed mending and then they went on mother's chair near the range for her to see to that night. Thursday was cleaning day and although it was only a small house, when there's an open coal fire there's a lot of dirt and dust about. The kitchen, especially, got very grubby and I don't suppose the fact there were six children helped, either.

The one place Mother enjoyed cleaning was our front room. It had a door which led straight out onto Napier Street. However, we never used this door. We always went down the alley to the back door in the yard and straight into the kitchen. The front room was sacred territory. It was mother and father's room and we never went in there without them. Mother was very proud of it. Not many people could boast of an extra-large rag rug and a red moquette settee and matching chair. I don't know where they came from. We'd all made the rag rug one winter. I'm not sure how much help I was at that time but I remember making quite a few rugs in winter time when I was older and able to use our big dressmaker's scissors. These days youngsters have to use plastic scissors with round ends.

In the front room there was a small, dark wooden table where father's wind-up gramophone was kept. You could buy records at Stead's down Leeds Road where we'd our 'account' which mother paid a few shillings into every week. Sometimes we'd all go into the front room, sit on the floor and father would play some First World War songs to us. He'd a Harry Lauder record which we particularly liked. It was 'Keep Right On to the End of the Road' and eventually we learnt the chorus so we'd all sing our hearts out when that started up. It was good fun. I think it's an anthem for a football club now. On these occasions father enjoyed a jug of beer which he'd bring home from the Lord Napier. Harry Lauder came from Scotland and his songs were very popular. They were the pop songs of the day, I suppose.

He was made a 'sir' which he probably got for his work raising money for soldiers and sailors who needed medical help after they had come home from the First World War. We also had a wireless which was kept in the corner behind father's chair, on a wooden crate. Father must have picked this up from the market where he'd been working. The crate, not the wireless. I don't know where that came from, either. It was dark brown and about the size of a large shoe box. He liked listening to the wireless, particularly if it was a detective story. It was woe-betide any of us if we as much as squeaked when one of those was on. As often as not a lot of knob twiddling went on together with strange squeals before the programme was found. We also had a tiled fireplace in the front room but I don't remember ever seeing a fire there, except on Christmas Day.

Friday's main job was to black the Airedale Range in the kitchen to keep it in good condition. The range, or 'Black Billy' as we knew it, was polished by mother with something called black lead, until you could see your face in it. The brass fender round the hearth got the same treatment. Not with black lead but some white stuff mother kept in a tin box. Friday was also the day for scouring the front steps with a special stone and then edging the steps in white. Most housewives took a real pride in the appearance of their house, no matter how little money they had and you never saw any litter or rubbish lying about anywhere. I suppose this was 'cos everything was used and nothing wasted. All scraps of paper went on the fire and, in our house, waste from the kitchen went to Grandad's hens. Everything else was put in a jam jar or box for further use.

Saturday was shopping day when mother would go out, sometimes with father, and buy what was needed for the following week. If it was one of us who needed something, such as a new pair of shoes, they went too, otherwise, they went on their own and we all traipsed along to Grannie Annie's. Then Jack and me usually went off to the allotment with Grandad and the girls had to amuse themselves as best they could. Sunday was a relative day of rest for mother as the only thing we always did was have a sit-down roast dinner together and, as we got older, she managed to organise this so she only had to see to the meat. Our Sunday roast could be chicken courtesy of Grandad Coble or, sometimes, a piece of lamb which was always a bit fatty. In those days, it was the thing to send children to Sunday School and we were no exception. This started at 3 o'clock in the afternoon in the church hall of the local Baptist chapel. It was about a ten-minute walk away down Leeds Road but it was still a bit of a chore for us as Mother always insisted that we all got washed and put on our best clothes. We went nearly every Sunday but I don't remember winning any prizes for good attendance. I do remember, though, that they had lots of social events especially for children, such as the processions at Easter time and someone organised a games afternoon every year at Whitsuntide on the Bun Field at Tyersal playing fields where we all raced each other in egg and spoon races or the three-legged race. That was where two folk ran next to each other with their nearest legs tied together. That gave them three legs between them. I don't think I ever won anything there, either.

We always had a cooked breakfast as mother believed, quite rightly according to today's advice, that this was the most important meal of the day. We'd have eggs and sometimes bacon, always with a thick 'step' of mother's tasty home-made bread, washed down with tea. Then, when we came home from school, we make do with maybe jam and bread and a glass of milk except in winter when there was always a hot meal waiting, usually a stew made with lots of vegetables from Grandad's allotment except on a Friday when we always had fish and chips.

I enjoyed school. It was about fifteen minutes away from home and across Leeds Road. There wasn't much traffic in them days. We usually walked there with our sisters. Lessons started at 9.30 am after we'd had the school assembly where we sang a hymn, said some prayers and listened to any news about what was going on. In the classroom we sat in pairs on benches at tables with inkwells. There were no biros. I often went home with blue hands. My first teacher was called Mrs Eastwood. We'd a break in the middle of the morning when we could have a drink of milk which had to be paid for. I think it was a halfpenny. We were lucky enough to be able to afford this but there were other children who had to go without. There was no free milk for schools until about 1946. Dinner time was 12 noon. The school didn't have a kitchen or canteen so we'd to do our own dinner. Sometimes I walked back home with one of my sisters and we had a bowl of soup or we could take what I suppose is the same as a packed lunch these days. This was often a potato with your initials carved into the skin and which was baked in the school's coke fired boiler. I don't remember anyone taking sandwiches. Then we went back to our classroom at 1 pm and finished at 4 pm.

I can still remember some of the children who were at school with me. There was Christine Baxter who had the same birthday as me. She belonged to a family who were so poor she'd to put cardboard inside her shoes to make them wearable. Then there was Michael Bell. I remember him 'cos of a most unfortunate incident. One day there was a terrible smell coming from his direction. He'd simply left it too late and had gone in his pants. We all had to move out into the assembly hall whilst Mrs Eastwood cleared it up. The headmaster, Mr Openshaw, gave us a right telling off the next day in morning assembly. We all thought this was very unfair as it wasn't our fault.

We didn't have a uniform. The boys wore short trousers with long socks and fancy jumpers and the girls had skirts and fancy jumpers as well. Hair had to be tied back 'cos of the risk of lice. We'd a school nurse and she inspected our heads, hands and finger nails very regularly for unwanted visitors. My best friend was Stephen Cartwright but we got put into different classes when I was about seven 'cos although I enjoyed going to school, I couldn't keep up with the rest of the them. This meant that I stayed in the same class for two years and Stephen made new friends.

In the 1930s I think schools were affected by what was a Depression in the country when there was a lot of unemployment and not much money for keeping up with things. There was a big hole in the ceiling in the assembly hall. It never got repaired. We just avoided sitting under it in case it decided to come down on us. In 1936 when unemployment was really high, especially in the north of England, a lot of unemployed men walked from Jarrow, which is near Newcastle, to London to hand in a petition asking for more industry to be created up there. A shipyard called Palmers had closed and a lot of jobs had been lost. They handed the petition in to Downing Street but I think they went home disappointed 'cos nothing was done. It was called The Jarrow Crusade and it was a lot of effort by honest working-class people which, in the end, was a waste of time. They must have worn out a lot of shoes walking all that way which they probably couldn't afford, either. I hope they had a lot of cardboard.

My father was born in Victoria Barracks, Beverley, in 1893 'cos his father, who was called Harry Lawton, was a serving soldier. My father's name was Harry too and that's how I came to be called Harry. I carried on the tradition, so to speak, being the first boy to be born into the family after my mother and father had managed to produce four girls. It's not short for Harold, either. It says Harry on my birth certificate. Now, I was actually born at home which was a little terraced house on the outskirts of Bradford, in an area called Laisterdyke. Our family came here about 1900 'cos my Grandad Lawton had died after falling off a horse somewhere in Africa during the Boer War. It must have been a very worrying time for my Grandma Lawton. She would have had to leave the army accommodation in Beverley and with five small children, including my father, she moved to Bradford, to an area where there was some family she could turn to. To be left with five children at that time would have been a disaster for her. The Social Services hadn't been thought of and there was nothing like the National Health Service. These were years in the future and people had to manage and help themselves and their own families, especially in working-class areas, which Laisterdyke certainly was. They moved into 53 Napier Street. Just nearby, at number 40, was a family called Coble and there were five children. One of these was a daughter called Caroline and she became my mother. Her parents became my Grannie Annie and Grandad Coble. So, that must have been how my mother and father met. They were neighbours.

Our little house was number 44 Napier Street. There were lots of streets with names like this at that time, 'cos it was the name of a famous general who'd won an important battle in the First World War. I believe there's a statue of him sitting on a horse in Whitehall in London. I've never seen it but my friend Alf, who I meet at the Day Centre, has been there and tells me it's a very nice statue. He goes down every year to be at the Remembrance Parade. I don't think he takes part in the marching or anything like that but just likes to put on his beret, be part of the crowd and remember all his pals who never came back from the Second World War. I watch it all on the tele. I think they're all in the Albert Hall. I've got a beret, too, which came in one of the black bin liners I keep being given. It's yellow and had a bobble on it but I cut that off. I know the colour's wrong but as I'm the only one there and I can't see it anyway when it's on top of my head, I don't think it matters. What does matter to me is that I always put it on right at the end of the programme when the poppies are falling. It seems respectful, somehow. I think about my pals in the Second World War who never came back, especially my best friend, Stanley. As well as that, I like to think that I'm doing something the rest of the country is doing, or at least some of it. I know lots of people don't bother these days. It all seems so far back, I suppose. Anyway, I like doing it. It makes me feel part of something.

Now, Napier Street was built about 1865, along with loads of other new streets. Like ours, nearby streets were named after generals or other military men. The streets near us were Raglan, Kershaw, and Dundas. There's a Wellington Terrace down the main road. We still do this today. I've read about a Falklands Court in the newspaper. What I don't understand is where really fancy names come from. Near me there's a little cul-de-sac of quite posh houses which were built only a few years ago and it's been called Venice Mews. Now what is that all about? We live in the middle of Yorkshire and to the best of my knowledge we are nowhere near Venice, which is in Italy. Who are these people who sit around a table and decide what a place is going to be called?

Nearly all the houses in Laisterdyke were small terrace houses like ours, built of mucky Yorkshire stone. Well, I suppose they weren't mucky when they were first built 'cos the stone would have been newly quarried but after lots of years of smoke and dirt from local factories, and there were lots of those near Laisterdyke, as well as a huge railway goods yard, they'd become dirty looking. Then there was the smoke from the coal fires everyone had. No- one had a gas fire in them days. The stone could have come from Tyersal which wasn't very far away. There's a pub there called the Quarry Gap so maybe that's a clue.

We'd loads of relatives living nearby. Everybody did. It wasn't like it is now when families live all over the place and only meet up at the proverbial christenings, weddings and funerals. Grandad Coble and Grannie Annie, as I've just said, lived opposite us and one of Grannie Annie's sisters lived with them. This was Auntie Nellie. I remember her very clearly 'cos she was always in the house whenever I went round there. She'd dark brown hair cut straight just under her ears with a fringe and always seemed to be wearing the same clothes – a black skirt with white dots on it and a bright blue jumper. She was always sitting in the same chair, as well. In fact, I don't even remember seeing her standing up so I can't tell you if she was tall or short. I remember her legs very well, though, not 'cos I looked at ladies' legs, I was too small to be interested in such things at the time, but because the holes in her black stockings were all sewn up with different coloured threads. We didn't have a lot of money but my mother would never have gone to such lengths to make a pair of stockings last longer. Auntie Nellie can't have changed her stockings very often either, if I think about it, unless it's my imagination that they always looked the same. Sometimes a new hole appeared and there were hairs coming out of it.

Anyway, whenever I went round there, she'd be sat in the same chair, near the kitchen range with her knitting. That was another thing. It was always the same piece of knitting in bright red wool. It could have been a scarf, I'm not sure, but I don't ever remember it being finished and a new piece started. She used to look at me over the top of her glasses but she never said anything to me. Her glasses were those with really thick lenses and wire frames. We used to call them bottle bottoms. Sometimes her fringe had grown and it hung over her glasses like a curtain. I couldn't be sure she could see me or her knitting. My mother always reminded me to say hello to her, which I did but I never knew if she understood me. As a youngster I was fascinated by her but at the same time rather frightened by her moustache. Grandad Coble had a moustache as well and they both looked the same to me. Maybe Grandad's was a bit longer. I also remember thinking she was trying to grow a beard too which was even more alarming. It seemed as though there were hundreds of whiskers on her face, some of which must have been several inches long. I didn't like to stare too much, though, as I'd been told it was rude to do that. I used to wonder every year if I should ask my mother to buy Auntie Nellie a shaving kit for Christmas. She obviously couldn't afford one but very probably at that time neither could we. Anyway, as young-uns did in them days, back in the 1930's, I just accepted her and didn't ask questions. These days young-uns ask every question there is to be asked and wouldn't be left wondering like I was.

Then, one day, when I went round to Grannie Annie's, Auntie Nellie wasn't there in her usual place. I got quite a shock when I saw the chair was empty and the mended stockings had gone. I wondered if this was the day I'd see her stood up and could work out how tall she was but, even though I waited in the kitchen chatting to Grannie Annie, she didn't turn up. Eventually, this was I decided, the time to ask a question and summoned up all my courage. Grannie Annie didn't seem to know what to say to me but then whispered that Auntie Nellie had gone to a better place. Having already asked my one question I couldn't bring myself to ask another so I just nodded as if I understood completely what had happened to her and got on with eating the jam sandwich she'd made for me. It was all very confusing and I never found out if she'd gone to heaven or a mental institution. I never saw Auntie Nellie again and no one talked about her. In a funny sort of way I missed her. She was the first person to go out of my life and left me with an unexplained gap. She was a sort of taken for granted presence which brings comfort and isn't noticed until it isn't there anymore. Looking back, I'm glad she lived with Grannie Annie and Grandad and the rest of her family as long as she did. These days everyone is so busy that it's not often that elderly infirm relatives stay with their families. They're moved into care homes which although a good idea on the surface, underneath there is nothing like being with your own nearest and dearest.

One of my mother's sisters also lived with Grannie Annie. This was my Auntie Lucy and she was my mother's sister. Now, she was the exact opposite of Auntie Nellie. Very chatty and full of fun. She was also tall and thin, slim, you'd say today and very much like my mother. She was always very helpful to me and, because they only had adults in their house, there seemed to be more time to do enjoyable things, like looking at picture books. Our house, on the other hand, was always full of my very noisy younger brother and my four sisters. Auntie Lucy was a great reader. She worked in the local library and was always bringing a new book as a surprise. I often sat on her knee whilst she read to me and she helped me a lot with my own reading which I found difficult to do. Looking back, she was very patient with me and together we read lots of classics such as Treasure Island, which became my favourite. She didn't have any children and she was always willing to give me some of her time which, looking back, she seemed to have quite a lot of. I still like reading, although now my eyesight isn't what it was, I don't do as much as I'd like to and my reading habits have changed too. I enjoy cowboy books by Louis L'Amour.

I think Grannie Annie had always been a fulltime housewife, looking after everybody. Grandad Coble, on the other hand, had worked on the railways, in the local goods yard. Well, I say goods yard, but Laisterdyke was a major junction and part of the London and North Eastern Railway. There were loads of tracks coming from all directions and joining up right under our noses. It was a very busy place. Grandad Coble had also been in the army, like my Grandad Lawton, and I suppose he got the railway job after that. I also don't know just what Grandad Coble did on the railways but he always had a sort of air of authority about him so I like to think he was a supervisor of some sort or maybe he just got that by being in charge of something in the army. I could just imagine him waving his arms about organising parcels being sent all over the country. Bradford had a thriving woollen industry right up to the 1950's as well as having big engineering works, some of which were very near to us. They all had to send off their orders somehow and the railway was used a lot back then to move goods. It's not like it is these days when almost everything goes by road and no one can get anywhere for traffic jams. But now Grandad Coble had retired and he spent as much time as he could on his allotment.

Anyhow, back to the relatives. Further up our street, at number 50, was my Uncle Frank and his wife, Auntie Lily, who was my mother's sister, and their two children Maurice and Alfred who were twins. There was six years between my mother and Auntie Lily, in which time Grannie Annie had another three children, making a total of five – nearly one every year. Uncle Frank also worked on the railways and was as thin as a beanpole. As Grandad Coble was thin as well, I used to think that all men who worked on the railways had to be thin. A sort of specification for the job. It was a wonder that Auntie Lucy didn't work. She was very thin, too and would have fitted in nicely. We also saw lots of the men who worked at the railway depot as they came and went off the various shifts and, to me they were all thin as well. Auntie Lily, on the other hand, was definitely not thin. She was, as we would say today, of generous proportions. Again, just as Auntie Nellie had fascinated me, so did Auntie Lily, or, to be precise, her bosoms did. We didn't have anything like them in our house and they were a continual source of amusement to me and my younger brother, Jack.

Jack and me did a lot of things together and we spent hours, or so it seemed, trying to work out how Auntie Lily managed to carry all that around with her. We would stuff things like shoes and oranges down our jumpers and try to see what jobs we could do when encumbered in such a fashion. Tying shoelaces, I seem to remember, was quite difficult, as was sitting at a table trying to eat as we'd to have our arms at full stretch. We got round that one by resting our bosoms on the table. Mind you, we could only try that one when mother had nipped out somewhere and we were in the house alone for a short while. But, we decided that it wasn't quite the thing to do as we'd never actually seen Auntie Lily doing that. Dancing, however, was the worst, or maybe the best, as they bounced around and the contents eventually fell out. We never stopped laughing.

One wet afternoon, though, when we were a bit bored, we'd another go at being Auntie Lily and, after stuffing everything we could lay our hands on down the front of our jumpers we'd a grand afternoon's fun. However, when father came home, we'd to try and find an explanation, as we sat at the tea table, as to why both our jumpers had been stretched and pulled out of shape at the front. We didn't have a lot of money to spare so clothes had to be looked after carefully and our jumpers were now shapeless and very baggy. I can't remember what we said but I know we were sent to bed very early. It didn't matter, though, 'cos we laughed ourselves to sleep that night and many afterwards, too. We never did another 'Auntie Lily' after that but just thinking about it still makes me smile.

My cousins, the twins, Maurice and Alfred, were four years older than me and five years older than Jack. When you're only six or so and someone else is ten, they think you're a baby and that they're grown up, so I didn't really have much to do with them, except that Jack and me were continually linked to them 'cos most of our clothes had been theirs at one time or another. This was, no doubt, the answer to my mother's prayers, as I think she'd a great deal of difficulty providing for six children from my father's wages as a council labourer. So, when the two boys could be clothed for next to nothing, she grabbed her chance. But, this had drawbacks for Jack and me. Maurice and Alfred took after Auntie Lily, which meant they were on the big side. I don't mean they had bosoms, or anything like that, but just that they were big. This meant that things which were passed down had to be stored under our bed in cardboard boxes waiting for a time when they would, more or less, fit one of us. I say our bed, 'cos me and Jack shared one. So, every now and then, mother would come up to our bedroom to see if there was anything which might be suitable. This always happened whenever there was something to go to, such as a Sunday School outing or we were having one of our rare trips to the seaside.

Hand-me-down clothes were part of life in Laisterdyke and probably many other parts of Bradford, too. No one really thought much of it, except, or so it seemed at the time, me and Jack. Because Maurice and Alfred were so many years older, the clothes had to be stored for quite some time and the getting out of the boxes was always a time of considerable anxiety for us, as to what would be chosen as our next 'new' item of clothing. Our house, like all other houses near us at the time, didn't have any modern conveniences such as central heating or even an inside toilet. In fact, upstairs didn't have any heating at all and most houses near us had gas lighting, too. If you wanted a warm bed in the middle of winter, you but a brick in the oven next to the fire in the kitchen, waited for it to heat up and then wrapped it in a piece of rag before popping it in your bed. It didn't keep its heat very long, of course, but it helped a bit. So, the clothes could have been there for ages in a damp house, which gave them the very distinctive smell of damp which could never be got rid of even though they were washed and hung outside to dry before we wore them. I think that was the worst thing about these clothes – the smell – otherwise we quite happily ran off to school decked out in brown and green checked shorts, red and white striped shirt and a blue and black striped jumper. A perfect clown's outfit but when everyone else is dressed like that you don't know any better and it all seemed perfectly normal to us. Sometimes mother would alter some items so they would fit Jack. But, at least we were clean. Some of the kids at school smelled of dirt and that's far worse. In the end, though, Jack actually drew the short straw regarding our clothes, as he was, so to speak, at the end of the line he got my outgrown clothes if they were still wearable. In other words, Jack got handed-down hand-me-downs.

My Grannie Annie was also tall like my mother and she tied her hair up in a bun on the top of her head. This made her look even taller. I once saw her before she'd put it up and was astonished at the length of her hair. It was very white and was nearly down to her waist. She didn't have a lot of wrinkles, though, and always seemed to be elegant and lady-like, at least compared to grandad. I think being in the army must have affected him 'cos he was always a bit abrupt with me, although he never complained when I tagged alongside him when he went down to his allotment. This was a short walk away from Napier Street and he just loved it down there. Sometimes Jack came too. He'd built himself a shed in which he kept his various tools, most of them home made and a wooden chair which he used to sit on and gaze into space, for what seemed to us, hours. The shed was kept very neat and tidy with a place for everything and everything in its place. It was a never-ending source of interest to me being filled with plant pots, wire netting, sticks, tools and all the other thousands of things which someone who has an allotment needs to keep just in case they come in useful. The next thing he was going to build was a greenhouse. To this end, he collected every piece of wood he could lay his hands on. It was all hidden behind the shed in case Grannie Annie came by and took it for the kitchen fire.

He grew lots of different things like peas, sprouts and cabbages. I still haven't ever seen carrots like he managed to grow. And, of course, it was what we call organic nowadays. He didn't use any chemicals that I can recall, just manure from the nearby piggery or, if he was lucky, the droppings of a passing horse. He used to walk over to the piggery with one of those big, shiny galvanised buckets, like the ones I used to use when I cleaned windows. Then he'd come back with it filled to the brim with something I couldn't bring myself to look at. I knew when he was coming back just by catching the smell on the wind. It was really terrible and it was a miracle to us that the vegetables never tasted of it. I think he was the only one brave enough to use the stuff. As well as putting it on the ground where he grew the vegetables, he also had a barrel where he always washed out the bucket, plus he used to throw a bit extra into the water to use as liquid manure. I suppose it was a clever thing to do but sometimes we took our dinner with us and it wasn't easy trying to look as if I was enjoying Grannie Annie's brawn sandwiches with the smell of the pig manure going up my nose. Grandad never seemed to notice.

As well as his allotment, Grandad Coble also had a hen run. I think all this outdoor activity was so he could escape from the house which was, of course, filled with women. This hen run was quite near the allotment so we didn't have to travel far between the two and the hens had the advantage of getting fresh greens. No wonder they produced lovely eggs. I think they were Rhode Island Reds and I enjoyed going to see them and having them come clucking round my feet when I threw grain down for them. And, of course, the hens provided even more manure for the vegetables. I suppose it was a very good system grandad had set up – a sort of working-class self-sufficiency. I was always sad, though, when mother made a roast chicken dinner and I would sit there wondering which one of the flock I was eating. I've never really enjoyed chicken since them days and the Meals on Wheels seem to use it a lot.

The piggeries that grandad went to for the manure were owned by a local businessman, Alfred Gill. He'd other concerns locally including a greengrocer's shop down Leeds Road where mother went when she needed something grandad couldn't supply. Then there was a lot of trouble with regard to Mr Gill. He went out to work on a Friday morning and his last call of the day would have been at the piggeries. By then he would have had more than £50.00 on him collected from his various businesses. That was a lot of money back then. When he didn't go home that night his wife and two sons went looking for him but didn't find him. His body was found next morning at the piggeries. He'd been battered to death. Eventually a man called Roberts, who helped Mr Gill out with his businesses was arrested and found guilty. Roberts was hanged at Armley prison. The executioner was Thomas Pierrepoint who later became famous for his trade, so to speak. Grandad stopped going to the piggeries after this and made do with his hen manure. It was sad about Mr Gill but I was happier eating my sandwiches without the smell.

The street next to ours was called Dundas Street and at number 11 lived my Auntie Shackleton and her husband, Uncle Willie. Auntie Shackleton was another of my mother's sisters, her real name being Sarah. Uncle Willie worked on the railways, too, and was also as thin as a beanpole, like the others. Auntie Shackleton, on the other hand, had the same generous proportions as Auntie Lily. I liked Auntie Shackleton a lot. She didn't have any children so every time I went round there she made a fuss of me, in the same sort of way that Auntie Lucy did but instead of books, Auntie Shackleton supplied food. She was always baking. I don't know who ate everything she made 'cos there seemed to be mountains of cakes and buns coming out of the oven all the time. Maybe this was the reason for her size. Anyhow, I'd enjoy some cake and a glass of milk whilst I was there and then she'd give me a bag of buns and maybe some bread to take home. But, mostly, but the time I'd got home the buns had all gone. I usually went back slowly and the very long way round on purpose. I was always hungry. Later, when Jack found out about the buns he insisted on coming with me so Auntie Shackleton used to give us double rations.

Across the street from Auntie Shackleton at number 26 Dundas Street, lived yet another of my mother's sisters and her husband and another two cousins. This was Auntie Craggs and Uncle John. I don't know why all my uncles and aunties were know in different ways, some by their Christian names and others by their surname. It's just how it was. Anyhow, my cousins were called Margaret and John and were more or less my age. Margaret was a bit older and John a bit younger. They were good fun and it was a convenient excuse to be able to go round to their house and then call in on Auntie Shackleton for a bun or two on the way home. They had a back yard, like we did. It wasn't very big and the outside toilet was there in the corner. But the yard was big enough for four nippers, as Jack usually tagged along to play and we'd loads of fun playing hockey with old broom handles and a piece of crumpled up newspaper. I think the broom handles must have come from Grannie Annie who gave them to us before

Grandad Coble could file them away in his allotment shed.

You'd to be quick with things like that 'cos if anything wasn't wanted by us then away it went to the allotment to be kept for some very important future purpose. It's what made the allotment shed so interesting. He even had a jar of glass marbles. There were little red and blue ones, ones with stripes and swirly things in them and then other really large ones which we called bolleys. These could be anything from speckled, striped to just plain bright colours. They were like huge gobstoppers. In case you don't know, gobstoppers were really large boiled sweets which totally filled your mouth when you popped one in. They took ages to melt down. The gobstoppers, not the bolleys. We didn't eat those. I don't know where the marbles came from but we'd hours of fun playing with them. A little later, when Jack was older and we started playing out together a lot more, the allotment shed marbles were always a big attraction. The funny thing is we never thought to take them home with us. They were down on the allotment and that's where they stayed.

Going back to our house, right opposite us at number 45 lived Uncle Leopold. He was my father's brother and he'd been born in Hull barracks as well. He was just a year older than my father. I didn't like Uncle Leopold very much 'cos he scared me by telling me tales of what he'd seen in the First World War. He was a career soldier, like Grandad Lawton, going into the army as soon as he could. He would have been about 26 years old when war was declared and he probably thought I was interested in that sort of thing, being a boy. I dreaded being sent over there. Anyway, whenever mother sent me over to Uncle Leopold's he took the opportunity of a captive audience to relive his war days. He was tall like all the others in the family. He also had a huge moustache and looked just like Kitchener on the First World War poster telling us that 'Your Country Needs You'. Uncle Leopold had also brought what was regarded in those days as a kind of shame on the family and, looking back, my mother was the only one who seemed to have anything to do with him besides his own mother, my Grandma Lawton. Well, I suppose she did, through me. I never actually saw her go over there herself but she used to send me with a bowl of soup or some baking which had made its way through the family from Auntie Shackleton.

After the First World War, Uncle Leopold went out to India with the army and fell in love with an Indian lady. They got married and then came back to England, setting up house in Napier Street, opposite us. I don't know how folk got houses in our area. We didn't own the house, just rented it. I seem to remember the rent man coming down our street every Friday evening, in the hope of catching tenants after the man of the household had been paid that afternoon. Every working man was paid in cash in them days and it wasn't unknown for the wages to be taken to the pub before they went home. I think we were the only family which didn't hide under the kitchen table at some time or another from him, which was a wonder taking into account my father's social habits. Anyway, Uncle Leopold and his wife, Sairah, that was her name, eventually opened up a crockery shop down Leeds Road which, according to family tales, was very successful.

Anyway, I don't think our family knew how to deal with her and it wasn't very long before things went wrong and she went back to India, leaving Uncle Leopold on his own. They didn't have any children. I don't remember her at all but one of my sisters does and she told me that Sairah had been very quiet and always dressed in colourful traditional Indian clothes. She must have found it really difficult being here in a strange land surrounded by customs and language she couldn't understand. Uncle Leopold apparently spoke to her in her own language. So, eventually, when I got to know Uncle Leopold, he was living by himself. He must have still had the crockery shop 'cos I can remember going there once. I think Grandma Lawton took me. It seemed a long walk to get there and inside were shelves piled with plates and saucers and bowls and jugs of every shape and size. It all seemed very colourful.

The little back room, where we went and talked to Uncle Leopold, was exactly the same. As well as more shelves filled with crockery there were more boxes and paper and lots of other things we'd to move, in order to sit down. It was the exact opposite of Grandad Coble's allotment shed. The whole place was what we'd call these days a shambles. Perhaps that's how people liked their shops 'cos, as I said, it seemed to be successful. Anyhow, Uncle Leopold, because of what had gone on before, kept himself to himself and I wonder, looking back, if the war had affected his mind a little bit 'cos once he got going with one of his tales it was a big mistake to interrupt him with a question, 'cos he'd start all over again from the beginning. It was best just to sit there and wait 'til he'd come to the end, which could be hours, or at least that's what it seemed like to me.

These days Uncle Leopold would be regarded as a hoarder. His house was just like his shop, crammed with everything you could think of. I don't think he ever threw anything away. The normal route into all our houses was by going round the back, through the yard and into the kitchen. The front door, which led straight into the best room from the street, was only used on special occasions or emergencies. But Uncle Leopold used his front door all the time. I don't know why. Maybe he couldn't be bothered walking all the way round. Anyway, once you were inside the front door, you were met by piles of newspapers and bags and boxes. They were all round the sides of the room and what furniture was in there was hidden from view by even more piles of whatever he was saving. I once went upstairs with him as he wanted to show me some pictures of India and it was the same up there. The houses on his side of the street were a bit smaller than ours. We'd three bedrooms and he'd only got two but I still couldn't make out which one he slept in. They were both filled with piles of clothes and even more boxes. I suppose some of the boxes could have been spare crockery for the shop but they looked as though they'd been there forever. Maybe he'd ordered too much once upon a time and had had to keep it in his house and just never got round to taking it down to the shop. I don't know, but it was the same in the scullery at the back, except here the place was filled, amongst a lot of other stuff, with pots and pans which were waiting to be washed up. It was a bit like those houses you see on the tele nowadays where they go in and help the owner to clean it all up. It certainly wasn't like our house or Auntie Shackleton's lovely warm, welcoming home on Dundas Street. And, I definitely wouldn't have wanted to eat anything there. Thankfully, it was never offered.

When Uncle Leopold did manage to corner me to tell me one of his tales, he perched on the edge of what looked like a small settee and I'd to make a space for myself on the floor between piles of papers. I remember him smoking a pipe and watching the ash fall onto the floor. It's a wonder he didn't set the place on fire. Then, when Jack started joining me on my outings, I was even more crammed in. We both tried to avoid going over if we could.

One of my father's sisters lived a little bit further away at number 10 Mortimer Row, down Leeds Road. This was Auntie Edna who lived with Uncle George and they provided three more cousins, Edward,

Thomas and Samuel. However, we didn't have much to do with them 'cos, as I've since realised, Auntie Edna and Uncle George weren't actually married. They got the cold shoulder like Uncle Leopold did. Not being married was really frowned upon in them days, not like now. If folk bother to get married at all these days, they have their children as bridesmaids. However, it appears that Edna was going to marry someone called Herbert who was, in fact, George's brother. All had been going according to plan and the wedding organised for the Methodist Chapel across Leeds Road. I believe they'd arranged to go and live with Grandma Lawton. This would have been around 1913 when Edna was 21 years old. But, no one had reckoned on Edna and George falling in love the minute they were introduced to each other by Herbert. As a result of all this, Edna left Herbert standing at the altar. The problem though, was that George was already married and had been brought up in the Roman Catholic faith, having attended St Peter's church all his life. Apparently, this was a cause for much amusement 'cos St Peter's was just yards from the Methodist Chapel. Anyway, George left his wife and set up house with Edna on Mortimer Row. He'd only been married to his first wife for a matter of months and, as far I know, they never got divorced. The First World War was just around the corner. Herbert went off to fight and never came back.

My last relative who lived not too far away was my Auntie Mary. She was another of my father's sisters and she lived at 23 Napier Terrace which was on the other side of Leeds Road. She worked at Bradford Moor Library, along with Auntie Lucy. Auntie Mary had been married but her husband had died in the fever hospital which was not too far away from us, again, down Leeds Road. A lot happened down Leeds Road! She didn't have any children but did have a lodger called Tom. They both worked at the nearby spinning mill. I think this was an arrangement that suited them both very well and didn't put them in any danger of being ignored like Edna and George were. Auntie Mary was very tall as well and she looked more like my father than any of the others. I'd have gone to see her more if I could but with her house being across the main road, I wasn't allowed to go that far. I did one day, of course, and that landed me in big trouble.

All the other relatives lived a long way from us. My mother's brother Alfred and his wife Hilda, lived in London. They were both killed in the London Blitz and one of my father's sisters, Lizzie, had moved to

Newcastle and married Albert Watson. We never met them or our three cousins, George, Beverley and Vera.

18:07:21 – 18:14:46

When he'd caught his breath again and, knowing his laces were secure, he steadied himself on the zimmer frame, making sure the brown plastic shopping bag was secured properly by the belt. He crossed the pavement and lowered himself slowly onto the road, one foot at a time, the zimmer frame giving him something to hold on to. He took great care to avoid the big puddle which was still there. The flats were in a cul-de-sac, the main obstacle being the large flower bed down the middle of the road. He smiled when he thought about the flower bed because there had not been any flowers in it for year. There were half a dozen small trees which had lovely pink blossom each spring and a few larger ones too but the ground under them was just bare earth with a few weeds sprouting up here and there. He liked the trees as he enjoyed watching the birds as they flew in and out of the. So, after shuffling over the first part of the road he lifted the zimmer frame up onto the flower bed.

He now realised he'd have been better going to the end of the road and avoiding the flower bed because, after the rain, it had become muddy. Now his boots pressed into soft black mud and the zimmer frame made little splashes as he put it down at each step. There were some stones, too, which made him even more unsteady as his feet slipped between them. Things would have been a lot better if the nearby street light had not been out, either. It took another nine small, shuffling steps to get across the flower bed and then the process was reversed as he went over the kerb and down onto the road again at the other side. He kicked the boots against the kerb to try and get rid of some mud but only succeeded in making a sharp pain shoot up his left leg.

He was nearly at the other side when he felt something soft under his right foot and realised he'd stood in a pile of dog dirt. He'd often seen people bringing their dogs down the cul-de-sac and, thinking that no one was looking, let them leave their doings on the flower bed. The council had put up a notice but it was ignored. So now he'd the result of this under his boot. He wiped it off as best he could on the edge of the kerb before stepping up onto the pavement and turning right towards the fish and chip shop.

You Can Choose Your Friends

With all these relatives living so close by, if any of us wanted any help or had a problem to sort out, or just wanted to talk to someone, there was always somewhere we could go. In them days lots of families lived near each other, not like nowadays when folks move all over the country at the drop of a hat and never see other 'cept at weddings and funerals. And, even then, they don't really want to see each other. They just turn up out of duty. They say you can choose your friends but not your family. I think, though, that I was very lucky 'cos I'd a very loving family when I was growing up. Mother had to work hard to keep us all going but we were never short of food and the house was kept clean. She was also very caring and always had time to help anyone who needed it. I remember there was a family just down the street from us whose father had been killed in some industrial accident. I don't know where he worked, maybe engineering, but back then the health and safety laws we have now hadn't been invented. As a result, accidents were often fatal and for the family concerned this was a tragedy. The Welfare State hadn't been invented, either, so the widow or what we would call a single parent these days, had to manage as best they could. This is where close communities came in 'cos families all helped each other in times of such need, even if they had very little themselves. And this is what my mother did. We were rich compared to some folk we knew, so she was always cooking a bit extra and it was often my job to pop down the street with a bowl of this or that for the fatherless family. I think Auntie Shackleton used to send stuff for them as well.

I was too young to think about the differences then but now I look back I don't remember them having much in their house at all. I used to play with one of the children. He was called John and if I was round there and it was raining, his mother would send us upstairs to play. It got us out of her way, I suppose. No one could afford carpets back then but there can't have been any lino or rugs on the floor either in their house, as I got splinters in my fingers a few times from the old floorboards. It was also a bit untidy upstairs 'cos all their coats were on their beds. We used to hang our coats up on hooks at the back of the kitchen door. But they were a bit short on doors and didn't even have a door between the kitchen and the front room, either. I'd once heard my father telling mother about people burning doors to keep warm because they couldn't afford to buy coal. Maybe he was talking about them.

John had two sisters who were both older than him, so John had the smallest bedroom to himself. They had a three bedroomed house like ours, so his sisters shared the second bedroom and I suppose their mother had the main one. John's bedroom was what we'd call a box room today or, to put it in more posh terms, a study. It seemed a large room for one person to me, as it was the same size that Jack and me shared back at number 44. He had a single bed with some boxes underneath where he seemed to keep his clothes, like we did. I don't think his had the smell ours had, though, 'cos he didn't get his clothes from his cousins like we did so they probably weren't in boxes for years on end. Anyway, one day, John's mother asked me if I'd like to stay the night. A sleepover it's called these days. This was an exciting prospect for a little lad who'd never gone much further than the allotment. My mother wasn't too keen on the idea but I'd a way of getting round her and I spent the night at John's house. That's how I know they didn't have blankets. The coats I'd seen on the beds were used to keep them warm. And that wasn't all. I'd shared the little bed with John but there were more than two of us in it 'cos in the morning I was covered in little red marks and they itched. John must have been immune from them 'cos he was ok. I went back home looking like I'd got the measles.

Mother was horrified but not as much as me 'cos I wasn't allowed out for a week in case someone saw me. She covered all those itchy bites with bright pink calamine lotion and then an even more dreadful discovery was made a few days later just as the blotches were going down. I'd creepy crawlies in my hair. So, my head was plastered with a paste made with vinegar and some sort of powder and I'd to keep this on for what seemed like hours before it was washed off in very, very hot water. This had to be done every day for a week. The worst thing was that everyone else had to do this as well. My two older sisters, Alice and Annie who were teenagers then were furious with me. No one spoke to me until all the lice had disappeared. After that, I started to play out a lot more with my little brother Jack and this turned out to be much better for me in the long run. We'd the sort of childhood that can be only dreamed about these days. We had freedom. No-one had heard of paedophiles and I don't think we'd many muggers or rapists living nearby, either, although there was possibly the Piggeries murderer somewhere amongst us, before he was caught.

Anyway, thinking back to home. My mother had long, dark hair which came down to her waist. Just like Grannie Annie, 'cept hers was white. I'd watch mother brushing it every day and sometimes she'd give me the brush and let me do it for her. In a house full of people there's always something to do and as we got older, we were all given jobs. My eldest sister, Annie, looked after the beds. Changing sheets was her job. My second sister, Alice, had to help mother with the washing. I always thought this was unfair 'cos it didn't take long to change the sheets but it took ages to do the washing. Anyway, that's how it was. My third sister, Norma, looked after the floors. They needed sweeping every day and once a week she'd to polish the lino and shake out the rugs. My fourth sister, Helen, had to do the vegetables every Sunday. This doesn't sound much of a job but as mother liked us all to sit down together, there were mountains of vegetables to do, especially when the allotment was in full swing and I'd been down there with Grandad Coble. Father had the job of bringing up the coal from the cellar which he did before he went to work and again when he came home. If we needed more during the day when he wasn't there mother used to go and get it. We also had what we called the coal hole in the back yard. This was next to the toilet but we didn't use it much for coal 'cos it was very damp and the coal got wet. The only time I remember it being used was when mother was expecting a baby and father put some coal in there so she didn't have to go up and down the cellar steps.

Then there was little me. My job became setter of the table which I liked doing. It didn't take too long and I could often chat to mother on her own as I did it. As my little brother Jack got bigger, we did it together and I eventually moved on to help with the washing up, whilst he took over the table setting duties. I became chief floor sweeper, too, and we all had to help to top up the water in the boiler which was something that seemed to need doing all the time. So, in our own ways, we all helped towards looking after each other by helping in the family. It was expected of us. Not like nowadays when, it seems to me, that youngsters can do what they like. Not that I know a lot of youngsters but I can't imagine any of those I do know spending a Sunday morning doing vegetables or bringing the coal in.

Not that there's coal to bring in with modern houses all having central heating which looks after itself but there are other things to do instead such as gardening. No, I think they'd rather be in their bedrooms playing computer games.

My father was very tall and a good-looking man. At least, that's what my mother said. He worked for the council as a labourer repairing the roads. It must have been a dirty job 'cos there was always a pair of his trousers drying in front of the fire. We didn't see much of him, except on a Sunday when we all sat round the kitchen table for Sunday dinner as, after his tea during the week, he usually went off to the local pub, the Lord Napier, which was just at the end of our street. He never came back the worse for drink, which was a great relief to us all, but he did spend money we could have used in better ways. Mother stayed at home to see to us. She never went with him. Years later I found out that he was a gambler as well as a drinker. I suppose the two go together. By all accounts, he was quite good at this gambling and his winnings must have helped to pay for his beer. When you're little you don't realise what worries and troubles anyone but yourself has. I don't remember any arguments or anything like that in our house, but I think my mother must have had constant money worries, especially with the drinking and gambling going on all the time. No wonder she was glad of the boxes of hand-me-downs under our bed. But, I think my mother and father were genuinely in love with each other and whatever faults they found were ignored. She always looked forward to him coming home at the end of each day and he greeted her with a hug and a kiss. They must certainly have been happy in bed, you might say, having produced all us lot.

As I said earlier, our rented house had three bedrooms. Some of the houses on the other side only had two, like Uncle Leopold, so we counted ourselves lucky. Some houses further down the street were known as back-to-back houses as they shared their back wall with another house which faced in the opposite direction, so to speak. That meant they only had one outside door. You got to the houses at the other side by going through passages between every four houses. The houses next to these passages had a third bedroom 'cos it went over the top of the passageway. We usually came into our house through the back door which led straight into the kitchen where there was a big fireplace. The water boiler was here and an Airedale Range with an open fire and an oven to one side with a place on top for pans and kettles. Topping up the water boiler was a constant job and hard work, especially on Fridays when we all had our weekly dip in the tin bath in front of the fire. The art of queueing was learnt at home from an early age! Our kitchen table was in the middle and, with seven chairs round it, this was our home headquarters. As there was always a baby in the house a high-chair stood in one corner ready for use until Jack got too big for it and then there were eight chairs. Most decisions and discussions happened around that table. And arguments, of course, although I don't remember there being too many of those. But I do remember one about rabbits.

It was my mother's idea. She thought it would do me good to have an interest and looking after a pet seemed to fit the bill, at least in her eyes. It was to be a present for my sixth birthday, which was on 7th June 1930. We didn't go in for surprises in our family but tried to get something the person in question actually wanted. Not that we could afford. I'd told my mother about someone at school having a rabbit, so she must have got the idea from me. I was thrilled to bits 'cos I didn't have much in the way of possessions and I liked the thought of having something all my own. On the other hand, father thought it was a complete waste of money. He counted any spare cash we did manage to have in pints of beer and just said no. Anyway, I don't know what happened after I'd been sent to bed or what my mother had said or done to win him over but I came home from school a couple of days later to find a rabbit hutch in the back yard with a little black bunny rabbit in it. I was so excited I told everyone I met. I think Grandad Coble had made the hutch. I called the rabbit Lucky and she became my best friend. I talked to her a lot and told her all my secrets.

Feeding her was no problem as there was always something from the allotment and she got our vegetable peelings and bits of dried bread as well. She seemed to eat anything. I loved cleaning her out and making her little house neat and tidy, just like Grandad Coble's allotment shed. I also enjoyed playing with her. I made an obstacle course for her in the back yard. She'd to go through a piece of pipe I'd found, walk up a ramp and across a bridge and then down another ramp so she could get back to her hutch. I used a carrot or something to encourage her and she learnt how to do most things. It was great fun for me and the hours I spent with Lucky were very happy ones. I suppose it also kept me out of mother's way during the long summer holiday. With me, and sometimes Jack, safely playing in the back yard, she could get on with everything she'd to do. One, and sometimes two, less to think about. The girls seemed to look after themselves.

But my happiness was short lived. The first thing I did on a morning after getting up and dressed was to visit the doings which was in the corner of the yard and, of course, I always looked in at Lucky on the way there. She was usually sat there watching out for me and stood up as soon as I called her name. But on this particular morning as I was making my usual dash, I saw there was no sign of Lucky and then I saw that the padlock was down on the floor. It must have been a Saturday 'cos I'd decided that I would be able to clean her out that day. She couldn't have got out on her own 'cos every night before I went to bed, I went to say goodnight to her and to make sure she was shut in properly. I always checked that the padlock was in place and that the gate to the back yard was shut as well. I couldn't put the bolts in place as my sisters needed to be able to get back in if they had gone out and my father definitely needed to after he'd been to see Lord Napier. My time in the doings was as short as possible and I flew out to see where she was, thinking she was still in the hutch on her little straw bed.

I'd taken to doing extra jobs around the house in the hope of a few pennies. Auntie Shackleton also helped out in this direction too. My main job for her was to sweep her kitchen floor. I don't think I did it too well but she always paid up. Grandma Lawton was also helpful in that direction, too. I swept her back yard instead of the kitchen. Grannie Annie gave me a few pennies from time to time and Grandad Coble, rather begrudgingly, paid me for feeding the hens. So, that's how I managed to buy straw for Lucky. I didn't want father going on about the rabbit being a drain on the few resources we'd. But, when I opened the door she wasn't there. She'd gone and I was beside myself with grief. I ran in to tell my mother and she'd to spend some of her precious time helping me look for her. The hutch was stood on four bricks to keep it dry and so I always put the key for the padlock underneath the hutch but when we looked it wasn't there. This would all have been around the middle of August. I'd only had her for a few weeks and I remember spending the whole of the following week going between crying and hoping she'd come back. I searched all the back yards, with the help of Jack, and pestered everyone in my quest to find her. I even asked my mother to go to the police but she didn't think it was important enough. No one owned up to having seen her.

On one of these searches, I wandered a bit further then I should have done and went down Thornbury Street. It was only a few minutes from Napier Street but where the folks in our street were poor, the folks in Thornbury Street were regarded as being even poorer. I'd to pass a bunch of older lads who I'd seen from time to time at school and asked them about Lucky. They all started laughing which I didn't understand. But, as I walked away one of them began singing a song about a rabbit, which included the word dinner. Lucky, had, of course, grown quite a bit so when the penny dropped and I realised what had probably happened to Lucky I was even more upset. I'd chosen the wrong name. This time my father got his way and the hutch soon disappeared. My only consolation was that it was only a week or so to go before school started again and I would be back with my pals even though my best pal had gone.

My mother, of course, tried to comfort me as best she could and Auntie Shackleton gave me all the buns and cakes I wanted until I was full to bursting. It was eating all these that probably gave me my nickname of Buster. Jack was upset at the loss of Lucky, too, but I don't remember any of my sisters being too bothered. And father certainly wasn't. Auntie Mary, though was very bothered by it all and after a visit to our house my mother said that I could go to Auntie Mary's house by myself, providing I took great care crossing Leeds Road. I think this was Auntie Mary's way of trying to make things better for me. The prospect of making that journey on my own certainly perked me up. After all, I went to school that way every day but then I went with my sisters and other children from our street and didn't cross Leeds Road by myself.

Anyway, as it happened, Annie took me to Leeds Road and saw me safely across with the usual warning to look carefully each way on the way home. At Auntie Mary's I had a lovely time looking at some books she'd been keeping for me and she helped me with a bit of writing, too. When it was time to go home, she gave me a book to take with me and I was so thrilled I couldn't wait to get back to show it to Jack. So, I ran all the way down Napier Terrace, straight into Leeds Road without stopping and straight into the path of a motorcyclist who swerved all over the road and then fell off. I tripped up and fell into road but then, as I didn't think I'd been hurt got up and just ran off as fast as I could. By the time I'd got home, though, my left leg was hurting and I sat hiding in the doings for ages worried that the motorcyclist was going to come and tell mother, or even worse father, what I'd done. Then I heard our back gate creak open. We never bothered putting the bolts on anymore since Lucky had gone. Anyway, looking out between the cracks in the door, I saw it was Trickie Dickie. This was our local policeman and he was known as Bobby Raistrick. His nickname was Trickie but as his first name was Richard he eventually became Trickie Dickie. It was quite a joke in our neighbourhood. We never bothered to put the bolts on now that Lucky had gone. He'd been on his pushbike nearby and had seen everything. After he'd gone, I crept out and went into the kitchen. Annie came rushing over to see if I was alright. She sat me down at the table with a glass of milk. Trickie Dickie had been to make sure I wasn't injured and told Annie that the motorcyclist had been going too fast. My left leg was never the same again. The book Auntie Mary had given me was The Boys Own Book of Astronomy.

Then a few weeks after that episode, I woke up in the middle of the night and needed to go to the doings. This was something I always dreaded. In our house we called the toilet the 'doings'. I don't know why we did but we just did. Maybe it's a Yorkshire expression. It seems to me it's been known by lots of different names. Sometimes it's a privy, from the French for privee meaning private, I think. At school we called it the bog and then in posh dance halls years ago the girl's toilet was The Powder Room. Then again, in some places it's referred to as going to the bathroom and if you are royal, you must say lavatory. A woman called Lucinda Lampton even did a series about toilets on the tele. My niece tells me there's a restaurant in Okinawa in Japan where the whole theme is bathrooms and the chairs are made out of toilets. I'm not sure I'd fancy eating anything in a place like that.

Anyway, in our house it was called the doings and it was in the back yard. It was a tippler toilet because of the way it worked. To get to ours you had to go out of the back door and down two steps. These were Yorkshire stone and very slippery in wet weather. There was a railing to one side of the steps but it was always loose. Just like the hand rail at my flat. Anyhow, father had fastened it together with a piece of strong string but one push and it would have fallen down. I don't think that DIY was his strong point and mother didn't have the time. They could have asked Grandad Coble, or even Uncle Willie 'cos he was very handy with a hammer. He was always doing things for Auntie Shackleton. In fact, he was probably one of the first men in the country to DIY. I remember going round one day when he was papering the ceiling in the front room. Auntie Shackleton was having to help him 'cos the paper kept falling down on his head. I don't know why I was there at that particular time, as I must have been in the way, but it was like watching a comedy show. They were both perched on step ladders and took the piece of paper upwards together, one at each end of the room. Then they lifted it towards the ceiling and Uncle Willie started brushing it on. But, as he came down his step ladder to move towards Auntie Shackleton the section that he'd just done always began to drop down and at one point he was all wrapped up in it. I must've left before they finished but I always made a point of looking at all the creases in the ceiling every time I was allowed into their front room.

Another time, poor old Uncle Willie tried to put some lino down in the kitchen. Although the floors of our houses were made of wood and most of us who could afford to keep fires going did so, the floors were cold and we often covered them up with rugs to keep the draughts out. Fitted carpets were unheard of. The nearest to a fitted carpet was a carpet square but these, when they could be afforded, were kept for pride of place in the front room, not a kitchen. Sometimes houses had stone floors and these would be even colder. To keep houses warm lots of people made rag rugs like we did. We made ours during the long, dark winter evenings and I helped my sisters do them. We used up old clothes, often mine and Jack's, tore them into strips and then tied them onto a backing sheet. I enjoyed doing that 'cos you could see the results of your efforts for the rest of the year. Anyway, Uncle Willie wanted to put down lino and must have decided to stick it to the floor. He'd been given a very large pot of very smelly glue and was apparently going to paint this on the floor before sticking the lino down. He'd cut the lino to size and had managed to position one end near the window and had put the pot of glue on the floor. Again, I don't know why I was there on that day but I shall never forget him stepping back and at the same time as he knocked over the tin of glue, he stood on the upturned lid which, of course, had glue on it.

First, he tried to get the lid off his foot. He did this alright but, of course, the sole of his slipper was still covered with glue and when he put his foot down again the slipper stuck to the floor and his foot came out leaving the slipper behind. He was so surprised at this that he put his other foot in the mess of glue which was slowly sliding out of the knocked over tin. Auntie Shackleton and me were doubled up with laughing but dare not laugh out loud as Uncle Willie had a temper which was, so I'd heard, a sight to behold. He didn't lose it very often but my mother told me that when he was angry it was best to avoid him until he'd calmed down. So, we tried to hide our laughter but couldn't. He suddenly turned on us, said some very rude words and marched out leaving his slippers and socks behind, all stuck to the floor. Auntie Shackleton and me laughed until we'd tears running down our faces. She made us both a cup of tea and I'd two buns. It didn't seem too long, however, before he was back. He'd a cup of tea and I went home leaving them to it. The next time I went round the kitchen floor had got its lino and the matter was never mentioned again.

Back to the outside doings. The doings itself was in a little brick building in a corner of the back yard which was split into two compartments. In one was the doings and we kept a couple of buckets of coal in the other. It's a wonder the coal didn't get stolen like Lucky did. Our main coal delivery went down the chute at the front of the house and straight into the cellar. Anyhow, both these compartments had wooden doors which were painted black and the doings had a small square hole in it at the top in the middle. There was no glass but was the only way light could get in. It was really draughty in winter and sometimes rain and even snow would blow in when you were perched there on the rough wooden seat. It wasn't unknown to find an icicle. The door didn't shut properly, either. In summer it turned into spider city. Occasionally one would come down on a thread to within inches of your face. Fortunately, those were the small ones. It was the ones with wire legs we didn't like. The flies weren't too nice, either. Mother kept putting up those blue flypapers. These were sticky strips of paper and if a fly landed on one it couldn't get off. but I think the flies cottoned onto this and avoided them. Sometimes we got proper toilet paper but at other times, possibly when gambling hadn't been very good, we'd to make do with old newspaper. Once mother got hold of some sort of very thin, bright blue paper which suddenly appeared in there. I think it came from Uncle Leopold's crockery shop. We didn't use it for very long, though, 'cos the blue came off not only on our hands but also all over our backsides as well.

So, if you needed to go in the middle of the night, you either had to hang on until dawn or else you made the journey in the pitch black out of the back door and across the yard. For some reason we didn't possess a chamber pot or slop bucket as they were known, so that wasn't an option, so to speak. I don't think mother liked the idea of carrying anything like that through the house each morning. She often told us the tale of how a neighbour had once found a dead rat in the slop bucket. Rats were everywhere in them days. Mind you, they are today so we're told. They say you're never really more than ten feet from one. The dustmen used to empty the doings in them days and once when the dustmen were busy emptying the privy of another neighbour, Mrs Illingworth, they heard a rat. Anyway, they didn't fancy dealing with it and help came in the shape of a little terrier dog, called Flossie, which the dustmen carried about in their cart for such an emergency. Flossie was a legend in her own lifetime, apparently, for she always got her rat. I think the dustmen used to hire her out when someone had a rat problem. I don't know who owned Flossie. Maybe it was the council.

So, that was why we didn't have a chamber pot and why I was having to go outside in the middle of the night. Somehow, as I've said, I'd always managed to hang on but that night it was impossible, so I set off. I crept down the stairs as quietly as I could and let myself out the back door. After seeing to my business in the doings, I found that the back door wouldn't open. It had been locked. I didn't know what to do. I did know, though, that I couldn't knock anyone up 'cos if father came down, I would have been in deep trouble. So, I stood there shivering. It must have been winter 'cos I was soon cold. I'd my pyjamas on and a pair of slippers but no dressing gown. We didn't run to such luxuries and I wished I'd put my coat on. But then, I hadn't been expecting to be locked out.

So, I decided to go to Auntie Shackleton's house. It was only in the next street to ours, Dundas Street. It seemed a better idea than trying to curl up in the doings until next morning. So, I set off. My slippers were very old and had needed replacing for ages. They had little holes in the soles which now let all the damp from the pavements come through. Mother had put some cardboard in them but it didn't work very well. I went through the back gate thankful we didn't use the bolts any more. Once in the back alley I walked as quickly as I could. There was no-one around and it was very scary. But just after I got to the end and had turned right towards Dundas Street, I saw someone walking towards me.

It was Tricky Dicky doing his night rounds, a beat it was called. I don't think they bother with all that these days. At one time they went around in black and white cars. They called them panda cars but you don't see them nowadays. Our local police station has closed as well. There's a telephone on the wall we can use if it's an emergency but as often as not it's broken. Someone enjoys trying to pull it off the wall. The next police station is only open part time. They probably think that everyone has a mobile phone but I haven't and if I was outside and needed the police, I'm not sure what I'd do. I've got a loud voice which goes with the rest of me so I suppose I could call out but that's no good if there's no one to hear. I've got a telephone in my flat now and if I need the police quickly, I can dial 999 if it's a proper emergency.

So, there was Tricky walking towards me. He didn't see me at first and I panicked a bit 'cos there was nowhere to hide. I'd passed all the backyards I could have nipped into. I knew I was in trouble when he called out my name. 'Harry, Harry. What are you doing here?' In them days when the policemen had the same beat all the time and walked around instead of being in cars, it wasn't unusual for them to get to know all the children in an area. That's how Tricky knew me. Knowing the children's names and where they lived probably kept crime down, as well. Anyway, I thought the whole neighbourhood would be looking out of their curtains any minute he shouted at me so loudly. So, it suddenly came to me what to do and I pretended to be sleepwalking. I didn't really know what sleepwalkers did but I'd seen a picture of someone with their arms straight out in front of them, so that's what I did. I'd to keep my eyes open, mind you, or I wouldn't have been able to see where I was going. I hoped he didn't know what a sleepwalker looked like, either.

I didn't answer when he spoke to me, just stared straight ahead. He didn't seem to know what he should be doing but he gently turned me round, got hold of my arm and led me quietly back home. He even took his jacket off and put it around me as I was shivering that much. My heart was thumping by the time we got to our house and I wondered if I should pretend to wake up. I began wishing I'd spent the night in the doings after all. When we got there, I stood on the back doorstep with him, trembling. I was cold and very frightened.

After waiting for what seemed like hours after Tricky had knocked on the door, it was opened. My heart was in my mouth in case it was father who'd heard us. I can still remember the relief I felt when it was Annie and the look on her face when she saw it was a policeman and me. I still couldn't pretend to wake up in case father appeared so, when Tricky had gone, after telling her why we were there, she took me in, led me up the stairs and I was soon back in bed, none the worse for my outing except my feet were still cold the next morning. I never, ever went to the doings again in the middle of the night.

18:14:46 – 18:20:02

With the smell of the dog dirt becoming fainter he continued along the pavement until he reached the corner where he turned left to go down the hill. He'd gone 100 yards. He stopped for a rest and sat for a moment on the low wall, realising as he did so that his right trouser leg was tight which meant the bag was full and needed emptying. He'd had lots of cups of tea today at the Day Centre and wished he'd done it when he'd got home this afternoon.

So, he got up and set off again. It was only a few steps before he could see the drain at the side of the road. This was a good place to stop because there were no windows in the sides of the buildings to his left and the windows of the houses across the road were hidden by trees. It was also between lamp posts which meant it wasn't too brightly lit, either. After checking up and down the road to see if anyone was coming, he bent down to pull up his right trouser leg. He'd to tug at it because the bag had expanded a lot and for a moment he thought he wouldn't be able to get at the valve to release the contents. However, the little valve appeared, so he lifted his leg over the kerbstone and put his foot in the gutter just near the drain, using the zimmer frame, which was on the pavement, to steady himself. He reached down once more, pulled at the valve and was pleased when he heard the trickle of water and felt the weight of the bag going down.

Just as the bag was nearly empty, a little white dog suddenly appeared and began sniffing round his legs. He tried to knock it away with his hand but it just ran round to the other side, looked up at him and then cocked its leg up against his left leg and ran off again. It had only been a small dog but it had managed to thoroughly soak his trousers. He could feel the warmth of the wetness. He made a mental note to wash his trousers in the bath when he got home. Anyway, there was nothing he could do right now so, once he felt that the bag had been emptied properly, he pressed the valve, shook his leg so that the trouser leg went down and lifted his foot onto the pavement. He was thankful that only a few drops had fallen onto his sock. Once, when he'd carried out this routine, he hadn't noticed where the valve was pointing and had managed to fill his boot with the contents. Now all he could feel was the wet trouser material clinging to his left leg. However, despite the dog, he felt rather pleased that he'd managed to drain the bag before anyone had passed by, apart from a few cars, which didn't matter. So, he set off again.

A Change of Circumstances

One Saturday it was raining heavily and mother and father had gone off shopping on their own. We usually went to Grannie Annie's on these occasions but that day me and Jack went to Grandma Lawton's instead. This made a real change for us, as we only usually went there with mother. I liked Grandma Lawton's house. It was cosy as she'd a liking for things which were pink. This gave the inside a sort of glow. Or so it seemed to me. Grandma was pink, as well. She'd a kind, round pink face with her white hair tied up on the top of head and she'd nearly always be wearing a pink jumper or blouse, often one she'd made herself. She was the proud owner of a Singer sewing machine which took pride of place in her front room. My sisters used it a lot as they got older and needed new fashionable clothes. Anyway, she was very good at making things and there was always some knitting in the chair by the fire in the kitchen, where she spent most of her time. She made jumpers for us and it was Grandma's jumpers which Jack and me pulled out of shape that time we were playing at being Auntie Lily. Anyway, there we were at Grandma Lawton's until someone came to collect us later that day.

There was always some fresh baking in her house, too, and Grandma's baking was not to be missed. She didn't run to icing or currants but for two ever hungry little boys Grandma's buns were a treat. We washed them down with ginger beer which she made herself with what she called her ginger beer plant. She kept this on her kitchen windowsill. I don't know how this worked but whatever it was, it was delicious and didn't seem to do us any harm. Not like today when everything is filled with chemicals and then we wonder why we all have allergies and get poorly so often. So, we wolfed down our buns and ginger beer and then Grandma suddenly asked us if we'd like to see something very special. She said she'd been saving this for us. She got out of her chair and waved at us to follow. We were going upstairs.

This was a revelation 'cos we'd never been allowed up there. This part of Grandma's house was regarded as the inner sanctum only to be entered on pain of death. A bit like the front room at home which belonged to mother and father. However, as Grandma was with us it was alright. It was the same with mother's handbag and purse or father's jacket. We'd been taught respect for other people's property both at home, Sunday School and school itself. It was a code most people lived by in them days. You could go out shopping or nip out for a gossip and not lock the door. Everything was safe, although I don't suppose many folk had anything which was worth stealing in the first place, except in our house we'd the treasured gramophone and a radio. So, this trip up the staircase was unbelievable to us. What an adventure!

Grandma Lawton's house was different to ours. It was a back-to-back so, when you came through her door there was a little hallway with the stairs right in front of you. There were two rooms downstairs, the one to the right was the kitchen where most time was spent and the other one, on the left, was known as the front room and always kept for best. This meant that it was hardly ever used except when Grandma wanted to go on her sewing machine. There were two rooms upstairs, too, one to the right and one to the left. The only windows were at the front, too. I don't know how Grandma Lawton and five children had fitted in there.

So, we followed Grandma up the stairs. She'd to stop twice to catch her breath so it was quite a long journey for two little boys wondering about the surprise in store for them. The stairs eventually led to a tiny landing which would have been really dark except one of the two doors up there was open so some light was coming from there. Both doors were painted a dark brown. Of course, that's all there was up there. No bathroom. It was all a bit spooky to me and Jack. The walls were a dark colour, as well. Green, I think. Magnolia and brilliant white hadn't been invented at that time. It would also have been lead paint which is now banned. Most of the houses, were of course, rented so decorating them wasn't very important. No point in using up good money to give it back to the landlord in improvements. You just lived with what you got when you found a house to rent. Unless you were Uncle Willie and DIY was your hobby. The colours in our house were more or less the same as at Grandma's.

So, back to the landing and its two brown doors. I managed to peep inside the open door and I could see this room was all pink, too. The walls were lighter in here but the cover on the bed was definitely pink. I'd never seen Grandma in bed but I imagined the sheets to be pink as well as Grandma's nightdresses. I think there was a little pink rug at the side of the bed, too. Anyway, we didn't go in there but Grandma opened the other brown door. Today this would be used as a bathroom. There was hardly any room to swing a cat but we all squeezed in. There was a very narrow single bed behind the door and nothing else except a very large, very old tin trunk under the small window and a little wooden stool in the corner.

Jack and me sat down on the bed wondering why we'd come up here. It ran through my mind that Grandma wasn't a nice person at all and that she was about to lock us up in the bedroom for the rest of our lives. However, Grandma sat down on the little wooden stool and pushed the tin trunk towards us. 'Here,' she said, 'is your surprise.' Well, it certainly was 'cos we couldn't understand why anyone would be interested in an old battered tin trunk. Then, suddenly, Grandma put her hand down the front of her pink jumper. I nearly fell off the bed. I just couldn't imagine what she was going to show us next. But I needn't have worried 'cos she pulled out a little key on a long piece of string. She'd kept that well-hidden, I thought. What a place to keep a key. I made a mental note to remember that for future use. Then she leaned over and unlocked the lid of the trunk.

Me and Jack looked at each other and hesitated. The last fifteen minutes or so had been so strange that there could have been anything in there. A dragon maybe, ready to come to life breathing fire. I wondered if she'd found Lucky and put my lost rabbit in there. Or, maybe coins or jewellery from a robbery. Perhaps toys. The big red bus I never seemed to get at Christmas could be there. Maybe food. A birthday cake with candles on but I couldn't think whose birthday it was. On the other hand, it could be a skull with big empty staring eye holes. I couldn't bear to think about that. I'd seen pictures of them in the books that Auntie Mary read to me but didn't want to see one in real life. I could see that Jack was as worried as me. So, we watched as Grandma lifted the lid up. It was a very anxious moment.

As the lid came up, the first thing I noticed was the funny smell. It wasn't a nasty smell but I'd not come across it before. We must have wrinkled our noses at the smell 'cos I remember Grandma telling us the smell wouldn't kill us as it was only mothballs. I hadn't heard of those before and my childish imagination suddenly told me that Grandma was breeding moths and that hundreds were about to fly out into our faces. I got ready to run. I couldn't stand insects flying or crawling and I still can't. If I come across a spider in the bath, I always give it a free ride down the plug hole as fast as possible. So, she pushed the lid all the way back and we saw a sheet of brown paper covering up the contents. My mind was still boggling at the thought of those moths about to fly out. 'Now,' she said, 'take the paper off and see what's in there.' Jack had to do that. I just couldn't in case of the moth things. But I'd no need to worry 'cos underneath was an army uniform.

Grandma helped us to lift out the top jacket which was very carefully folded. By this time Jack and me were kneeling on the floor at the side of the trunk. We laid the jacket carefully on the bed and Grandma unfolded it. It was bright red and had gold buttons. There was some gold braid round the neck and the sleeves. It was, to our eyes, the most beautiful thing we'd ever seen. After that we looked in the trunk again and brought out a white belt, some white gloves and a pair of black trousers, again with gold braid down the side. I don't remember seeing a hat. At the bottom of the trunk there was a small cardboard box which Grandma lifted out with tears in her eyes. Inside were a lot of papers. I think they were letters. She picked up an envelope which had black edging but didn't open it. Then she told us the story of how Grandad Lawton had been a soldier and was killed when he fell off his horse during the Boer war, at a place called Colesberg which, she told us, was in South Africa. All these had belonged to Grandad Lawton. Jack wanted to know if Grandad had been killed in the red jacket but Grandma said that they never sent him back so she never got to bury him properly. She'd kept his spare uniform 'cos that was all she had to remind her of him.

She put the envelope with the black edge back in the cardboard box with the other pieces of paper and we put everything back into the trunk very carefully, folding all the clothes exactly as they had been. Then we closed the lid and I was given the important job of locking the trunk and handing the key back to Grandma. It disappeared down the front of her jumper where it had come from. Grandma stood up, put the little stool back in the corner, pushed the trunk back under the window and wiped her eyes on her sleeve. Then she went downstairs and we followed, our heads full of what we'd just seen and been told. We were both given a big hug when we got to the bottom and Grandma gave us a cup of tea and a slice of cake. We'd just about eaten all our cake when Annie called in to collect us. When we got home, we told mother all about Grandad's trunk and she said that it was the anniversary of the day Grandad had been killed. That was why Grandma had chosen that particular day to show us the trunk. She'd asked mother to take us there specially. We never got to see the trunk again though. Grandma died a few weeks later. Father found her sat in her chair with her pink knitting in her lap. I can still feel that last hug she gave me. I didn't go to her funeral and I don't know where she's buried. I sometimes wonder what happened to the red uniform.

Not far away from Laisterdyke there's a place called Tyersal. This is where Annie and Sam lived after they were married and there's a street there called Arkwright Street. This is one of those streets called after someone. In this case it was the inventor of the spinning frame. The big mill at Tyersal was W & J Whitehead's and it was a spinning mill using the same machinery that Arkwright had invented. Arkwright came from Lancashire where they spun cotton which had come all the way from America or India 'cos we couldn't grow cotton. But here in Yorkshire we were able to grow wool on our own sheep. At Whitehead's they took in the fleeces from the sheep and at the other end woollen yarn came out. A lot of this was used for military uniforms in the first and second world wars. I suppose some of it was used for knitting wool and maybe that's where Grandma Lawton's wool had come from. Cotton wouldn't have been any good for uniforms, although I suppose it would have been alright out in the desert.

Now, not far from Arkwright Street there was a big house called Coronation House and that was where our coalman, Mr Shuttleworth lived. I remember him as a really nice man. He'd a red face and a large moustache and always wore a flat cap. Sometimes if mother was a bit short of cash, he'd still deliver our coal and told her to pay him the next time she saw him. Whitsuntide was a very important time in our annual calendar. Not only did we get new clothes which didn't come out from under the bed but we also got to go to the Bun Field riding on Mr Shuttleworth's coal cart on Whit Monday. One year we went on Mr Callendar's cart. He was the local greengrocer and anyone riding on his cart got to hold cabbages and cauliflowers. He was very generous and let his young passengers keep what they'd been holding. His was the most popular cart even if you only got to hold an onion. The carts were pulled by horses which were dressed up in ribbons and bows and the carts themselves were decorated with flags and bunting. I remember it as being very colourful.

As I've said, we'd plenty of shops nearby. In fact, you could buy almost everything in Laisterdyke. We'd plenty of entertainment right on the doorstep, too, 'cos we'd pubs, social clubs and the Lyceum Cinema. Then, of course, there were lots of churches and they were always having social do's to raise money. I suppose it's still the same today with churches running jumble sales and Christmas Fairs in their church halls. Anyway, mother paid into a weekly account at Stead's shop down Leeds Road. That meant that when we needed anything such as a pair of shoes, all we'd to do was go down and get them. Father's records from there, too. It was a sort of savings scheme, I suppose. Mind you, that wasn't to say that when a pair of shoes was worn out it wasn't passed down the line until they were completely gone. This concerned the girls more than Jack and me. Jack was lucky in that way, 'cos I've always had very large feet and my old shoes were always far too big for him until he was a lot older so he was taken to Steads when he needed new shoes. Then, just before Whitsuntide we'd all traipse down to Steads to be kitted out. Jack and me usually got new short trousers, a new shirt and a jacket. That's each, not between us. The girls got new dresses. Then on Whit Sunday itself, we would parade round our relatives in our new clothes before setting off to Sunday School. I liked that bit 'cos Grandma Lawton and Grannie Annie always gave us a penny each. We weren't a very church minded family and I don't remember mother or father ever going but we were sent every week unless we were too young or were poorly. I think they were glad to have the house to themselves.

It was quite a walk from our house down Napier Street to Arkwright Street on Whit Sunday. Grandad Coble used to take us. I think Grandad went on to the allotment after he'd delivered us. All six of us went together with Annie left in charge after Grandad had gone. We all wore our new clothes and used to get very excited at the prospect of riding on one of the carts. There was always a Whit Queen and one year Alice was chosen. She didn't have to go on the coal cart or hold onions but had a cart all to herself with some attendants. This cart came from Whitehead's mill and they all sat on bales of wool waving to everyone. I think Granny Lawton made Alice's special dress on her sewing machine from some old curtains. After she died the sewing machine went to Granny Annie. Anyway, we all met up in

Whitehead's yard and Mr Shuttleworth or Mr Callendar would put as many children as they could on the carts. Everyone had a flag to wave unless you were on Mr Callendar's then you waved your cabbage or cauliflower. The procession went the long way round so people came out of their houses to watch us go by. Then we'd go along Arkwright Street to Driver's Field which was part of Driver's Farm. It's a football field now. Anyway, the farmer's wife, Mrs Driver would give everyone a cup of tea and a long bun. I suppose that's why we called it the Bun Field. They didn't grow buns there. It was just grass. There were games and races with little prizes, maybe an orange or a banana or a small bar of chocolate but we didn't mind 'cos we all had a lovely afternoon. Then after all that, every Whit Monday there were fireworks in Peel Park which wasn't far away, either. Mother and father took us to this and we all walked to a bit of a hill nearby and watched them from there. By the time we got back home we just fell into our beds dizzy with the excitement of the day.

As well as the annual event at the Bun Field, we enjoyed going to the Lyceum Cinema or the Lyceum Picture House, as it was at that time. That's now been turned into a night club. They get the acts that are at the end of their careers and who people only go to see because it reminds them of their youth. Anyway, the Lyceum was on our side of Leeds Road, right next to Mortimer Row where Auntie Edna and Uncle George lived. It was near the Model Milk Company factory where they made sterilised milk. This lasted longer than ordinary milk and came in long tall bottles but we didn't use it as none of us liked the taste of it. So, we went every Saturday we could and Jack and me eventually used to try to do extra little jobs, such as sweeping the back yard, to pay for our tickets. During the time I'd Lucky I'd to try even harder to find these little jobs but Auntie Shackleton knew all about our Saturday jaunts and often helped us out. Again, it was nearly always Grandad Coble who escorted us there and waited for us when it was time to come out. Sometimes one or more of our sisters would come with us and then, of course, we didn't need Grandad which never failed to disappoint us as he always gave us a penny or two for sweets.

We loved the cowboy films with John Wayne and Buck Jones in them. All the local kids went. We always had to queue to get in and then everyone rushed to get to the front row first, including us, especially if it was a morning of Mickey Mouse. Every year the

Lyceum put on a children's party at Christmas, usually on the Saturday afternoon before Christmas itself. This was instead of the film that day. You had to buy a ticket for this in advance but it wasn't very much. Auntie Lucy usually got them for us as Christmas presents. Again, it was very good fun with funny hats and lots of games. Everyone got an apple and an orange to go home with. It was a nice start to Christmas which was always a time of fun and merriment in our house. Christmas 1930 is the one I remember with lots of affection.

Father, as I've already said, worked for Bradford Corporation, repairing the roads. I don't think he earned a lot of money although later on he became a foreman. Mother, however, must have made the most of what he gave her after he'd had his social life at the Lord Napier pub. In them days there wasn't such things as joint bank accounts. Most transactions were cash and on pay day it was quite normal for the man of the house to give his wife an amount out of his wages. This was known as Housekeeping Money and each wife had this to run the household. Some men were mean with this money and others were generous. If the husband was mean then the wife had a hard job making ends meet. There were a few of those down our street, and it was often the ones who had even larger families than ours to see to. It was usually the rent which didn't get paid and folk hiding under the kitchen table when the rent man was on his way, wasn't unheard of. It wasn't unknown, either, for a house to be suddenly vacated in the middle of the night with the Landlord discovering that there were no doors in the house as they had all been burned to keep the family cooking range going. Like the family I stayed with one night.

My teacher that year was Miss Allott and she helped us to make Christmas cards for our families. I always enjoyed doing that sort of thing. We made decorations at home, as well, and for weeks I would be sat at the kitchen table with some of the others pasting strips of paper together to make paper chains. We used any paper we could including newspapers and sometimes father's old betting slips and brown paper bags from the shops. We made our paste from flour and water. We hung these all around the kitchen and in the front room they were hung from the centre light to the walls and corners so it was like being inside a big top at the circus. Grandad Coble brought us one of the biggest chickens from the hen run and mother seemed to be baking mince pies every day. On Christmas Eve me and Jack were in such a state of excitement we couldn't stand still, so mother sent us round to Grannie Annie's for an hour or so.

When we got back, escorted by Grandad Coble, as usual, everyone was in the kitchen and me and Jack were told to shut our eyes. We did this and we were led into the front room. When we opened our eyes we could hardly believe what was there. A Christmas tree! We'd never had one before, making do with a branch from the local woods and decking that out with more paper chains. It turned out that father had been working in the centre of Bradford and, as he was passing the market which was closing, there was this Christmas tree lying in the gutter. He'd looked around but no one was taking any notice of him so he picked it up and brought it home. Mother was horrified at first, as she thought this was stealing and told him to take it back. But everyone protested and, eventually, mother gave in and we kept it. So, we'd our first Christmas tree and it stood in pride of place on the little wooden table vacated by the gramophone which had now been put on a wooden box I'd previously seen in Grandad Coble's allotment shed.

We didn't care that our tree was only about two feet high, was a little bent over and didn't have any branches on one side. To us it was simply beautiful. My sisters stood it in a bucket filled with coal so it didn't fall over. We decked it out with some paper chains we took down from the kitchen and some bits of silver paper. We always had silver paper 'cos we saved it out of father's empty cigarette packets. It came in useful for all sorts of things and it was just the job for making little bows for the tree. Alice had made more red fancy bows with some of her old hair ribbons, too. They looked wonderful. That Christmas Eve me and Jack even talked Mother into allowing us to go into the front room after tea with a mince pie each just so that we could sit and look at the tree. Father had already gone to the Lord Napier to start his own celebrations. Before he set off, though, he helped us to put a small glass of beer out for Santa Claus and a carrot for Rudolph. Mother eventually got us to go to bed and I remember me and Jack whispering in the darkness about the tree and, of course, wondering what Santa Claus was going to bring us that year. I went to sleep and dreamed about the big red bus, which I'd wanted every year but had never got.

When we woke up, we found that Santa Claus had been and he'd left us some packages in the pillow cases which we'd left at the end of our bed. Jack and me shared a bed as the bedroom wasn't big enough for two single beds. We were thrilled to see that Santa Claus had even labelled them with our names. I don't know what time this would have been but I dashed in to tell mother and father the good news and then dashed back to help Jack unwrap everything. There was a lot of tearing of paper, most of it plain brown and some newspaper but I don't remember any of the presents I got, except one. I got a big red bus. That day me and my new red bus saw all our relatives and then we sat round the kitchen table and had a feast. I didn't even think about which hen we were eating. Afterwards we went into the front room and father played us his new record. I think he now had a grand total of five. This was his present from mother. It was Springtime in the Rockies and we all sat on the floor and watched in astonishment as he and mother danced to the song. I went to bed with the sight and sounds of that day spinning round in my head and if I close my eyes I can see and hear it all over again. I think I went to sleep with the big red bus clutched safely in my arms, too. What a Christmas it had been. The only sad note was that Grandma Lawton wasn't there to share it all with us.

After the excitement of Christmas, though, the new year of 1931 came and I was soon back at school and sitting in Miss Allott's classroom. I hadn't moved up in the previous September but stayed at the same desk in the same classroom. I didn't mind too much 'cos, though my friend Stephen wasn't there any more, as he'd moved up, I was now in the same class as Jack. I liked school even though I still wasn't very good with reading and writing or sums for that matter, and couldn't wait to get home each day to tell mother what I'd been doing.

I can't remember much about the rest of that year until our lives changed forever in October. We'd all gone back to school after the summer holidays and I'd moved up with Jack. I was still struggling with reading and writing but I suppose they couldn't keep me in a class of six-year-olds for ever. So, a couple of weeks after we'd gone back to school, we walked home with Annie only to find that mother wasn't there. Grannie Annie was waiting for us and she told us that our new little brother had arrived that morning but mother and the new baby had been taken to hospital. When father came home, he went straight out again to see mother. When he got back, he told us they'd decided to call the new baby Stephen and it wouldn't be long before they were out of hospital. I think they called the baby after my Grandad who fell off his horse 'cos his middle name was Stephen. Anyway, none of us got to see baby Stephen, 'cos he died the next day. We'd got an orange box all ready for him as a cot and I remember that all the sheets and blankets were pink so they must have come from Grandma Lawton's. Nothing was wasted. It seemed strange that they had called the baby Stephen when my only friend at school had been Stephen too and he disappeared from my life as well.

It didn't seem very long, though, before mother was back home with us but she wasn't well and stayed upstairs in bed. The doctor came to see her and I remember that father had to go and borrow some money to pay him. In them days there was no National Health Service. It was Pay as You Go. And, if you couldn't pay then the chances that you did actually go, so to speak, were very high. It was nice having mother home even if she was away from the rest of us upstairs but she wasn't home long before she went back to hospital. It was all very confusing for me. Auntie Shackleton came to look after us but after a couple of days my sisters seemed to take over, especially Annie who was the eldest. No one told me what was wrong with mother but father took me and Jack to see her one evening and I remember wondering why she'd tubes sticking out of her all over.

I wasn't one for asking questions so I just stood there looking at her. She didn't say anything to me, just smiled. I held her hand and just blurted out the usual list of what I'd been doing that day. I couldn't hug her what with all the glass tube things, so just gave her a little kiss and we went home. I didn't get to go again and I missed her at home. The day after I'd been to see mother, I told Miss Allott all about it and when the bell went for home-time she asked me if I'd stay behind for a little while. We usually walked home with Norma so I told Jack to go and find her and to go on without me. I was very anxious 'cos I thought I'd done something wrong but it turned out that Miss Allott thought it would be nice if I wrote mother a Get Well letter. She gave me some paper and I copied from the board as she wrote it up. I always had a bit of trouble with my writing so it took quite a long time but Miss Allott had a lot of patience. I don't know what it was I wrote as I couldn't read much at that time. She got out an envelope, addressed it and even put a stamp on it telling me to put it in the post box on the way home. It would get to mother the next day. I was really pleased with myself for doing all this but I was also longing for my tea so, after popping the envelope in the post box, I ran like mad all the way home, making sure I looked both ways loads of times before I crossed Leeds Road.

I was looking forward to having something to eat and hoped Annie would have my tea ready for me but instead of all the everyday noise and chatter, after bursting through the back door, I found that all the family were sat around the kitchen table in silence. All the girls, and Jack, too, were crying. Grannie Annie was there with a handkerchief held up to her face and Grandad Coble was stood in a corner staring at the floor. Auntie Shackleton and Uncle Willie had their arms round each other. Father was standing just near the stairs door and when he saw me, he scooped me up and held me tightly to him. He'd never done this before and I couldn't understand what was happening so I started crying too, even though I didn't know why. He put me down onto Grannie Annie's knee and told me that mother wouldn't be coming home again 'cos she'd gone to heaven to be with Stephen and Grandma Lawton.

I knew a little bit about dying 'cos of Grandma Lawton. I'd also heard Auntie Shackleton telling mother about an old lady somewhere near us who hadn't been seen for a day or two so Uncle Willie and another neighbour had broken into her house and found her sat at the table with a knife and fork in her hand, ready to have her dinner which had gone cold on the plate. She was sat there, stone dead. I've often wondered why she hadn't fallen off her chair or forwards so her face would have landed in her dinner. She would have had mashed potato up her nose, whilst I've got it between my toes. Anyway, there she was. The funniest thing about all, though, was that she lived in a house with a front and back door like ours and the front door hadn't been locked. There had been no need to break down the back door at all. It was a good job she hadn't been burgled or the thief would have had a right shock.

Anyway, at least I'd visited mother just the once with father even though I'd seen the tubes sticking out of her. It's the tubes I remember most about our visit. In them days they were made of glass, not plastic like nowadays. She'd been in one of them long wards with two rows of beds facing each other. I think they were called Nightingale wards. It was all women too, mind. Not like these days when men and women are all mixed up. The last time I was in hospital I'd a woman at each side of me. I suppose it makes a change but it isn't the same. I find it easier talking to a man. So, mother was in this long ward with her bed facing the tall windows opposite. I don't know what actually happened 'cos I wasn't there but from what I've been told since, all of a sudden something fell past the window opposite mother. She was so surprised that she sat up, a glass tube broke inside her and she died. So, she never got my letter. That was 3rd October 1931.

18:20:02 – 18:26:11

Progress after emptying of the bag was slow but sure. Unfortunately, there was another side street to cross and he was becoming aware that his boots were starting to hurt. When he reached Laburnum Grove he was very careful stepping down from the kerb onto the road. There was no flower bed down the middle here but it seemed to take a long time to reach the other side. All this effort had made him feel tired. He could go no further so he stopped by a blue wooden gate and leaned on the zimmer. After a few moments, he was just about to set off again when there was a deep growling sound from the other side of the gate and a very hairy dog with huge ears jumped up on hind legs to bark furiously at him. It startled him, especially as it looked as though it was going to come over the gate and attack him. He shuffled off as fast as he could to get away. He didn't think he could cope with any more dogs tonight.

There was a bench just a bit further on and, even though he was only a few yards from the fish and chip shop, it was important to sit down again and rest not only his legs but his heart which was thumping away after the incident with the barking dog. After a minute, he felt strong enough to continue. The sight of the fish and chip shop was a great relief. However, there were three deep steps to negotiate before he could get inside the shop. He went down these steps cautiously, clinging to the black metal handrail to his left.

He was glad when he reached the bottom in one piece. He'd forgotten that there was another way in without steps just a bit further round the corner on the pavement. His mind was somewhere else tonight. He pushed open the heavy glass door and joined the queue.

The Coming of Doreen

I didn't go to mother's funeral. Instead, me Jack and Helen went round to Auntie Shackleton's house. Funerals in them days could be grand affairs. The hearse was often a big glass box on a cart, so you could see the coffin, pulled by big black horses wearing black plumes and with the drivers sitting high up at the front wearing top hats and tails. I've no idea if this is what mother's funeral was like but I don't expect it was. We didn't have the money to spend on such things. A few years ago, I thought I'd try to find out where my parents were buried. I don't know what made me think about it. It was just one of those things that comes into your head and doesn't seem to go away until you've dealt with it. So, Christina got in touch with the council for me. She's my niece, in case you've forgotten. They were very nice and she found out that mother was buried in Bowling Cemetery. There was no record of father so I don't know what happened to him. No one knew anything about Stephen, either. I wondered if he'd been buried with mother. He wouldn't have taken much room up.

Bowling Cemetery is a long way from where I live so Christina took me in her car. We went there one lovely sunny afternoon. I was quite excited at the prospect of seeing mother's grave after all this time. The cemetery is huge, with loads of graves, some with big stone memorials. We parked near the gate and set off to look for the plot. The man from the Council had given us the plot number and explained where it was but it still took some finding. We walked up and down the rows of graves for ages without any luck. Graves usually have the number of the plot on them and sometimes the name of the stone mason or undertaker who arranged the grave. These numbers were often hard to find as they were hidden by weeds or stones. Then we came across a large grassy stretch with a few small headstones here and there. Some of these had fallen over. The whole area looked neglected. We found a grave which had a headstone and saw that it was plot 231. We were looking for 238, so we tried to count seven graves along. That wasn't easy, though, 'cos you could hardly see them. They were all grassed over and the mounds were hardly there at all. Our family obviously hadn't had enough money to put up a headstone, so we left a bunch of flowers where we thought it might be. I was pleased with myself for having made the effort to come and see where mother had ended up but it also made me sad as I sat in the car going home wondering what life would have been like if she hadn't died at that time. Why is it always cold in cemeteries even on a warm day?

So, when everyone had come back from mother's funeral, we all went home together from Auntie Shackleton's. It was one of the few occasions I can remember walking holding father's hand. Jack was on the other side. When we got back the house seemed cold and empty even though the fire had been banked up before we left and was going well. Annie put the kettle on and made us all a cup of tea which we drank in silence. It was the most awful time. Father eventually stood up and told us he was going out for a while. I don't remember what we did after that but I do know we were woken up by a loud bang in the middle of the night, followed by some shouting. Curious to know what was happening, I crept out of bed and onto the landing and down the stairs. I opened the stairs door a bit and peeped through just in time to see Annie and Alice opening the back door through which came father. He fell down, landing in a heap just inside the door. My sisters tried to pull him further into the kitchen but he was quite a heavy man and they only managed to move him a few inches. I heard Annie tell Alice to stay with him whilst she went off to get some help. I sat on the stairs and kept as quiet as a mouse. She was quickly back with Uncle Willie and together they managed to pull him to his feet and started to walk him towards the stairs door where I was. So, I made a dash to the top and watched from inside our bedroom. They were too busy to notice our door was open a bit.

It seemed hours before they got him to the top of the stairs and by that time father was saying all sorts of funny things but I couldn't understand any of it. I also heard Uncle Willie saying he'd be alright in the morning and told Annie to take his shoes off but leave him in his clothes and just cover him up. Alice went downstairs and came back with the galvanised bucket. I was really upset when I saw this and went out onto the landing. Mother only put the bucket in a bedroom if one of us was really sick, just in case we needed to use it. So, I was terrified that father was really sick. Then, Alice saw me on the landing and packed me off to bed straightaway. The others were just coming out of father's bedroom. Jack was still fast asleep so she tucked me in on my side of the bed. I wanted to know if father was going to have to go to hospital. After a big hug she said father would be alright but would probably have a headache in the morning. That was the first time I'd ever seen a drunken man.

It wasn't very nice at home without mother. No one knew what they were supposed to do. We all had our little jobs to do which mother had organised but other major things had all been seen to by her. At that time Annie was thirteen and due to leave school the next Easter when she would be fourteen, Alice twelve, Norma eleven, Helen was just eight. I was seven and Jack six years old. As it was quite normal to leave school at fourteen in them days, it seemed natural that Annie should take over mother's duties. So, everything was reorganised. Looking back, it was a lot for a lass of her age to take on but I don't suppose there was much choice. Auntie Shackleton came round every day and helped out by making our tea but gradually Annie stayed at home more and more trying to keep up with everything. We'd an awful lot of fish and chips. Me and Jack were always running round to the fish and chip shop if Annie was in a rush to get something on the table in time for father coming home. But most of all I missed mother tucking me up in bed, telling me she loved me and wishing me sweet dreams.

I suppose everyone did their best and gradually life took on the sort of routine we'd had before it had all happened but it was a long time before I forgot that, on bursting through the kitchen door after school, mother wouldn't be there. She'd taught both Annie and Alice how to bake bread and make stews and roast but, somehow, no matter how they tried, nothing tasted quite the same as it had done. The washing was still done on a Monday but on an evening not during the day. It seemed to take all week before it was dried and put away. We still had our big wooden kitchen table which was scrubbed every week by Norma, who hated doing it. She said it spoiled her hands. I offered to do it but Annie wouldn't hear of it so we'd to put up with Norma's complaining. I used to wonder what the table would tell us if it could talk. It'd come with the house so must have been very old. Everyone gathers round a table when there's something important to talk about so ours must have heard some interesting things. Besides being a table where mother had baked and plucked chickens and where I'd practised my hand writing for hours, it had also been a ship for me and Jack on rainy afternoons when we'd put an old sheet over it and gone underneath. Sometimes it had been a little house and sometimes we even had our tea sat under there in our tent in the Sahara Desert. We didn't know where that was but had heard Uncle Leopold talking about it.

The kitchen range was still cleaned every week, the floors were swept and the rugs shaken out. Annie was always first up and last to bed. Helen was the dark horse of our family. We discovered that she liked sewing and she surprised us all by repairing our sheets when a hole appeared and turning collars to make them last longer. We'd inherited Grandma Lawton's sewing machine. She could also use a hammer and repaired the rail in the back yard and she made the door to the toilet close properly. We were astonished at what she could do, especially when it came to hammering home a nail. When I found out about that I wondered if she might get a job with our cousin Margaret's Uncle Bernard who was an undertaker. I think mother's coffin probably came from there. I hope we got a discount.

We'd never had much to do with our cousins, Margaret and John but after mother died they started calling in. Uncle Bernard was really their uncle, not ours, as he was their father's brother. It was their father who was our uncle. Anyway, we'd met Margaret's Uncle Bernard just before the summer holidays. Margaret said she'd a message for him from her father and she'd like us all to go with her, so we all traipsed down Leeds Road. It was a long walk to Uncle Bernard's but eventually we stopped at a big black door with a brass plate at the side which I couldn't read. Just before she knocked on the door Margaret told us to watch out for Thomas. I thought it was a cat or a dog and as Margaret's Auntie Maisie let us in, I was ready for being attacked. However, all was quiet and Auntie Maisie was very friendly. We followed her through to the kitchen where we enjoyed a piece of cake and orange juice. It was a big house compared to ours and seemed really posh to me. She sent us through the back door to the yard to find Uncle Bernard. Now, what Margaret hadn't told us was that Uncle Bernard was an undertaker. That was why she'd wanted us all to go with her. As we turned into the yard, the first thing we saw were two coffins stood up against the wall. There was another one on a bench to the side with a lid on. I imagined a dead body in it. It was beginning to get dark and the place was scary. As we got there a young man walked out of a workroom to the left. He'd an apron on which said Thomas on it. I knew that name 'cos I sat next to a boy at school who was called that and I'd seen him write his name lots of times. I wondered why Margaret had warned us about him, as he was very friendly.

Now, just a couple of weeks before, Auntie Lucy had read some stories to me. One of these had been about a ghost and I was at an age when these things could prey on a young mind. I'd already had trouble with skulls in Grandma Lawton's tin trunk. So, when I saw those coffins that was bad enough but when Thomas suddenly lifted up the lid of the coffin on the bench and made the sound of a ghost I just stood there and started screaming. Uncle Bernard came running out of his office thinking one of us had had an accident. Thomas ran back to his workshop laughing his head off but I went home and slept with my head under the covers for weeks after that.

Eventually Christmas 1931 arrived and I think it was the saddest time of all for us. None of us felt like making decorations and the thought of a Christmas tree was too much. The day was saved, though, by Auntie Shackleton. She invited us all to their house for a Christmas Day dinner. It was their way of trying to make Christmas without Mother a bit better. It worked in a way, as we'd a lovely chicken and then some games afterwards with Uncle Willie. They had even wrapped up a small present for each of us. I got some pencils. But we all still went home with heavy hearts. Father went out to see Lord Napier and then came back to sit the front room by himself. It wasn't long before we heard 'Springtime in the Rockies' being played.

So, life carried on, as they say, but there was one fly in the ointment and it was father. I'm sure he loved us all but he didn't show us much affection. I often wished he'd cuddle me like mother had done. He'd a good job, went out to work every day to provide for us and I think, as far as he was concerned, he thought that was his role in life. He'd gone shopping with mother on Saturdays but I wonder if it was to make sure she didn't spend too much. Now Annie and Alice went by themselves. We'd never seen mother and father quarrel, not like some homes down our street. No one took much notice, though, 'cos we all knew these things soon blew over but there was one incident concerning a family, who lived at the end of our street, which left a deep impression on me. They were called Smith and there were five children, one of them being called Moira. We were in the same class at school. I once had to go round to their house for some reason I can't remember but what I can recall is Moira's father sitting at the table having his evening meal whilst her mother was standing by the sink.

They were arguing and didn't even notice us. Suddenly, her father stood up and threw his plate at her mother. The food splattered as it hit the pot sink just missing her mother. I got out of there as fast as I could. Moira told me they were always arguing and sometimes her father hit her mother, too. Well, we didn't have anything like that. I think it also explained why Moira had such a sad look on a face many a time.

Then there was the evening I went with Annie to take some baking to the family who'd moved into the house where Grandma Lawton had lived. Annie knocked on the door and a voice from inside shouted for us to go in. We found ourselves in the little hallway and saw a man standing at the top of the stairs in his pyjamas. He was holding a pair of crutches which he flung down the stairs. One of the crutches hit Annie on her leg and she dropped the teacloth which she'd wrapped the baking up in. No sooner had the scones hit the floor than a thin dog, with a lot of its hair missing, appeared from nowhere and started eating them. The man then slid down the stairs on his backside shouting at the dog. He only had one leg. That's the man, not the dog. The dog bared its teeth at him but turned and went away. By this time, I'd hidden behind Annie's skirt. The man said he was sorry, picked up his crutches and we all went into the kitchen. We'd to leave the scones on the floor. His wife was sat at the table holding a baby. When she saw us, she put the baby on the floor and it started crawling towards us with a dummy in its mouth, which soon fell out. She bent down and popped it back in the baby's mouth. It was covered in dog hairs. I can't remember what happened after that but it was one of the reasons I tried very hard to keep our kitchen floor properly swept. Grandma's house was no longer pink.

So, I was thinking about father being a fly in the family ointment. As time went on, he started coming home a bit later every night and hardly bothered to talk to us. Annie turned fourteen in the April, left school at Easter and found herself a job at a local jeweller's shop. But this meant that she was now home a lot later than when she'd been at school. So, she was always rushing round to get father's meal ready and sometimes he didn't turn up for it. As often as not we'd have gone to bed before he got in. We hardly saw him. We all thought he was lonely and missing mother, finding comfort in his pint of bitter, although he never came home drunk again. I don't think it ever occurred to him that we were missing her too. Every now and then I would go and sit in the doings and have a good cry. Anyway, as a result of our change of circumstances me and Jack had a summer of freedom 'cos there wasn't anyone to answer to anymore. We felt that although Annie had taken over, she wasn't to be obeyed in the same way as mother had been. We soon realised that as long as we turned up for meals either at home or somewhere else, like Auntie Shackleton's, then nobody seemed to mind. We discovered a place where some of the wall had fallen down and where, if we climbed up a bit, we could watch the trains coming and going. We spent hours there.

Father, I said, had become more and more distant. Then, one teatime, he suddenly came home early. It was a surprise to us all. I can even remember what we were having. Alice had made us bubble and squeak, which I've always liked. It was a cheap dish to make and I think we'd a lot of meals like that. Anyway, there was Alice, Norma, Jack, Helen and me all sat round the table when the door opened and father came in. Annie hadn't got home from work. It was the beginning of November as Annie had taken us to a bonfire just round the corner the night before. Apart from Annie and Alice and sometimes Norma, the rest of us were usually in bed by the time father came in, so, this was very unusual. He came in smiling, told us that he'd like us to meet a friend of his and turned back to wave his hand at someone who was waiting in the back yard. The next thing we knew was that this woman walked into our kitchen. He said her name was Doreen. She smiled at us but I don't think any of us smiled back. There was complete silence broken only by Jack dropping his spoon on the floor.

Alice was the first to say something, asking Doreen if she'd like a cup of tea to which father said it wasn't necessary as they were going out to the Lord Napier. He went upstairs to get changed which took us aback even more 'cos he didn't usually bother coming home, but went straight to the pub in his working clothes. He disappeared, which left Doreen standing in the kitchen staring at us whilst we all stared back at her. The moment father appeared they were out of the door and gone. None of us spoke for a few minutes until Norma suddenly asked who we thought the woman was and Alice remarked she thought father had smartened himself up a lot recently by having more regular shaves and brushing his overcoat. She'd put it down to her imagination but now she wasn't so sure. Jack asked if Doreen was going to be his new mother at which we all shouted at once, 'No.'

But, in the end, we were to be proved wrong and Doreen became a regular visitor to our house. She and father would sometimes sit in what we regarded as mother's front room, talking and laughing and having a beer together. I suppose he enjoyed the company but to us in the kitchen it was very upsetting. Once or twice, she came to our house before father was home and didn't even bother to knock, just walking in. I was doing some sums on the kitchen table one day when she did just that and she and Annie had what is called 'words' over it. I think Doreen tried to be friendly to us all but, somehow, we couldn't take to her. Father had already told us that her husband had gone somewhere else, we never found out where, and that she was on her own, like he was, with two little girls, Nellie and Mabel who were twins and eleven years old. Gradually, though, I suppose we got used to her so that when father announced they were going to get married, it didn't come as too great a surprise to anyone. Annie, Jack and me had already met Nellie and Mabel when we'd come across them with Doreen unexpectedly in the Post Office. Apart from staring at each other, nothing was really said but I think there was an instant and mutual dislike between us and them.

Doreen was as near to mother as anyone could be in height and build. She even had the same hair colour but there the similarity ended 'cos Doreen liked to be glamorous and wore a lot of make-up which mother never did, except for lipstick every now and again, such as if we were going into Bradford. We never saw Doreen without makeup and she always had her fingernails painted bright red to match her lipstick. She also had her hair done in what they called a bob which was very fashionable whilst mother had kept hers long and pinned up on top of her head. Doreen also usually wore a tight sweater and skirt and, although these things meant nothing to me at the time, my sisters were often whispering about her. The other thing was that father wouldn't tell us what job Doreen did, which led to more whispering.

This state of affairs lasted until we were well into the new year of 1933. We'd our Christmas without father as he chose to spend it with Doreen. It was another very sad Christmas for us but probably better than the one we would have had if father had been there with Doreen. Then, in the middle of February, one Saturday morning, father chose to tell us that we would be leaving Napier Street on Monday and moving to a place called Eccleshill. It sounded like the other side of the world to us and it meant an enormous upheaval for us 'cos we'd have to change schools and leave our friends behind. Annie had already been working for nearly a year and now Alice was due to leave school too and bring some much needed money into our household. So, on a damp, dreary morning we went off to school and all our worldly possessions were taken on Mr Shuttleworth's milk float to our new home in Eccleshill. At the end of our school day father was waiting for us at the school gate and we actually got on a bus to our new home. Nellie and Mabel were already there and we'd no sooner got through the door when father announced that he and Doreen had been to Bradford Register Office that morning and had got married. He hadn't bothered to tell us, as he thought it would be a nice surprise.

Well, it certainly was and the house we were moving into made it a day worth remembering, too. It was on Victoria Road, a typical Victorian terraced house and very near the coal depot. From our bedroom window, we could see the trains coming in with the coal wagons loaded up and the coal merchants going into the yard with their horse and carts. In fact, the house was rented from Mr Varley who was the local coal merchant. The house had a little hall with those brown and blue tiles, a front room with an open fire and a back room with what we called a scullery off that. That's where there was a pot sink and wooden draining board plus a couple of shelves where we put the plates and pans. We lived in the back room 'cos it had an Airedale range like the other house, where there was always a fire and where all the cooking was done. There was an oven at the side. There was a cellar too but it was damp and there was often a puddle in the middle of the floor. We kept the coal in the coal hole which was in the back yard and it had a lock on the door to keep it safe. Upstairs were three bedrooms and a bathroom with a toilet in it. That was a sight, I can tell you. No more creeping down the stairs and out into the cold night. Then, there was another staircase up into the attic. It seemed like a mansion to us coming from our humble little house off Leeds Road. Of course, there was no central heating or double glazing in them days and the house was freezing cold. It also needed painting and some of the lino had holes in it. There was a particular place on the stairs where you had to be very careful not to catch your foot. Helen tried to repair it with some lino father brought home but it kept coming off. Eventually she took the lino up and we just had bare floorboards. At least it was safe.

Apparently, Mr Shuttleworth had helped father to unload our furniture and Uncle Bernard had sent Thomas to help carry it into the house. It had seemed like a big house when we first went in but with ten of us living there it soon became very small. Father and Doreen took the big front bedroom and Nellie and Mabel the large bedroom at the back. Me and Jack were given the small bedroom over the stairs at the front and found that father had managed to get two small single beds which meant that me and Jack no longer had to share a bed. We were thrilled to bits, although we still had to keep our clothes under the bed in cardboard boxes as there was no room for anything else in there except a wooden crate which we used as a bedside table. I kept The Boys Book of Astronomy on there.

The girls drew the short straw, though, and all four of them were consigned to the attic which, whilst big enough for two large beds had a sloping ceiling which meant you could only stand up in the middle bit. Annie still had her job in a local jeweller's shop and after she came home about six o'clock there was a lot of crying and banging as the girls tried to sort themselves out. We celebrated father's second marriage with fish and chips eaten in silence round the kitchen table. Annie, Alice, Helen and Norma were very upset at being pushed into the attic where they probably had less room than at Napier Street. The fact that Nellie and Mabel were sniggering didn't help. The highlight of the day came when me and Jack were sent to bed and we enjoyed ten minutes looking at The Boys Book of Astronomy before climbing into our little beds and falling asleep straight away.

The silence of the fish and chip supper continued for as long as I can remember. Father went off to his job and kept telling us how lucky we were because there were millions out of work but as he was a council worker his job was safe. There was always a road which needed repairing. After Alice left school, she got a job at a local café on Tunwell Street, known as the Sunshine Café. Doreen seemed to have lots of friends and was never at home. So, the four of us, Norma, Helen, me and Jack, had to let ourselves in when we got home from school. We were known as latch-key kids. With Alice working in a café, she was often able to bring home a few teacakes which was useful 'cos no one baked bread in our house anymore. Doreen enjoyed going to the pub every night with father and, as Nellie and Mabel kept themselves to themselves we were, in effect, like two separate families living in the same house. Father never noticed.

As it turned out, we didn't have to change schools at all and continued at Killinghall Primary by going on the bus. When the weather was good, we sometimes walked home and spent our bus fare money on sweets at the corner shop just near school. However, the summer came and went and we all went back to Killinghall Primary School in September except Alice who was still enjoying her job in the café. I was still in the same class as Jack. We were both pleased about that. So, time moved on and another Christmas without Mother was not far off. It was difficult not to get excited 'cos at school we'd been making Christmas cards and decorations for what seemed like weeks. Father brought home a little Christmas tree one night and after tea we all sat round the table, not Nellie or Mabel though, and made our own decorations. It was just like old times, except it wasn't. I missed mother a lot. Sometimes me and Jack sat on our beds and talked about her and then had a good cry. Doris didn't do mince pies like mother had done. In fact, she didn't do mince pies at all.

On Christmas Day itself, me and Jack woke up really early expecting to find a few parcels at the end of our beds which Santa Claus had left for us but, to our dismay, there was nothing there. We decided that maybe he'd left them under the tree this year, so we crept out of our beds with our feet on the bare floorboards and made our way downstairs. Yes! Under the tree was a pile of parcels. Just as we were about to have a look at them, father came in. We hadn't been as quiet as we thought. He said it was too early to be opening parcels and sent us back to bed which we thought was mean. We laid in bed until father put his head round the door, told us to get dressed and then go down for us all to open our parcels.

When we got downstairs, we found that a coal fire had been lit in the front room which made it nice and warm and then Doreen began to hand round the parcels. Father was first. He got a blue waistcoat. He brought out a parcel from behind his back to give to Doreen. It was a bottle of scent. He'd never given mother anything like that. Nellie and Mabel were next and they each got a long white scarf with tassels on the ends. Annie and Alice each got a head scarf and Helen and Norma a pair of thick woollen gloves. That's a pair each, not one glove each. By this time, I was almost dizzy with excitement and couldn't wait to open my parcel. I tore it open with shaking fingers to find that it contained the red bus I'd been given three years before by mother. I couldn't believe my eyes and burst into tears. I was older now and didn't play with red buses any more. It'd disappeared when we moved but as I still had my Boys Book of Astronomy, I hadn't been too bothered. Father started saying something about there not being much money this year to which Annie shouted that there was enough money for silk scarves and perfume, so it ended up in one big row. To this day I don't know what Jack got. Christmas Day dinner was eaten in much the same way as father's marriage fish and chip supper had been.

So, the new year of 1934 arrived and it wasn't too long before the coal hole punishments arrived too. As I've said, Annie was already out working in a local jeweller's shop and Alice was enjoying being in the café. Norma, Helen, me and Jack were all still at school. This meant that Doreen had to do more housework and it didn't do her temper any good. Annie and Alice tried to help out when they came home but the rest of us just didn't want to help Doreen at all, especially as her own two daughters were never asked to do anything. One day I came home from school earlier than usual. I can't remember why. The key wasn't in its usual hiding place so I knew someone was already inside. I went into the house and forgot to wipe my feet. It had been raining and my shoes were a bit muddy. I was really hungry and wanted to see if there was anything to eat. I never gave the muddy shoes a thought.

Suddenly, Doreen appeared in the kitchen shouting at me and pointing at the muddy footprints. She was very angry, stepped towards me and slapped me across my head. After that, despite my protests and apologies, she dragged me through the back door, down the steps, opened the coal house door and pushed me in, slamming the door and turning the key in the lock. So, there I was in the coal hole, in the dark. There was a little chink of light over the door but not much. I was cold, miserable and hungry and my head hurt. I'd to sit on the upturned coal bucket which wasn't comfortable 'cos it had a rim round the edge. I don't know how long I was in there for, probably wasn't all that long, but it was a scary experience. When she came back for me, she just opened the door and thumbed for me to get out. I think she let me out then 'cos she knew the others would be home soon. After that, the coal hole punishment was always in the back of my mind and it was inflicted on me on a regular basis, often for something and nothing. I didn't dare tell Annie or Alice or even Jack in case Doreen found out and invented something even worse.

Looking back, I wish I'd had the courage to tell someone.

The 4th of June 1934 was my 10th birthday. Although we'd moved away from Napier Street and the many relatives we'd over there, Annie and Alice had managed to keep in touch and would often walk over, taking us with them. Sometimes I went by myself and sometimes with Jack but it was quite a walk and though there wasn't the traffic there is nowadays I still had a fear of crossing Leeds Road. I did go to see Auntie Mary, though, as we now lived on her side of the main road. I sometimes took the Boys Book of Astronomy with me and I loved listening to her explaining all the pictures to me. I was getting better at reading and Auntie Mary would listen as I read out something to her. She'd a lot of patience. I was getting a lot better in the writing department, too, but I was still the slowest in the class at everything else. Anyway, I enjoyed going over to see her and also to see all the others, especially Grandad Coble and Grannie Annie. They always made me and Jack welcome. Sometimes Annie would go over there on her own to see someone or have errands to run and so she'd leave me and Jack with Grandad Coble and Grannie Annie for nearly a whole day. Grandad would take us down to his allotment which was still such a treat. He was so proud of his new greenhouse. He'd eventually built it himself out of the pieces of wood which he'd been saving for years.

It wasn't far to the allotments from Napier Street and me and Jack were always aware that we were going somewhere near the scene of the Piggery Murder. We often wondered if we'd find a clue which the police had missed. So, one day when Alice had to go over there for something, I went with her and it was arranged that I'd go to the allotment with Grandad. I don't know where Jack was that day. I was looking forward to doing a bit of detective work. Anyway, as well as his vegetables Grandad had hens and it was always my job to go and collect the eggs. I still got a few pennies for doing this, too. The hen run wasn't far away. When I got there, I went into the hen hut with the little basket we used for the eggs. It was easier for me to do it, anyway, 'cos I was smaller than Grandad. There were nine large brown eggs. I was really happy at finding so many 'cos I knew that I'd get to take some home which would please Doreen. I was always trying to find ways to avoid the punishments. So, I backed out of the hen hut and went to show Grandad what I'd got. I couldn't see him at first but as I went into the greenhouse he was lying there on the floor.

I didn't know what to do. He'd told me he was feeling tired as we'd walked down to the allotment so I wondered if he'd decided to have a nap but it seemed a funny sort of place to choose. He wasn't moving and when I crept over to have a better look, I could see that his eyes were open. I dropped the basket of eggs and ran back without stopping to tell Grannie Annie. There was a lot of commotion after that and I never saw Grandad Coble again. I don't know what happened to his allotment. Something else had changed in my life forever.

I can't remember much else happening for the rest of 1934 except Norma left school and went to work in the office of Pollard's, which was a mill just a short walk from our house. She started going to classes to learn shorthand and typing. Father came home with an old typewriter one day, much to our surprise, and she spent a lot of time practising on the kitchen table. We still had family rows and we were all still in second place behind Nellie and Mabel. All except Norma, that is, 'cos she'd made friends with them. I don't know if this was 'cos they were all the same age and all girls but it had a good effect for me 'cos the nasty tricks and teasing gradually stopped. I think Norma must have had a hand in this. I don't think she liked them any more than the rest of us but by making friends with them she protected us younger ones from them. One trick they played on me, Jack and Helen was that when we'd come home from school on a very hot day, there was some lemonade waiting for us with a note that Nellie and Mabel had made it specially for us. As I've said, it wasn't unusual for us to come home to an empty house, as Doreen was always out, so we looked after ourselves until Annie or Alice came home from work. Anyway, the lemonade looked very nice in the glass jug on the kitchen table so we got some cups, poured out the lemonade and all took a drink. It wasn't lemonade at all but soapy water, which made us all rush to the sink as fast as we could so we could spit it out. We told Annie when she got back and there was another row that evening.

Christmas came and went with the usual carry on that was, by now, normal for our family. Presents would be bought and wrapped but no one ever got what they really wanted or needed. The spirit of Christmas never visited our house at all. It only came to Doreen and father when they went out to the pub every night. I was always glad when New Year's Eve had come and gone 'cos it was the start of a new year and it always brought me hope that things would get better.

And, in a way, they did but only for a very short time.

The rows were a regular happening in our house and one night there was a lot of shouting between father and Doreen, at least more than usual. It must have been a Sunday 'cos father had been home all day except when he'd gone to the pub at dinner time and then had gone again at night with Doreen. Sunday roasts and dinner round the table were a thing of the past. We often had to make do with sandwiches and, during the week, fish and chips. Anyway, that night, me and Jack were asleep in bed and were woken up by a lot of shouting and door slamming. The next morning there was no sign of Doreen, Nellie or Mabel. It was Annie, not Doreen, who woke us all up to get ready for school. That was a nice surprise. Doreen usually opened our bedroom door and shouted that it was time to get out of bed. She didn't do things quietly where we were concerned. Helen was already in the kitchen eating some porridge so we joined her at the table and then Annie said she'd something to tell us. She stood in front of us and, taking on a posh voice like the newsreader on the radio, announced that Doreen had gone, taking Nellie and Mabel with her. We all burst out laughing. I'd a lovely day at school thinking that they wouldn't be there when I got home. And, so it was for the rest of the week. Anyway, my state of excitement wasn't to last, 'cos when I got home on the Friday, there they were, all sitting in the kitchen as though nothing had happened.

But then something did happen shortly after this latest upset. It was just before the school holidays had started in the summer of 1935 when we'd a sudden move from Victoria Road to Norman Lane. We'd gone to school that morning as usual, but when I got back to Victoria Road, I found two men talking to Doreen on the front door step. She was crying. When I went into the house, I found that mother's settee and chairs were gone, along with father's gramophone and radio. The kitchen table and chairs were still there but everywhere else was bare except for all our mattresses on the bedroom floors and our wooden bedside crate. By the time I'd looked around and gone back down stairs the two men had disappeared and Doreen was sat at the kitchen table wiping her eyes.

It turned out that she'd had been spending the rent money on herself and Nellie and Mabel, buying clothes and make-up, instead of paying the rent. Our landlord, the coal merchant, had given us one week to pay the arrears which hadn't happened. So, the two men were bailiffs who'd come to take our few possessions as payment for the rent. There was nothing of Doreen's to take, as she hadn't brought anything other than clothes with her when she'd married father. We were allowed to stay for one more night in much reduced circumstances and somehow father managed to secure us another house on Norman Lane by going to see Uncle Bernard who had a friend who rented out houses. He was another undertaker. So, we moved to Norman Lane. Father eventually got another settee and chair for our front room from someone he worked with, whose mother had just died. They were old and battered and not as nice as what we'd had. I was just thankful I still had my Boys Book of Astronomy as I'd taken it to school that day to show my teacher.

Again, we stayed on at Killinghall Primary, going on the bus every day. Alice and Annie had a bit further to go to their work but it didn't make any difference to Nellie or Mabel 'cos they'd both left school and found jobs at Lingard's, which was a department store in the middle of Bradford. The rooms in the new house were a bit bigger than those in Victoria Road except there wasn't an attic bedroom which made it, I suppose, smaller. So, whilst father and Doreen had the big front bedroom, again me and Jack had the front little bedroom, which we now had to share with Helen and Norma. There was just enough space for four little truckle beds. These were sort of camps beds on wooden legs. Not very wide and not very comfy, either. I had to keep the Boys Book of Astronomy under my bed. Even worse, though, was that Annie and Alice had to share the third bedroom with Nellie and Mabel. It was the move from Napier Street to Victoria Road all over again with lots of crying and banging. I never went into their room and it wasn't until several years later Annie told me that they'd divided the room into two. One half for Nellie and Mabel and the other for herself and Alice, like enemies facing each other. They'd put a chalk line down the middle of the lino and a thick pencil line up the wall, across the ceiling and down the other side. A sort of Berlin wall was made by hanging a piece of old curtaining on a washing line from a nail in the window frame to the light fitting in the ceiling. And woe betide anyone who crossed that dividing line.

Me and Jack always tried to keep out of Doreen's way as much as we could, so that summer we started to go fishing. This was something we would do on a regular basis right up to the Second World War. It was a long walk to the canal but worth it. We didn't have fancy rods but used a garden cane with a line dangling from it. We found a feather as a float and a piece of bent metal for a hook. At that time, there were some fish called gudgeon in the canal. They're only little things and we used worms as bait. We only ever caught one fish which I think was a roach. I kept pulling on the line and it kept pulling back. But our hook didn't have a barb on it so it eventually fell off and swam away. We never caught anything again but it was great fun for us. I think we both enjoyed just sitting in the peace and quiet with our sandwiches.

There was one more funny episode I can think of around 1935 and it concerned Jack. I was usually the one who was on the receiving end of Doreen and her bad temper but now and then she went for Jack. That particular day, I'd be about eleven years old which would make Jack ten, and it was during one of the school holidays, maybe the half term in autumn 'cos it was getting dark quite early. Anyway, we'd been over to see Grannie Annie. Auntie Lucy had been there as well and we did a bit of reading with her. Then, we'd called in at Auntie Shackleton's. We'd told Doreen where we were going and that we'd be back for tea but we forgot all about that and had our tea at Auntie Shackleton's. After that we'd called in to see Auntie Mary for a while and by the time we got back, which wasn't all that late, Doreen was beside herself with anger and by that time father had arrived home, too.

The problem was that father always believed everything she told him, mostly leaving the disciplining of us to her. This is what he'd done when our own mother was alive and so he just thought, I suppose, that Doreen would do the same. The difference was that we weren't her children and, basically, she didn't like us. She favoured Nellie and Mabel all the time but father could never see this and if Annie or Alice tried to explain or make excuses for us, he always took Doreen's side. Anyway, this time, when we got back, we found out that Doreen had told father we hadn't said where we were going or when we'd be coming home. This wasn't true. Father had never been violent towards mother, or any of us but, egged on by Doreen, he got hold of Jack and gave him such a mighty swipe across the head that Jack fell over and hit his head on the table leg. Father said a few choice swear words and stormed out of the kitchen and up the stairs. Alice had just arrived home and he shouted at her to see to Jack. Doreen ran after him. And left us to it.

Alice picked Jack up and had to put a plaster on his head. There was a small cut and some blood but it didn't last long. Then we heard the front door open and bang shut and knew that father and Doreen had gone out. Annie came home soon after they'd gone. She was now seventeen and, a few weeks earlier, on a day trip to Blackpool, she'd met someone called Sam. So, as she was in a hurry to go out to meet up with him Alice offered to sit with Jack. Annie quickly made us some cheese on toast, which was one of Jack's favourite meals. However, Alice had also made arrangements to see her young man, Frank, which meant that Jack, me and Helen were left in on our own. Norma, who was now 16, had gone out with a girlfriend to the pictures. Nellie and Mabel weren't at home, either. They'd gone straight out from work and were going to catch the last bus home. So, Helen went to read on her own in the bedroom and me and Jack looked at The Boys Book of Astronomy. After a while I went up to see if she wanted to join me and Jack in a game of Ludo but she didn't and when I went back into the kitchen, Jack was nowhere to be seen. I checked everywhere, even behind the settee in the front room. Then I checked the coat hooks near the back door and found that his coat had gone along with his shoes.

I opened the back door and shouted for him but there was no answer. I did the same with the front door with the same result. Helen had heard me shouting and came to find out what was going on. I told her about Jack and, as we didn't know what to do, we just sat there, near the range in the kitchen wondering where he might be. It was very much like the one we'd had at Victoria Road and it was always nice and warm, except it didn't keep me warm that time and I found myself shivering. It must have been the worry. Helen wanted to go out and find Jack but it was dark and we would have been in trouble with father and, more importantly, Doreen. As there was nothing more we could do, Helen went to bed and I stayed up.

I sat there for ages before I heard someone coming through the front door. I'd been to both the front and back doors calling for Jack quite a few times but there was no reply. I'd left the front door unlocked in case he came back. I jumped up hoping it was Jack but whoever it was had gone straight upstairs. I hoped it wasn't a burglar but then I heard footsteps coming down again and father came into the kitchen. He was on his own with an odd look on his face. When he saw me he wanted to know why I wasn't in bed and said something about wanting to see Jack. I just blurted out that he couldn't 'cos Jack was gone. At this, he turned, went to the front door and started shouting for Jack like I'd done. Although it was getting late by this time one or two people were passing by and one of them was someone father knew from his workplace. He stopped and asked if anything was wrong. I was standing behind father at this time and I don't think father wanted the man to know what had happened 'cos he told him that he was calling for the family cat.

Father then said he'd go and look round the streets for him and that I was to go inside and to bed. Well, I went inside and got ready for bed but didn't get into it 'cos just then Annie and Alice arrived home, together with Nellie and Mabel. Nellie and Mabel just ignored us and went straight up to their half of the bedroom. They'd all come back on the same bus from Bradford. Someone said Norma was staying overnight at her friend's. However, just as Annie and Alice were about to go out and look for Jack, there was a banging on the back door and when Annie opened it there was father holding Jack in his arms. Jack had been hiding in the coal hole all the time and his eyes were red with crying as well as his coat being covered with coal dust. I've never understood why I didn't see him in there when I'd checked it earlier. I think everyone was ready for the biggest row our family had ever had but, instead, father just hugged Jack and I'm sure he'd tears in his eyes too. I think father was ashamed of himself for hitting Jack and had come back from the pub early to see him. He sent us both upstairs to bed and then came up to read to us from one of Jack's favourite books, Robinson Crusoe which, this time, had come courtesy of Auntie Lucy. Neither of us could ever remember him reading us a bedtime story before. Doreen had stayed in the pub. She wasn't interested.

After this episode our lives calmed down again, with Doreen, Nellie and Mabel more or less still ignoring us. I can't remember Christmas 1935 at all, but in January 1936 the King, George V, died. I think it was at Sandringham. He was succeeded by Edward VIII, who was actually called David. I don't know why he wasn't King David. Anyway, he was seeing an American woman called Wallis Simpson and wanted to marry her. But, she wasn't thought of as being suitable material for the royal family as, not only was she American, but she'd already seen off two husbands, so the Prime Minister said he couldn't marry her. I don't mean that the prime minister couldn't marry her, just the king. There was a real kerfuffle over this. In the end Edward, or David, decided he wanted her more than he wanted us so he abdicated and they became Duke and Duchess of Windsor and went off to live in Paris.

So, his brother became King instead. This was George VI and his wife was Elizabeth. They are the parents of our present queen. Their coronation was in Westminster Abbey on 12th May 1937 and it was party time in Great Britain. Down Norman Lane tables were set up in the road for a street party. Everyone was encouraged to bring something to eat and it seemed to me there were mountains of sandwiches and piles of buns. I met up with Jack and we rushed home to pick up some sandwiches we'd made the night before, as our contribution, and then rushed out to join everyone else. Helen came along and the three of us enjoyed the singing and laughter all afternoon. Then we went down to Peel Park where there was a band playing and loads of people dancing. We didn't see Father or Doreen. We didn't care, though, as we were having the time of our lives. We'd met up with Annie, Sam, Alice and Frank and we all watched the fireworks together later that evening. The whole country had celebrated in a similar fashion. Of course, no one near us had a television. These days that's where everyone would see what had been going on. The coronation was the first outside broadcast but only the richest few would have had a television. Mind you, it didn't do them much good, 'cos when war was declared in September 1939 the television was shut down and didn't come back on until 1946.

Annie had met Sam Harris at the Blackpool Winter Gardens. He lived in Bowling which was on the other side of Bradford but that didn't seem to matter to them. She was always so full of joy at the prospect of meeting up with him. Sometimes he came to our house so he'd met father and the rest of us. I don't know what father or Doreen thought of him but I liked him a lot as he always seemed to have a smile on his face. Doreen seemed to be at home more often now when we came back from school but we didn't get many home-cooked teas from her, like we did with Annie or Alice. As often as not she'd wait until the three of us were in and then send me down to the fish and chip shop. Father usually came in about six o'clock and got the same. Meanwhile, Annie was still seeing Sam and it came as no surprise when he came to our house one night and asked father if he could have a word with him. It turned out that he'd asked Annie to marry him and, of course, she'd said yes straightaway. In them days you'd to be twenty-one to get married without your parent's consent and, as Annie had only just turned eighteen, there was a bit of an argument. It turned out that father didn't want to lose Annie's wage and she was only allowed to get married 'cos they promised to pay father five shillings a week.

So, at the end of August 1937 Annie walked down the aisle with Sam. I say walked down the aisle but it was, in fact, at the Register Office in Bradford. We all went, of course, and it was nice seeing Auntie Shackleton again and the rest of them. Doreen and her daughters didn't come, of course and father wasn't invited. Only two of Sam's four brothers came, Fred and Ronald. He'd no other family there for him. As we came out, I noticed a man in a doorway on the other side of the road. It was father. I didn't say anything. Afterwards, we all went to Collinson's Coffee House on Market Street where we'd a meal in an upstairs room. This was the first time I'd ever been in a proper café. I thought it was lovely. Sam and Annie had arranged to move into digs on Heath Street, just down the road from Napier Street. Sam had a good job as an overlooker at Whitehead's Mill which was only a ten-minute walk away from Heath Street. Annie found another job in a new department store in Bradford, called Brown and Muffs which was known as the Harrods of the North. It was a very posh shop. They had a small department just for selling fountain pens and that's where she started. Marrying early was Annie's way of escaping the constant rows our family always seemed to be having and years later, she told me that Sam had experienced the same sort of problems. I think it was love at first sight. Sam came from an even larger family. He'd four brothers and three sisters and his father was in and out of work all the time. This created loads of problems and, even when the older ones had started work and bringing in money, things hadn't got any better. When Sam met Annie, he'd already moved out and was living in digs in Bowling.

Now, there had been enough of a to-do about Annie leaving and getting married to Sam, but only a few weeks after that it was Alice's turn to leave the family nest. She'd been seeing Frank for nearly the same length of time Annie had been seeing Sam, except Alice wasn't leaving to get married but to go and live with another family. She rented a room in a house off Leeds Road and was able to share some of this family's life together. She couldn't put up with sharing a bedroom with Nellie and Mabel any longer, plus, after Annie had left,

The One Hour Thought

Alice had found herself having to do the lion's share of the household chores. Doreen was enjoying her trips out again and had slipped back into her old ways. The arguments between Doreen and father were still going on and, as Nellie and Mabel had discovered The Lyceum which was now a dance hall, Alice must have felt like Cinderella.

Anyway, one night she came home from work and went straight up the stairs to her room without speaking to us. This was very unusual 'cos she always came into the back room to see what was going on. It must have been a Wednesday, 'cos that was the day Doreen didn't come home until much later. When Alice did eventually come back down, she came over and gave us all hug and a kiss before sitting down at the table and explaining she was going on a little holiday for a few days and that we must manage without her and help each other. I just knew that Alice was never coming back. She then made us the nicest tea we ever had. It was sausages and mash and those bright green mushy peas followed by the remains of the apple pie she'd baked the day before with loads of custard. I can't remember her actually going out of the door but I can remember us all sitting there after she'd left wondering what would happen when father got home. Nellie and Mabel would now have the second bedroom all to themselves whilst the four of us were still squashed up in the front little bedroom. We should have swapped over but, of course, it was never mentioned.

Alice left father a note which she propped up on the shelf above the range. He saw it as soon as he came in, opened it and then turned on his heel and went back out of the door, without a word, like he always did when there was a problem he didn't know how to deal with. The answer, more often than not in his eyes, was to be found in a pint of beer. Or, at least he thought it was. It did mean, though, that there was even less money coming in now Alice had gone. She left the café and went to work at Whitehead's Mill at Tyersal. Years later she told me father had gone to see her at work and demanded that she give him five shillings a week like Annie had had to do. I don't know what was said but I don't think the money was ever paid. Norma was now almost eighteen and seeing her young man, Laurence, who worked in the local Post Office. She seemed to spend a lot of time round at his house. She still had a nice job working in the office at Pollard's, so they were busy saving up to get married and she kept as much of her money to herself as she could get away with. That meant that me,

Helen and Jack still had to more or less look after ourselves. Helen was now fifteen and after leaving school she'd gone to work in the Sunshine Café, more or less taking over from where Alice left off, I suppose. I don't think she was paid very much but she did bring teacakes home, like Alice had done.

As for Nellie and Mabel, how much they contributed is anyone's guess. I only know that father became even more remote after Alice's departure and we barely saw him except at weekends when he would often go into the front room and just listen to the radio. It was just like the time after mother had died. He and Doreen didn't say much to each other, either, and, looking back when they did it was usually with raised voices. I'm not saying that Doreen didn't do anything at all. She did the shopping and bought food and paid the rent and other bills from the money father gave her. I think the shock of the bailiffs at Victoria Road made her a lot more careful with money but she still did the minimum for us. She managed to do the weekly washing but I'd to help her with the mangle to wring the clothes out before they were hung on the line to dry. She'd never been able to cook like mother or Annie or Alice, either, so homemade pies and bread became distant memories to be replaced with fish and chips.

Towards the end of May, the following year, 1936, my days at school were numbered and I began thinking about getting a job. I would be fourteen in June. Father had mentioned it a few times and so I went to see Mr White, who was now the headmaster at school. I didn't know anyone else who could help me. I'd enjoyed being at school even though I'd always been in a lower class for my age and had found reading, writing and arithmetic difficult in the early days. I'd never caught up with everyone else. No-one at our school would ever have thought about going to university, no matter how clever they were. University was for rich people, not the likes of us. Anyway, Mr White was a kindly old man, at least he seemed old to me but was probably only 50 or so at that time. He just looked old. He'd a little moustache and always wore a brightly coloured tie with a matching handkerchief in his jacket pocket. His secretary was called Miss Jones and she was as wide as she was high. Her desk was just outside Mr White's office so you had to walk past her to get to him. I don't know why but Miss Jones had always taken an interest in me and she'd arranged for me to see Mr White. In the normal course of events, you only saw the headmaster at morning assembly or if he was walking down a corridor. It was quite a scary experience to be going to his office. However, there was no need for me to have worried at all as he seemed very happy to listen to my hopes of being a motor mechanic and told me he would try and see if he could find something for me.

So, it wasn't more than a week later when Miss Jones came to our classroom and asked our teacher if I could go and see Mr White. Now, it was unusual to be called to see the headmaster, the normal reasons being that you'd either done something wrong or there'd been a tragedy of some sort at home, which wasn't all that uncommon at that time, as the Health and Safety wasn't what it is nowadays. Accidents happened all the time. So, everyone's eyes were on me as I got up and followed Miss Jones. Jack pulled a face at me as I went past him. When I got to Mr White's office I went in, sat down and he smiled as he told me he'd got me an interview with the manager at Pollard's, where Norma worked. There was a possibility of them taking me on as a doffer. Well, he might have had a smile on his face but I didn't have one on mine as I left his office. I knew that a doffer was the lowest of the low in the mill and, although I also knew that any job offer couldn't be turned down, it was a disappointment I couldn't hide so I made my way to the boy's toilets, locked myself in a cubicle and had a good cry. My dreams of being a motor mechanic were not to be. It had been easier for Mr White to get in touch with Pollard's than start looking for more interesting possibilities.

So, on a lovely sunny day on 7th June, 1938, which was my fourteenth birthday, I started at Pollard's Mill as a doffer.

18:26:11 – 18:30:51

As he went through the door, he breathed a sigh of relief as he saw there were only five people ahead of him. It was a very popular fish and chip shop and sometimes the queue went right outside. He'd only been there a few seconds when the owner of the shop spotted him and called out that he would put the usual order on for him. This consisted of a fish special, which was an extra-large fish, plus a fish cake and an extra sized portion of chips. He was quite hungry but if he couldn't manage to eat it all tonight, it would do for his breakfast in the morning. The microwave was useful for that sort of thing. He'd done this a few times before and the chips had always tasted alright.

He looked at the people in front of him. One woman, a workman in one of those bright green vest things and three scouts in uniform. That reminded him it was Tuesday because the scouts always met in the church hall on Tuesday evenings. The lady at the front was served and, as she turned round to leave, he realised that it was the woman who had recently given him all her husband's clothes. She said hello and then hurried away, giving him a broad smile and saying she would see him later. He hoped not.

As he stood there patiently waiting, leaning on his zimmer frame, he became aware that his right foot was hurting him. This was a worry and the only cause he could think of was that the neighbour had tied the laces too tightly. His leg was bad enough without having to deal with a painful foot as well. The left foot seemed too tight too. He wondered about asking someone to tie the laces again for him but decided to do it for himself when he got outside. He could sit on the little wall again and try to reach down. This would be better because he knew exactly how he wanted the laces to be.

A Working Lad

Bradford has always been a wool town. It started off with little stalls in the city centre hundreds of years ago, selling wool that had been brought down off the moors on pack horses. Then, during the Industrial Revolution in the 1800's, Bradford grew and grew until the city was more or less surrounded by mills. It wasn't a city back then, of course, but a town. It became a city in 1937. Bradford, at one time, had more millionaires as a percentage of the population than London had. They were called wool barons and built lots of big houses, some of which are still standing today.

However, nothing lasts forever, so they say, and Bradford's rise to affluence started to slide during the 1920's as a worldwide recession began. What became known as The Great Depression arrived here in 1929, going on into the 1930's and leading to the misery of high unemployment and widespread poverty. The north of England bore the brunt of the depression 'cos most of the country's heavy industries were here, such as coal, steel, mining and ship building. At the start of 1930 there was 70% unemployment in some areas. Families began to depend on government handouts which were called the dole. The problem was that the payments were according to how much the worker had contributed so those in low paid employment didn't get very much at all and, in any case, it was only paid for 15 weeks. After that the family had to rely on their local authority for help. This often meant that many of those who were long term unemployed were virtually destitute. I think this system changed in 1931 when unemployment benefit became means tested but this wasn't very nice, either, as the applicant had to answer lots of questions to prove they didn't have any savings or other form of earnings. All this was very humiliating for a lot of very poor people.

So, as a family, we counted ourselves very lucky indeed. By the time I left school, father had risen to the dizzy heights of being a foreman for the council road repairing teams. This meant that his job was safe and there was a weekly wage coming in even though it had to go a long way. He worked outside in all weathers and often arrived home with muddy trousers, boots wet through and a soggy overcoat which created an awful smell as it dried in the kitchen. Sometimes, if he'd been involved more with the labouring side of the work such as laying tarmac, then his clothes would smell of tar and if one of us had a bit of a cold we were told to sit next to his coat or jacket and breathe deeply. I don't think it did a bit of good.

Although a lot of Bradford mills had closed in earlier years due to the Great Depression, there were still some on the go near where we lived and so my first job was to be at Pollards. Norma had got there first and was working in the office. I was to be a doffer, the job arranged for me by Mr White, the Headmaster. Starting at the mill was quite a shock. I'd have liked to have been a garage mechanic but it was all out of my hands at the time and I wasn't given any choice in the matter. For a start off, now I'd to get up no later than 5.45 am 'cos my shift started at 6.30 am and even then, it was a rush most mornings. I finished at 5.45pm so I'd been on the go for 12 hours. That was Monday to Friday and we worked on Saturday mornings as well from 7.30 am to 11.30 am. After all the years of not seeing a lot of father, it was strange having breakfast with him, not that it consisted of much, just a thick slice or two of bread covered with dripping, known as doorsteps, and a big mug of tea. It was quick, easy and very filling. We got another breakfast at work about 8 o'clock which I was always pleased about 'cos I was forever hungry. I suppose I was a growing lad. Sometimes I ate my sandwiches for that breakfast and then I'd to buy something for dinner which used up my spare cash. One of the girls used to go out with the orders and bring back whatever we wanted. She went to the Sunshine Café where Helen was working. There was a small area just off a corridor where we could get hot water so, provided you took your own pot, tea and sugar, you could make tea. We all shared a bottle of milk. The treat of the week came on a Friday when we all ordered fish and chips for our dinner. I don't know if recipes for batter have changed much since then or maybe it was 'cos they came wrapped in newspaper, which also gave us something to read, but I'm sure they tasted better than they do nowadays.

As Doreen didn't go in for much home cooking, the sandwiches which I sometimes ate at my work breakfast time, were what I'd made the night before from whatever was about. I once took sandwiches filled with cold porridge 'cos there wasn't anything else. Those were the days before everyone had a fridge, so we kept things like cheese and eggs on a shelf down the cellar steps. People usually went shopping every day for bread and fresh food 'cos there were plenty of small family-owned shops like butchers, bakers and greengrocers. Maybe there were some candlemakers, too. Anyway, they seemed to be on every corner. These days its supermarkets everywhere instead. They're alright, I suppose, but you can't chat to the assistant on the till like you can to someone who's there all the time in their own shop. These assistants are forever changing, as well. You never see the same one twice. It's getting like that at the doctors. I used to see Doctor Gray every time, as he knew all about me. Now they've changed the system and you've to see whoever is available. This means that you don't get to see the same doctor very often and so you've to start explaining yourself all over again. And some of them are so young, you feel that they're guessing. The older doctors always applied some common sense. Now they send you away with a prescription for some pills. I've loads of them and it takes me ages on a morning to take them all.

Anyway, my shift started at 6.30 am. I only had a ten-minute walk so that wasn't too bad but it often turned into a five-minute run as sometimes I just couldn't get myself out of bed. When I'd been for my interview at Pollards, I'd met Mr Mitchell who turned out to be the works manager. He was there on my first morning, waiting just inside the main door and he showed me how to clock in, as it was called. Everyone had a card which was kept in a slot on a board near the time clock. As you arrived you had to find your card and then put it into the machine which printed the time on it. This way, at the end of the week, the wages department could work out how many hours you'd worked or to put it another way, how much time you'd missed by being late. At some places a buzzer sounded at the start of the shift and this gave you five minutes to get through the gate. If you got there after the gates had been locked then some mills made you wait until breakfast time before they would let you in. This meant that you'd lost two hours and that was why I often did the five-minute run to work.

Some people paid a man to wake them up every day. He was known as a 'knocker-up' and came along at the time you wanted to be woken up with a long stick with wires on the end which he bashed against your bedroom window. Some of them used a pea-shooter. It was often done by an elderly man or woman but sometimes it was the local policeman as he did his beat. This gave them a bit of extra pay as it cost about a shilling a week. I don't think Trickie Dickie did it, though. Anyway, we never had to bother with anything like that 'cos the house next door used one of these 'knockers-up' and he was so loud I think he woke the whole street up. So, after I'd done my first clocking- in, Mr Mitchell took me through to where I was to work. It seemed a very large place to me and, after walking through enormous rooms with high glass ceilings and huge looms rattling away, we eventually reached Shed 6 where the noise of the machines was so loud it was impossible to hear what the person next to you was saying. The air was filled with dust and the floor was greasy with lanolin from the wool. These glass ceiling were called northern lights. Not because they were multi coloured but 'cos they were found in the north of England. They doubled the natural light coming in. Looking up, they were like the inside of tents with one glass wall going straight up and the other sloping down. Our room had about twenty of these all across from one end to the other. It was ok in winter but got a bit hot in summer. The supervisor, or overlooker, as they were known, was Mr Parry and, after Mr Mitchell had gone, he called over another lad about my age and told him to show me the ropes. His name was Billy. He worked on four machines and I was destined to have the other four. They seemed enormous to me. He'd to shout at the top of his voice 'cos of the noise and I learnt how to lip read like everyone else 'cos it was impossible to have a normal conversation in there. I never forgot how to do this and I could often make out what people were talking about at the other side of the pub, in later years. No one knew I could listen in to their conversations.

So, I learnt how to be a doffer. I don't know why taking the full bobbins off and putting back empty ones was called doffing but it was. Maybe it's to do with taking things off 'cos when you doff your clothes or your hat, you take them off. There was a long row of spinning machines down one side of the room, or I really should say shed, 'cos that's what each of these places was called. There were eight of these machines and the spaces between them was called a gate. Each machine had two sides – front and back, with 44 bobbins on each, which both ran at the same time. The machines were driven by long leather belts which were fastened with metal clips. If any of these clips came off, the leather belt whipped into the air and could cause serious injury, especially if it caught you in the face. When all the bobbins were full the machine automatically stopped and that was when these full bobbins were taken off, put into an empty wicker basket on wheels, and the new empty bobbins put on. After that had been done there was a steel bar called a monkey which had to be lifted up to the top of the machine so it could be re-started. Then again, when a thread broke, I'd to take the wasted thread off and fasten the good thread back onto the bobbin. This gave me blistered fingers until I found out how to do it properly. A poorly repaired knot is called a slub and we got into trouble if there were a lot of these. The ladies in the burling and mending department dealt with these faults and managed to make them disappear.

Cleaning the machine was very important as well and it was best done while everything was still going, cos we were all on piece work, which means that we were paid for how much we did. If the machine wasn't running then we weren't earning anything. I was fourteen years old when I started doing this but before that, during Victorian times, children as young as five would be going under the machines to clean them and to collect fluff and fibres which had fallen onto the floor. These children were often seriously injured and many of them lost fingers or limbs in accidents with the machinery. As well as that, they could be badly treated by the overlookers and could be beaten quite brutally for some small offence such as talking. Billy told me he'd heard of a girl who had once had nearly all her clothes ripped off but no one could hear her because of all the noise and another time a young boy had three fingers torn off. Apparently, a girl fainted when she saw the blood on the floor but the overlooker told the others to pick the fingers up and carry on, to keep production going. There were no laws to stop this happening until the Factories Act of 1939 changed all that and made it plain what mill owners had to do to make sure their workers were safe. I know all about this 'cos there was a big poster at one end of the shed and I'd to pass it every time I wanted to visit the doings.

Anyway, on the first morning after Billy had shown me what to do, I was on my own. I got a bit muddled up the first few times and Billy wasn't pleased that he'd to keep breaking off his work to help me. After our breakfast at 8 o'clock we were allowed another short ten-minute break in the morning and our dinner time was 12 noon. By this time, I was worn out. Just before this, though, a few of the other lads came to the end of a gate, pushed me near a wall, pulled down my trousers and poured some oil on my twiddly bits. I didn't know what was going on and wondered if Doreen had put them up to it. But, when they saw how frightened I was, they pulled me and my trousers up and, still laughing, told me I'd passed the initiation test by not shouting out. Apparently, this happened to all new lads in the sheds. Sam told me later that at Whitehead's mill an initiation ceremony for new lads there often meant being trapped in a wicker basket with the lid down and pushed over the cobbles for five minutes. At least mine was over in a few seconds.

There was a canteen in the factory so, on that first day, I went there. However, by the time I'd queued up for my meal, eaten it and gone back to work, the whole half hour was gone, so after that I generally took sandwiches and ate them near my machines where I could at least have a proper sit down even if it was only on a wicker basket. It was a lot cheaper doing that, in any case. We got another ten-minute break in the afternoon. The machines had to be kept running at all times so Billy and me had to go on our breaks at separate times. Looking after eight machines was very hard work. Four was bad enough.

As nearly everyone left school at fourteen in them days, there were quite a lot of other boys my own age and, if we'd eaten our sandwiches quickly, we sometimes played marbles which was good fun. I made friends with a boy called Stanley, who was a bobbin sorter, which meant that he sat down all day picking bobbins off a conveyor belt. As they came down the chute, he'd to throw them into various tubs. It looked a lot easier than what I'd to do. Stanley and me tried to have our breaks and dinner together whenever we could. We got on really well. In later years we went to the local dance halls in search of young ladies and even joined the same regiment in the army on the same day some years later in 1942. Anyway, I finally finished my first day at 5.45pm but it had been so hard and I was so exhausted that when I got home, I could scarcely speak and went straight up to bed without having anything to eat.

However, I was woken some time later by Jack who told me I'd to get up quickly and go downstairs. I thought something had gone wrong again and went down feeling sick. But I needn't have worried as Alice and Annie had both come back to see me and were in the kitchen along with Helen and Jack. They were all standing round the kitchen table which had been set out for a birthday tea. Norma had gone out with Laurence. Annie had brought a birthday cake and it even had my name on it and one candle which had come from the candle box in the cellar. We all sat round and had our potted meat sandwiches. Then Alice lit the candle, I blew it out and they all sang Happy Birthday to me. I went back to bed the happiest lad in England.

So, thinking back to work, when the wicker basket was full, I'd to push it to the other end of the shed and out over the cobbles to another building where it was kept, along with all the others, until it was wanted in the weaving shed. Some places had bobbin laddies who pushed the full skip out but we didn't have any of those so we'd to do it ourselves. When those baskets were full they were very heavy and it soon built up my muscles. I don't think I'd had any before then. After doing that I'd to bring back another basket filled with empty bobbins to use up again. They were recycled, just like we're supposed to do with everything today. All this had to be done as fast as possible. It was like that programme on the tele called Beat the Clock, except we'd to do it every day. Back then a 48-hour week was standard for a lot of manual labourers, of which I was now one.

It seemed a long week to me but, as I queued up to get my first wage which was twelve shillings and sixpence, I was quite proud of myself. Particularly as I hadn't been late once. It would have been nice to have kept this wage to myself but I knew this wouldn't be possible and had to hand over my unopened wage packet to father, later that night, just like Annie and Alice had had to do. He'd always given them something back and I was quite pleased to receive three shillings. Up to then Father had given us all a few pence now and then so pocket money was something I'd never really had, except when the Aunties had given Jack and me pennies and I'd done those extra jobs to pay for Lucky. The trips over to see the relatives had always been the best way of getting some money and it was nice being given a threepenny bit. We said this as a thrupenny bit as we lived in Yorkshire. It was worth three pennies and I spent a lot of my money on comics. They were easy for me to read as the story was told by the pictures. I particularly liked The Rover and Alice had made a point of getting me an old copy of The Rover Annual for my birthday. This liking for comics carried on for years and later I became a fan of The Hotspur and then moved on to The Dandy. I think it came out about the time I started work and I used to take them to work for something to read at break times. I must have had quite a collection. I wish I'd got them now 'cos some of them are rare and change hands for hundreds of pounds. I shared all my comics with Jack. We kept them in a cardboard box under my bed along with The Boys Book of Astronomy.

One of my favourite things whenever we went back to Napier Street was to call in and see Auntie Lucy. She'd been one of my mother's sisters and she still lived with Grannie Annie. She was also very good friends with Auntie Mary and one of the saddest events of that year was that Auntie Mary died. She'd been poorly for quite some time but it was still a shock to hear that she'd passed away. Again, this was a funeral I didn't go to but I did benefit from her demise as Auntie Lucy got all her books. So, if me or Jack wanted another book, we'd go over to Grannie Annie's and look on Auntie Lucy's book shelves. I'd already got The Boys Book of Astronomy and Jack had Treasure Island and every time we went over we came back with a few more. We kept them under our beds. I loved books even though my reading was still slow. The Boy's Book of Astronomy was still our favourite, though, 'cos it had loads of pictures in it. I don't know what happened to Tom the lodger.

At the time I got my job at Pollard's Norma was still working in the office there, although I never got to see her. They had different hours to us and I think she didn't like to admit that her brother was a doffer. The twins, Nellie and Mabel were still working at Lingard's department store in Bradford so, although Alice and Annie had now left home, there were, in theory, five wages coming in. I don't think Helen's amounted to much, though, except in teacakes. I don't know how much all this added up to and, although Doreen had been married to father for over five years, she still treated us all like second class citizens. If we'd chicken then she made sure that Nellie and Mabel got the best white meat whilst we all had to make do with the legs and other bits and pieces. I don't know why father never said anything but he didn't. It had been the same with the hair washing for the girls. There was always an argument going on about whose turn it was to commandeer the sink for half an hour and it seemed to me that Mabel always got there first. It was no wonder that Alice left home as soon as she could.

In the September of 1938 Alice married Frank. They had been courting for over a year and had decided not to wait any longer, especially as there were rumblings of a war in the offing. They got married at Bradford Register Office. Frank had a good job and worked in a wool merchant's office down in Bradford. I don't know exactly what he did but he was always very nicely dressed whenever he called at our house. I think Frank must have earned quite a good wage as Alice and Frank managed to buy a little house. This was a bit further on from Sam and Annie who'd left Heath Street and bought a small terraced house on Tyersal Road. Alice had been working at Whitehead's since she'd moved in with the family down Leeds Road, so, she didn't have to change her job. She worked in the canteen. I suppose her experience in the café had come in useful.

Again, Doreen and her daughters didn't come, so it was up to Jack, Helen, Norma and me to go to their wedding instead. Alice hadn't spoken to father since she'd left and so he wasn't invited. It was a rainy Saturday morning. Sam was Frank's best man and Annie stood in as Maid of Honour. As we came out of the register office, I saw a man standing in a doorway opposite. It was father, watching another daughter getting married. I didn't say anything. Then we all walked down the road to the Midland Hotel. I can't remember what we had to eat, but I do remember Helen and Norma crying as Annie, Sam, Alice and Frank all went home together to Tyersal, whilst we had to get the bus home to Eccleshill and Doreen.

18:30:51 – 18:36:58

After being served and carefully putting the fish and chips into the brown leather bag, he left the fish and chip shop and turned right. He was about to go up the three deep steps when he was met by a man coming down who stopped and helped him.

Once at the top, he sat on the low wall and put the zimmer frame with its precious cargo next to him. It seemed a long way down to his boots but, using the zimmer frame for balance, he managed to undo the laces of both boots. He'd been taught in the army how to fasten laces so they could be undone quickly with one tug but the army, however, didn't teach you how to fasten them up again if you only had one hand. So, he sat there wondering what to do.

Then, the man who had helped him up the steps came out of the fish shop. Although Harry had told himself that he wasn't going to bother anyone, he asked the man if he could please fasten the laces up for him. There was no hesitation and, whilst Harry held the warm parcel containing the man's supper, following Harry's directions the laces were soon tied exactly how he wanted them. The man wished him good night and went on his way.

So, he set off again, stopping every few yards to get his breath back. He approached the blue gate with utmost caution. He stopped and listened. No growling. No dog. It must have been taken inside. What a relief. Another few steps and the left leg was beginning to be painful again. It had seemed a lot better whilst he was in the queue but now it was aching again. He comforted himself that at least he didn't have to stop and empty the bag in the drain and the boots were more comfortable now the laces were looser. By the time he reached the wall at the corner of Laburnum Grove he just had to sit down and rest. He could smell the fish and chips and couldn't resist putting his hand in and taking out a few chips. They tasted so good he was tempted to eat them all just where he was. However, he was beginning to get very cold. So, he pushed himself up, grabbed hold of the zimmer frame and turned to cross Laburnum Grove. It wasn't far now.

And What Did You Do In The War?

There'd been a lot of talk and gossip in the mill for a long time about the possibility of a war with Germany and, in fact, some gas masks were actually given out in 1938. Father came home with six one night in a big brown box. Jack and me had great fun trying them on until Doreen intervened and made us put them back in the box. She didn't have much of a sense of humour. I don't know why he only got six or why he got them at all but maybe council employees were given priority. So, after the Prime Minister at the time, Neville Chamberlain, came back from a meeting with Adolf Hitler waving a piece of paper telling everyone it was Peace in our Time, we all thought that was that and there wouldn't be a war. Doreen had already covered our windows with strips of sticky brown paper to stop the glass flying in, in case a bomb dropped nearby, although we never thought that our house would be hit. It was always going to be someone else's. Father also brought home some pieces of wood and we kept these propped up on the back wall of the kitchen so that if there was an air- raid we could all get under the table and shield ourselves with the wood. How on earth he thought that we'd all fit under the table I don't know. And we only had six gas masks.

Jack was fourteen in May 1939 and had found a job at Pollard's, like me and Norma. He'd never wanted to work as a doffer, or anything else on the shop floor for that matter. So, when he'd been sent round to see Mr Mitchell, like I was, apparently, he did some sort of written test which got him the job of office junior in the same office as Norma. He seemed to do a lot of filing and running all over the place with messages. Sometimes, though, when there wasn't much to do I expect, he would appear with a sweeping brush and we would have a bit of a chat. In them days, of course, there were no computers, just pens and paper. There was a telephone service but it was very limited. If you wanted to make a call you went through to the Post Office telephone operator who would dial it for you. Although Norma did most of the typing in the office Jack said he'd like to learn so we rescued the typewriter father had brought home for Norma. We found it under her bed. Jack put it back on the kitchen table and taught himself. He eventually did letters and invoices and this skill came in very useful when he joined the police force. So now we were all working, except Doreen. None of us could ever work out what Doreen did all day. She didn't punish me anymore, as I was quite tall by this time, but I always felt that I was at the bottom of the pile, as far as she was concerned. She never once gave me a cuddle.

However, on 3rd September 1939, which was a Sunday, at 11.00 am whilst father was listening to the radio in the front room, he called us all in 'cos the Prime Minister was going to make an announcement. A few weeks before this, Jack, Helen and me had decided that we'd like to have Sunday dinners again so, we put down our knives and peelers, stopped preparing the vegetables and went in to listen. We only had enough seats for four people so Helen, Jack and me had to stand in the middle of the room. We listened as the Prime Minister came over the radio telling us, in what was a very sad and tired voice, that we were now at war with Germany. I began to be glad that we'd the wood near the kitchen table, after all. We would need another two gas masks, though.

One result of this announcement affected me directly and quickly. I'd been at Pollard's for over a year now and had made friends with a lot of people including a set of lads my own age, one of which was Stanley. Another lad, who always came over to join us at dinner time, was called Chillo. He and Stanley were my best friends at Pollards. He'd been born here but his father was from Spain. His father had a cobblers shop just down the road from Pollard's. Anyway, it wasn't long after war had been declared that there was an announcement that anyone who hadn't been born in Great Britain, as we called ourselves then, were regarded as enemy aliens. Tribunals were set up around the country to try and find anyone who could harm our national interests and some of them were sent to internment camps. These were all over the place. The Lake District, the Isle of Man and the Isle of Wight were all used to keep these people away from our secrets. Others had restrictions put on them as to where they could go. One of these was Chillo's father. I can't remember the exact details but I know that Chillo had to leave Pollard's and go and work with his father instead. There were another three or four foreigners working at Pollards, and it wasn't long before they disappeared too. I don't know what happened to them.

Although we lived a long way from London and other big cities, father was busy at work helping to build defences for Bradford just in case Hitler decided that we'd be a target. In fact, we still lived not far from a big railway junction and it was known that such junctions were targets 'cos they helped to supply the country with what it needed. So, father filled sandbags at work and then again when he came home at night. A spirit of camaraderie built up and most police stations and public buildings had piles of sandbags outside them very soon. Another thing that happened was that road signs were taken down so that any invading troops wouldn't know which way to go. The Welsh Nationalists used to do that to the road signs in Wales years ago. It was a proper nuisance to holiday makers. Sometimes they moved them round to point in the opposite direction.

As well as the sandbags, we were also ordered to keep a blackout. Doreen had brought a sewing machine with her so that came out and she made us some blackout curtains with special material that Nellie or Mabel had managed to get from Lingard's. We hung these pieces of cloth from poles suspended above the windows. They'd to be put up as soon as it got dark and then taken down in the morning. It was a nuisance so we put up some heavy curtains downstairs which father got from the market. We continued with the blackout hangings upstairs and eventually just left them there all the time. As well as sandbags and blackouts there was the dreaded air raid warning siren. This was a screaming sort of sound which scared the life out of you when they tested it. You never knew if it was the real thing or not until they started testing it at the same time every week. Usually Friday at 12 noon. I used to wonder what people would have done if there had been an air raid at exactly the same time as they were testing the siren.

Anyway, everyone had to make arrangements about what they were to do in the event of an air raid and to this end Anderson Shelters were given to households earning less than £250.00 a year. I don't know what anyone earning £260.00 was supposed to do. These were made out of curved pieces of corrugated iron which bolted together. They were meant to go in back gardens and Annie and Sam got one. You could either just stand them on the ground or dig a three-foot deep hole for it and put the soil from the hole over the top as an extra precaution. As father was in the right occupation, being with the council road working gangs, he brought a pick axe home one day and spent a whole weekend digging up the stone flags in our back yard ready for our Anderson Shelter which never came.

Just before war had been declared something called Operation Pied Piper happened. With the threat of being bombed by the Luftwaffe, the government decided that it would be safer if children were sent away from towns and cities. So, over four days, hundreds of children were taken to railway stations with their gas masks, food ration books, clothes and a label pinned to their chests stating who they were and where they were going. They were literally moved across Britain to live with strangers. Some villages hadn't prepared for these children coming and so when they arrived the children were stood in lines and the people who had volunteered to take them in walked up and down the lines until they found a child they fancied taking home. The phrase 'I'll take that one' comes to mind. Life for some of them was pleasant I suppose if they were lucky enough to go to a farm or a house with a large garden. But many were unhappy, filled with anxiety at being away from their real homes and often mistreated, although it has to be said that lots of them probably went to much better living conditions than they had left behind. Some adults were also evacuated and in the end over three and a half million people were affected by this situation.

Anyway, Christmas came and went and life just continued on in Eccleshill as if nothing was happening in the rest of the world. There were a few precautions made at work when a lot of buckets arrived which we'd to fill with sand and put at the end of our machines and volunteers were asked for to go up on the roof as fire watchers. We all thought it was best to be prepared, just in case. Jack always finished before me but he didn't mind waiting for me so we enjoyed walking home together many a time, although it wasn't very far. Sometimes Stanley would join us as he lived our way too, near the White Hart, which father and Doreen frequented.

About the time of my sixteenth birthday in June of 1940 every household in the country got a leaflet with the terrifying title 'If the Invader Comes' which gave advice and hints on what we'd to do if the German army came marching down Norman Lane. Rule number one in the leaflet told us to stay put if the Germans came by parachute, plane or ship. They must've thought we'd be machine gunned down from the air. I don't know why they bothered, though, 'cos most of us would have automatically run away as fast as we could across the fields. We wouldn't have stopped at home to make them bacon and eggs. The second rule was that we hadn't to believe rumours and we hadn't to spread them, either. The leaflet said that the Germans told lies and if we were stopped by a British Officer, we'd to ask a policeman to verify the officer in case he was a German pretending to be British. And so it went on. I don't think many folk took much notice of it.

But, suddenly, on 8th August 1940, all our efforts to defend ourselves seemed to be worthwhile when the Luftwaffe, which was the name of the German air force, began attacking ports on the south coast. They also targeted shipping convoys, then moved inland to bomb aerodromes and the Thames Estuary and Kent but had heavy losses. We had a very efficient defence system. However, they kept on targeting the south coast despite more high losses. It was as if they just hoped we'd suddenly give in. There was a lull in these attacks for a few days at the end of August but then they changed tactics and made London their main objective. These attacks on started on 7th September at 4 o'clock in the afternoon. Large formations of enemy aircraft came flying over, dropping their bombs. Our Royal Air force defended every night in their Spitfire or Hurricane planes.

This first day became known as Black Saturday. On that first night they managed to bomb right across London setting it ablaze, the miracle being that although all the surrounding buildings were alight, St Paul's Cathedral remained undamaged. The Docklands in the East End, in particular, were targeted. This was a very densely populated area and hundreds of people were killed, more wounded and even more left homeless. This battle for the skies became known as The Battle of Britain and the bombing campaign on London is known as the Blitz. When it finally finished on 5th October, over 43,000 civilians had been killed, one in six was homeless and thousands of houses had been destroyed. In London, as well as the Anderson Shelters, lots of people went down into the underground to get away from the bombing. There are loads of old photographs showing them all sleeping on the platforms. None of this was near us, of course, but we listened to the radio every day for news of what was happening. There was no television in them days. We were thankful we didn't live in London.

Anyway, by this time, as father kept telling us, the island of Great Britain had been turned into a fortress. I think he tried to make us feel safe. Pillboxes, tank traps, gun emplacements and miles and miles of barbed wire had been put all around the coastline. There were even gun emplacements on the banks of the Leeds and Liverpool canal, as it was thought that the water, shining in moonlight, could lead the bombers to Liverpool, which was a very important port for us. There are still the remains of one or two of them today. All this was, of course, in case there was an invasion which everybody was convinced could happen any time. I suppose this was where the leaflet would have come in handy.

There was talk of nothing else at work where I was still a doffer. We'd blinds fitted over the roof lights and windows and everyone was very careful to turn lights off when they could. The firewatchers were still on the roof every night and we looked after our buckets of sand very carefully. If there had been an invasion by sea right at the beginning then I suppose the Territorial Army would have had to deal with it but in May 1940 a new force was announced to help defend us. It was called the Local Defence Volunteers. They were supposed to be on the lookout for parachutists coming down and invaders landing on the beaches in rowing boats but, as we were 80 miles from the coast, it all seemed a bit useless to us. This Local Defence Force was made up of men who lived locally and me and Stanley joined them as soon as we could. I think Jack was a bit too young. The television series Dad's Army which was based on a town on the south coast, makes fun of what they did but, at the end of the day, the idea was that if there was an invasion then the LDV would be able to hold the situation until regular troops arrived. We knew the LDV as the Look, Duck and Vanish brigade.

One night I met up with Stanley and we went to Eccleshill Congregational Church Hall to sign on, as that was where the Headquarters of the LDV was. Quite a few other lads of our age were already there. As you couldn't sign up for the regular army until you were 18 the LDV was seen as a start. I suppose we thought we were helping in some way. Well, we'd have had to help if an enemy parachutist had come down in Eccleshill. There would have been about two hundred of us waiting there, I suppose. We didn't have uniforms or guns. Instead, we were given an armband to wear and we'd to practice marching up and down with broom handles for rifles. But, we were taught map reading, first aid and how to do the semaphore with a torch. I showed Jack how to do this and we used to send each other messages in the dark after we'd gone to bed. Anyway, at weekends we used to go on what were called route marches and it wasn't unusual for us to be out for several hours at a time. We often had to run through fields, through Ravenscliffe Woods, down rough cart tracks and then defend a barn with our broom sticks.

In July the LDV was renamed the Home Guard which is what you see in the Dad's Army programme. Eventually we all got proper uniforms of a blouson jacket and trousers which made us look and feel like proper soldiers. By now, though, I'd got long arms and legs and so my trousers and jacket were too short. I'd to make do. There still weren't enough rifles to go round. Some of us were still using the broom handles and no one knew what we'd do if the Germans turned up. Defending Eccleshill with broom handles didn't seem like the best idea, but we did look nice in our uniforms.

We were split into platoons and every two weeks each platoon was on duty and we'd to report to the Church Hall at 6 pm for our orders. Unfortunately, it was sometimes an all-night duty and two of us had to stand at the church gate facing Harrogate Road, as there was Fisher's mill opposite which we also had to guard. It was spooky standing there in the cemetery in the middle of the night. It was two hours on and four hours off with a good supper somewhere in between duties. What we were all scared of was German parachutists suddenly coming down. Some of us started taking spade handles as these were more robust than broom handles, together with garden forks and rakes. As well as the route marches, we also did physical training in the yard consisting of jumping up and down and running on the spot for what seemed like hours. Occasionally we'd to go over to the nearby fields and crawl about in the long grass which always seemed to be wet as we often went home soaked. All this seemed too much for us sometimes but it all came in handy later when me and Stanley were in the real army.

As well as being in the Home Guard, I was also picked to be part of the team of workers who were on Fire Watch at Pollards. There was something called the Auxiliary Fire Service which did fire watching too but I think they were there to look after public buildings such as Town Halls, so we did our own. Anyway, I did fire watching one night every two weeks which meant that sometimes I didn't have any sleep at all for forty-eight hours if it came the same week as the overnight carry-on in the cemetery. I have to say, though, that Pollards was well organised up on the roof. There loads of those galvanized buckets which we also had near our machines, filled with water or sand in case the hose, which the maintenance men had fixed up, didn't work. Of course, we all knew that if the mill went up in flames everyone would lose their job so it was up to everyone to join in and help. As well as the Home Guard there was another organisation called the ARP which stood for Air Raid Patrol. These Wardens, as they were called, were often women or, like the Home Guard, men who were too old to be called up, and went round making sure that everyone had a proper blackout. You got into trouble if even the smallest chink of light was showing. I think it was a criminal offence.

There were all sorts of other organisations crying out for volunteers, as a lot of the original employees were going off to join the services. Ambulance drivers and first aid workers were all needed as well as rescue teams. Besides volunteering for Fire Watch duties, father had joined the Heavy Rescue Squad. As he was a foreman and in charge of a team of road-repairers they probably used the equipment they'd with them all day. One night at the end of August, there was a knock on the door and I opened it to find it was Fred, who was a friend of father's and was in the Rescue squad too. Father was in the front room in his armchair fast asleep, having already called at The White Hart on his way home. We could hear him snoring from the kitchen. He'd forgotten that he was meant to be on duty and it was only by chance his friend had called for him. Seeing father asleep Fred shook him by the shoulder to wake him up and told him to get a move on or they'd be late. Father replied that he'd be ready as soon as he could find his teeth to which Fred said that Hitler would be dropping bombs not sandwiches. Father left the house without his teeth.

The following day, father told us that the Heavy Rescue Squad had had to go down to Bradford that night as the air raid siren had gone off and it'd been likely they would be needed. They travelled there in an ambulance, along with ten other members of the squad. The centre of Bradford was in complete darkness as everything was blacked out but the cinemas were all emptying as they got there and everyone was shining their torches on the ground to see where they were going. Father reckoned that it was these little lights that the Germans spotted as they flew over. We'd heard the planes and it wasn't long before we'd scuttled into the air raid shelter under the table pressed up against Nellie and Mabel. Norma was hunched up in a corner with Helen pressed up against her. We enjoyed pulling faces at Nellie and

Mabel, once we'd got our gas masks on, 'cos they couldn't see what we were doing. Doreen didn't get a gas mask as she was the last one in. Helen had screwed some handles to the pieces of wood so we could hold them up like shields just as the knights of the round table did. Except our table was square. Anyway, we all sat there in our gas masks listening to the droning noise of the planes as they circled above Bradford. We missed seeing the bombing.

The centre of Bradford had been hit as well as houses up Leeds Road. We were glad we'd moved from Napier Street as a bomb dropped on Tyersal Road but didn't explode which was very lucky for the people living there, especially Annie, Sam, Alice and Frank. Father reckoned it was a target 'cos Tyersal Road is very long and straight and would have looked like an airstrip. We were under the table for hours that night. We hadn't ever spent so much time with Nellie, Mabel or Doreen. It must have been a Saturday night, as I think we all slept late the next morning. On the Monday Nellie and Mabel found they no longer had jobs 'cos a bomb had fallen on Lingard's. It was a good thing they'd got the blackout material when they did.

Just after all this had happened, though, father had come home one night and announced we were moving to yet another house. This one was on Mount Street which wasn't far away at all but we were excited at the prospect of having three bedrooms, a cellar and an attic. It was a middle terrace house and we couldn't wait to see an end to living like sardines. The thought of another night under the kitchen table with Doreen, Nellie and Mabel filled us with horror. We'd be able to go down to the cellar instead. At that time, we were all out working, except Nellie and Mabel who'd recently lost their jobs due to Lingard's being bombed. Doreen was still an unknown quantity. So, we all perked up thinking about the forthcoming move but then things took a very unexpected turn.

Doreen had started to be unwell about the same time that the London Blitz had started at the beginning of September. At first, she'd complained about having headaches and took to her bed. Then she started feeling sick and didn't want anything to eat. Father called the doctor one evening who took one look at her and went back to telephone from his surgery for an ambulance. No one down our street had a telephone and, of course, mobile phones were something related to science fiction at the time. The doctor thought Doreen should be in hospital so she was taken to Bradford Royal Infirmary.

Father went with her and came back just before 10 o'clock to tell us that Doreen had died in the ambulance and they'd never got her to the BRI at all. Nellie and Mabel were out at the time, which wasn't unusual, so father had the job of telling them when they got in. Me and Jack went up to bed. Helen was already fast asleep. We couldn't quite believe we'd never see her again. She'd only brought misery into our lives. Norma waited up with Father.

I seemed to remember that our own mother was buried very soon after she died, unlike Doreen who had the honour of being in her coffin in our front room for three days, mostly with the lid off. A neighbour lent us two chairs and she was balanced on them. There always seemed to be someone coming to have a look at her. They call it paying your respects. I don't know if Norma went in to look but me, Jack and Helen didn't. Coming round when they knew father would be out, Alice and Annie had called in to see us but neither of them had wanted to see Doreen. They brought us all fish and chips. As we sat round the kitchen table, with Doreen lying in state in our front room, we all said how thankful we were that she'd gone. Nobody knew where Norma was. We all agreed that the thought of seeing a dead body was too awful for words, especially that of Doreen although I suppose it would have confirmed that she'd really gone if we'd had a look. Our experience at Uncle Bernard's years ago had not been entirely forgotten, either. Over the next few days, the door to the front room was kept firmly shut. Helen spent a lot of time in our bedroom and Jack was still practising his typing on the kitchen table. I read out passages from the Boys Book of Astronomy for him to type. This had the advantage of helping to improve my reading, too. I don't know about Helen but me and Jack couldn't get to sleep for the thought of Doreen getting out of her coffin and coming to tell us off about something. We hardly saw Norma and father just came in and out as fast as he could before rushing off to drown his sorrows in a pint of beer.

In them days when someone died, it was usual for all the nearby houses to draw their curtains on the day of the funeral, which they did for Doreen. Her death was all muddled up with us moving house and we actually moved out the day after her funeral. Anyway, everybody pulled their curtains on for her. Just as I hadn't gone to my mother's funeral so I didn't go to Doreen's, neither did Jack nor Helen. Annie and Alice didn't bother, either. In fact, to this day I don't know who went, apart from father, Norma, Nellie and Mabel. I don't even know where she was buried and, at the end of the day, I'm not that bothered. There's a cemetery just round the corner near Mount Street, where we moved to. I don't mean we moved into the cemetery, just that it was near our new house. Anyway, she might have been put there but I never went to look and no one told me. I was at work at the time of her funeral. After losing our own mother we'd all had to more or less bring each other up, Doreen caring more for her own two daughters than she ever did for us. Nellie and Mabel never actually came to Mount Street with us.

On the morning of the move, which was a Saturday, they came down stairs with a battered old suitcase each and just walked off. I'd been given permission to be at home that morning, rather than going into work. I wasn't paid, of course but just wanted to be there this time. I think Nellie and Mabel must have had a word with father 'cos he told us they'd found lodgings in Manningham but, we didn't care and we were all as pleased as Punch that they'd gone. The new house would have been better for us whilst we were all there, but now two had suddenly gone, it meant even more room for us. It had been too late to stop the move. Helen and Norma now could have their own bedrooms whilst me and Jack now had the longed-for attic. We didn't hear anything about either Nellie or Mabel until years later someone told me that Mabel had eventually married but her husband, who was in the Royal Marines, had been killed and Mabel had committed suicide shortly after that. They didn't know anything about Nellie. Father had the main front bedroom to himself.

However, that state of affairs wasn't to last too long, either, 'cos Norma married Laurence towards the end of October 1940. He'd come home on leave from the navy and I think it was a last-minute arrangement. Norma was just 20 years old. So, once again, we all traipsed down to Bradford Register Office except this time we didn't go to the Midland Hotel or Collinson's Café but to Kirkgate Market where we enjoyed pie and peas. There was no sign of father this time. I think they spent their first night as a married couple at the Midland Hotel. Laurence had to return to his duties so Norma came back to us for a couple of weeks and then she went to live with Alice and Frank. Sam, who now was a manager at Whitehead's, had got Norma a job there, so she left Pollard's and Eccleshill.

So, as fast as Norma packed her suitcase and left, Helen and me moved round. Helen went to the larger back bedroom, vacated by Norma, and I came down from the attic to the smaller front bedroom. Although I liked sharing with Jack, I was glad to be coming down as I hadn't been looking forward to a freezing winter up there. Jack decided not to move. We now had spare beds we didn't need so we dismantled them, selling them to the family next door, together with one of our little truckle beds, for seven shillings and sixpence. We put that towards two chests of drawers and two chairs from a second-hand shop round the corner. Father had given his approval for this and, much to our surprise, had given us some more money so we could get what we wanted. I'd also been over to see the aunties at Laisterdyke, just after the move and came back with a rag rug and a small rickety wooden bookcase, which I carried on my back. It'd been donated by Auntie Lucy. I put the rag rug next to my bed and the bookcase next to the chest of drawers. I can still remember the pleasure I got from filling the bookcase with my books, pride of place being taken by The Boy's Book of Astronomy. Jack had managed to talk father into buying even more furniture and ended up getting a little table for the attic, and a typist's swivel chair, where he constantly practised his typing. Father had managed to replace the radio taken by the bailiffs and came home one night with an old bedside cupboard to put it on. We'd been very short of furniture since the Doreen and The Bailiffs episode.

It was wonderful to have my own room and the chair was always useful as I put my clothes on there in reverse order every night, so I could hop out of bed and get dressed quickly every morning. I also managed to find a small wardrobe in the second-hand shop for next to nothing and Stanley helped me to carry it round one Saturday afternoon. This was where I kept my coat and jacket, with my boots on the shelf at the bottom. I couldn't get over having so much storage space to myself as I only had five shirts and these, along with my underwear, were placed carefully in the chest of drawers. In the attic we'd kept our things on a nail at the back of the door with smaller items like socks and underwear in boxes under our beds. Helen felt the same about her room, talking father into getting her another small wardrobe. Jack had to make do with his little typing table and swivel chair and boxes under his bed, as we couldn't get anything bigger up into the attic.

Now at the beginning of the war in 1939 conscription had begun and we counted ourselves as very lucky that none of our family had been called up. However, they must have got to the letter H 'cos in the middle of December of 1940 Sam got his call up papers. His surname being Harris. By some unfortunate cast of fate Alice's husband, Frank, got his the following week, just before Christmas. His surname was Collins and we all thought he'd been forgotten. We were glad that father was in what was called a reserved occupation 'cos the ages for conscription had just been extended to include men up to the age of 50 and father was just 48 years of age.

Christmas soon arrived and we got an invitation from Annie and Sam to go over to their house for Christmas Day Dinner but it was made clear that father would not be welcome. That created a problem for me, Jack and Helen so in the end we decided we couldn't leave father sitting alone in the house on Christmas Day. We found a little tree and put up some decorations and on Christmas Day we gave each other a small present. We even managed to cook a decent Christmas Day Dinner for us all which was a minor miracle 'cos rationing meant that a lot of foods weren't there. But we might as well not have bothered. Father was sullen and took himself off to the White Hart. When he got back, we had our Christmas dinner but it was eaten mostly in silence. We pulled our home-made crackers and put our silly hats on but it didn't do any good. He went up to his bedroom as soon as he could and left his presents unopened under the tree. We all decided to go over to Annie and Sam's where we'd home-made mince pies and a lot of laughter. The following week Sam and Frank had gone.

So, the year turned and 1941 arrived. Gradually, for some reason we couldn't work out, father seemed to becoming happier in himself and now there were only four of us we saw him talking and laughing more than he'd done for a long time. The war was, of course, still under way, the mess of Dunkirk and the Battle of Britain having been and gone the year before. Dunkirk was where over 400,000 British troops who were trapped on the French coast were rescued by hundreds and hundreds of little fishing boats, civilian cabin cruisers and barges. They ferried the troops from the beaches to the larger ships offshore but despite the Royal Air Force protecting them a quarter of all these little boats were sunk by the Luftwaffe. All this began on 26th May and was known as Operation Dynamo. Anyway, that was 1940 and here we were in 1941 and still at war. We got news of what was happening from the War Report on the radio every night and there were newsreels in cinemas as well, although a lot of this news was censored to stop vital information passing into enemy hands. By keeping bad news from us, I suppose in a way it helped to keep our spirits up. It wasn't unusual to buy a newspaper with blank bits in it which had been censored out. At Pollard's, as with many other mills and factories all over the country, we were entertained every day with music, one particular programme being called Worker's Playtime when people could write in for requests to be played. After listening to the news on the radio with father in the front room, we sometimes listened to Tommy Handley. Father liked the Brains Trust, as well. I listened to this once but didn't understand any of it.

Dance Halls were popular, too although the dance hall in Laisterdyke, The Lyceum, was now a cinema again. This was where we'd gone as young children on Saturday mornings. Now it was a short bus ride away and the three of us would sometimes go to see the latest film. I remember one night we went to see Citizen Kane which starred Orson Welles and we'd to walk all the way back in total pitch darkness due to the blackout 'cos the buses had stopped running. In between fire watching and Home Guard duties, sometimes I went out with Stanley to the dance hall in Eccleshill. We were always hoping to meet someone. Stanley, besides being a good-looking young man, was also a good dancer so always had a girl on his arm. I got left behind in the good looks department. I also had two very large left feet. But I didn't mind and enjoyed sitting at the side just listening to the music and watching everyone.

It was during one of these sittings out that I got talking to a girl called Elsie who said that she'd two left feet as well. Although we didn't dance, we chatted a lot. She lived at the bottom of Leeds Road and we went to the Odeon Cinema a few times although her job as a trolley bus driver and my long shifts, the fire watching and the Home Guard, meant that meeting up was often difficult. I'd also got an allotment. It wasn't far from Mount Street and I enjoyed going there on a Sunday morning. It was completely overgrown when I started on it, as the man before me had joined the army and gone. Jack came and helped me and eventually we started growing things. It reminded me so much of the happy days we'd spent with Grandad Coble. I hadn't realised how much I'd learnt from him.

Back at home, we stuck a map on the kitchen wall so we could find places being mentioned in the news. It was a good lesson in geography. So, the war carried on and so did we with our everyday work. Father kept on repairing the roads, Helen kept on running the Sunshine Café, Jack kept on being the office junior at Pollard's and I kept on being a doffer.

Having practised for hours at home, Jack had become very good at typing and when he eventually joined me and Stanley in the Home Guard he proved useful at meetings 'cos there was a typewriter in the church hall office. He typed anything that was needed and when the minister of the church found out he began to ask Jack to type things up for him, as well. This made Jack think he was being taken for granted so, even though he was only sixteen, he started to charge for doing things for other people and actually made quite a good little income out of it. He was often on the typewriter in the evenings copying from some handwritten piece he'd been asked to do. It was on one of these evenings when we were on our own, that Jack confided in me that he'd like to join the police. I don't know where this came from as none of the men in our family had ever done anything but manual work. Anyway, that's what he was going to do when the opportunity came by.

So, at this time, most men had gone off to war, except those too old or, like father, in essential occupations. Suddenly, women from all walks of life were needed to support the war effort when there was a shortage of working men. They found themselves working in heavy industries such as steel making and hundreds were employed in munitions factories all over the country. They worked in engineering, chemical plants and did lots of the jobs previously done by men. They became postmen, or post ladies as we called them, they worked on the railways as train drivers, porters or ticket collectors or anything else which needed doing. They became bus or trolley bus drivers, like Elsie, and lots of women worked in big warehouses making parachutes and barrage balloons. These were enormous balloons, at least fifty feet long, which floated up in the air on long ropes. They were used to protect ships when they were in a convoy and passing through channels or narrow seaways by stopping dive bombers from attacking the ships. They were also used to protect ships while they were in port unloading much needed goods.

At Pollard's we found that there was more and more work to do 'cos material was needed to make military uniforms. Suddenly, overtime was available and sometimes compulsory, to meet demand, I suppose. My wages went up but as father didn't ask for an increase in my contribution to the household so I began to think I could save some of it. I went to see Mr Mitchell for some advice and he told me to open an account with the Prudential where I could put away a few shillings a week away. A man would come to the house to collect it every week. So, that's what I did. For the first time in my life, I'd money in the bank. I was still seeing Elsie and began to see a bit of a future for myself.

Now with four of us working I suppose we were, again, quite well off compared to some families on our street and with rationing coming along there wasn't much to spend our money on. We'd bought everything we needed at the second-hand shop and the house was more or less fully furnished. I thought about trying cigarettes but didn't fancy the idea of my hard-earned wages just going up in smoke. Father had given up smoking cigarettes soon after Doreen died. He'd never smoked a pipe, either, which I think was unusual back then. I don't think Jack or Helen ever smoked and Norma had been so fastidious about how she looked I can't imagine her wanting to be seen with a cigarette dangling from her mouth. This was a bit strange, when I think about it, 'cos lots of the film stars of the time were always photographed with a cigarette dangling from their mouth and Norma liked to think she was keeping up with the fashion of the day.

I've already mentioned rationing and this became more and more of a problem as the war progressed. Fresh fruit, butter, meat and vegetables became scarce. We were allowed one orange a month to begin with but this eventually went down to none 'cos there weren't any. Father even talked about taking the flag stones up in the back yard just like he'd done at Victoria Road, so we could grow vegetables until I reminded him that I'd an allotment. Loads of households dug up their back yards or gardens to grow cabbages. I often wondered if the Anderson shelter had ever arrived. We were never offered one on Norman Lane. Anyway, the allotment proved to be a real lifeline for us and the posters which said 'Dig for Victory' certainly applied to us. I was always running down the street with a bucket and spade if a horse and cart came by and there were horse droppings to be had. There was a horse at Pollard's, too, but there was a lot of competition for the droppings it made and I often missed out but I did take home wet straw which I put on the compost heap. I knew how to do a proper heap 'cos I'd watched Grandad Coble. So, with help from Jack and sometimes Helen, we did a lot of digging and I managed to take something home most weeks. Before the allotment arrived and had got going, we seemed to have fish and chips all the time, so the fresh vegetables were lovely. We'd lots of vegetable stews. Every so often I got a hen given from a man at the allotments but we didn't really like this 'cos we'd to pluck it and it was usually really old. We reckoned it had dropped dead from old age and the thing had to be cooked for hours before it could be eaten, especially by father with his false teeth.

As the war continued the food shortages got worse and it was a good job that the Women's Land Army had been formed. When volunteers were asked for over 80,000 women applied even though they knew they'd have to work at least 50 hours a week and get paid next to nothing. I don't think they did much in the way of cattle or sheep rearing as meat was always in short supply. A sausage was a treat. And no sooner had people dug up their gardens, they started keeping hens. You could keep all the eggs if you had less than 20 hens which was really good for those with these hens when the rest of us were rationed to two eggs a week each. Some terrace houses with long gardens at the back organised themselves so that each house grew one sort of vegetable and one had the hens and then they shared it all. Bread was never rationed, though, along with offal or fish which often turned out to be whale meat.

Helen was still working in the café but, as she didn't want to spend the rest of her life doing this, she'd been going for what would now be called private lessons to a woman two streets away to learn shorthand and typing. She'd practice on Jack's typewriter and though paper was in short supply too, she got by on the paper Jack was able to bring home from Pollards office. One day he'd been asked to clear out a cupboard and he found about twenty pages from an old accounts book just lying there at the bottom. They were very yellow and had all those lines on for accounting but Helen used every square inch of them. I think she worked hard at getting good with shorthand and got Jack to read passages from books out to her. I was still slow with my reading. Then she read them back to him from her shorthand and typed them up. He didn't always tell her he was going to use The Boys Book of Astronomy and I think this tested her to the limit.

But, then at the beginning of summer, just as Helen was going to look for a job as a shorthand typist she became poorly. She'd had a bad cough since the previous winter which hadn't got any better. The doctor had said it would improve but it never did until one day when she'd coughed so much, she simply couldn't get out of bed. As it happened, our doctor had gone off and joined the army so another doctor came on this particular day when she couldn't get out of bed. He asked loads of questions then said he thought Helen had TB, which needed special care. During the next few days Helen didn't leave her bed so father, Jack and me looked after her as best we could but as we were all out at work during the day, I went over to see Auntie Shackleton who came over every day until we got home. By the end of that week the doctor had managed to get Helen into a special home in Ilkley so an ambulance was organised and she was carried down the stairs to go and get better fifteen miles away in fresh country air. Ilkley's on the edge of the moors and there were no factories or mills like we'd all round us in Eccleshill. It was much healthier out there. But it was very awkward going to see her which we could only do at weekends when there was no Home Guard or fire watching duties. We ended up by each of us going one weekend in three and Annie, Alice, Norma and everyone else going whenever they could. I walked up to The Sunshine Café and explained what had happened to Helen. A lady called Mrs Shuttleworth had taken over where Helen had left off. Helen got better very slowly and eventually came home just before Christmas 1941 having spent over six months in Ilkley. As there was no National Health Service, I don't know how we paid for all this. I think father must have been making quite a profit out of me and Jack. Or maybe he'd got very good at gambling on the horses. He'd had enough practice. He still went off to the White Hart every night.

Doreen had been dead now for just about a year. As I've said, father always called in for a pint or two of beer, sometimes more, on his way and suddenly the name Vera began to be mentioned. Me and Jack were very curious to know who this was and we'd visions of another strange woman coming to live with us. We were very happy as we were and wanted none of that again. By chatting to father in the most casual way we could manage, we gathered that Vera worked at another local pub, The Royal Oak, as a barmaid. We didn't even know he went in there. So, me and Jack hatched a plan. As I was over six feet tall and looked a lot older for my age, I was to go to the pub and see what this Vera looked like. So, one evening, off I went. I'd never been in a public house before and didn't really know what to do.

Anyway, when I'd got through the door it turned out to be quite empty and just as I was wondering what to do a woman's voice rang out asking me what she could get for me. As I'd never bought beer before I said the first thing that came into my head which was a pint of best. I didn't even know what that was. So, I went over to the bar, paid for the glass of beer and very carefully carried it over to what I thought was a good position to hopefully see Vera when she came in.

There was only one person serving on and she seemed very efficient. She'd curly, bleached blonde hair, red lips and was very bosomly. Then, I overheard someone call her Vera and I nearly knocked my pint of beer over. I just couldn't imagine father with someone like that. In later years whenever I watched Coronation Street, every time I saw the barmaid called Bet Lynch, I was reminded of Vera. Having identified her, I was just about to go when father walked in. Luckily for me though I'd got a table behind the door so when he walked over to the bar, I was able to escape without him seeing me. I left the pint of beer untouched on the table. I just couldn't get home fast enough to tell Jack.

Christmas 1941 looked as though it was going to be just as strange an affair as 1940 had been, with just the four of us. I think father was still feeling the loss of Doreen, despite the coming of Vera, 'cos he suddenly announced he'd asked Annie, Alice and Norma to come over for dinner on Christmas Day. Laurence was away with the navy and Sam and Frank were away with the army. This seemed a very odd thing for father to suggest but we went along with it. Looking back, though, it ended up being a good idea 'cos rationing was taking quite a hold and lots of things were in short supply, so we all contributed something. Father, Jack and me were still in our jobs but Helen was just at home recovering from the bout of TB. She was definitely on the mend, though.

Recipes were always being given out on the wireless and special leaflets were printed with ideas for meals. Some of these were things like Baa-baa turnovers made from a sheep's head or lentil roast or liver and oatmeal pudding. Sugar was always in short supply so carrots were used in tarts, diced beetroot in puddings and custard was made with parsnips. Our Christmas Day feast had an awful lot of grated carrot, grated apple and grated potato in it. These ideas were necessary to get food on our plates. Nowadays, these sort of dishes are found in so called posh restaurants who take pride in presenting the sort of things we'd to eat during the war because there was nothing else. Anyway, I still had the allotment so I supplied sprouts, turnips, potatoes and a very chewy chicken from the man at the allotment for which I'd paid by digging his plot one Saturday afternoon. Annie and Alice brought some mince pies which tasted quite nice but no one asked what was in them and some Christmas cake which, again, had strange ingredients in it. There was no marzipan or icing which were the bits I liked best. I can't remember what Norma contributed.

Father had even brought home what served as a Christmas tree. It was actually a branch from a tree with no leaves on and we stuck it in our bucket of sand. This was kept handy in case of a bomb dropping but I don't know just what we'd have done with it. There wasn't much sand in it. Anyway, we decorated the branch like we had done all the others, with bits of paper and milk bottle tops. We made the most of being a family again and Annie and Alice went out of their way to make sure we spent a lot of time laughing. Norma continued with her superior attitude to us all and Helen spent most of the day gazing into space dreaming about Phil Cooke, who she'd met whilst recovering from TB in Ilkley. He was training to be a doctor.

We didn't know if father enjoyed himself or not. We knew he'd enjoyed the beer he'd brought home and after dinner he took himself off to bed for a rest. The others made their excuses to leave before it got dark saying they didn't want to walk too far in the blackout. Helen got herself ready to meet Phil and so me and Jack were left to our own devices. We decided to look at The Boys Book of Astronomy. We hadn't looked at in a long time and we'd a really good time spotting the stars from the attic window. As we were both taller now it was a lot easier. We eventually heard father go out about six o'clock so we went downstairs and finished off the chicken and the pudding. It wasn't much for two growing boys and I remember chewing the bones for ages to get every last bit of meat off. So, Christmas Day 1941 came to an end. It hadn't been as strange as we thought it was going to be. It had been good with us all sitting around the kitchen table again. I never found out how father had persuaded Alice and Annie to come to our house.

Helen went back to work in the Sunshine Café until she could find a job as a shorthand typist and in May of 1942 the cheese ration was cut back to one ounce a week. That's a piece of cheddar that would fit in the palm of your hand. It was hardly worth having as we could just about make one piece of cheese on toast if we all contributed our ration. Mine's a big hand so I suppose they were talking about medium sized hands. Then Helen began complaining that cosmetics were becoming very scarce. I brought a beetroot from the allotment for her and she tried rubbing the juice on her face instead of rouge but didn't do it again when she'd to go to work looking like a clown as it had stained her skin and she couldn't wash it off. In the same way, nylon stockings were not available so ladies began to stain their legs with strong tea. They used it before they put any milk in. Then they drew a line up the back of their legs to look like a seam in a stocking.

Anyway, later in the summer I'd a really bad cold and was told to go home and get better. I was sneezing and coughing everywhere. They must have thought that I'd infect the whole workforce, what there was left of it. So, I went home. It was a lovely warm sunny day but I thought I was dying. I couldn't wait to get into my bed and go to sleep but as I went up the stairs I heard laughter coming from father's room. It was a woman's laugh and I was certain that it was Vera. I stood on the landing a few minutes wondering what to do. For a moment I thought of bursting in on them just to see the look on their faces but fate took a hand and I'd a sneezing episode instead. Suddenly the laughing stopped, the door opened and there was father looking like thunder. I ran into my room, slammed the door shut and got into bed expecting father to come in and shout at me. But he didn't and it wasn't very long before I heard them going down the stairs and the door banging shut behind them. Like before, when I'd seen Vera behind the bar in the Royal Oak, I couldn't wait to tell Jack.

Life continued much the same for the rest of the year until the beginning of November when Stanley came to tell me an army recruiting office was going to open in Bradford Town Hall for a few days. I still hadn't quite got over discovering father and Vera so this was my chance to get away. The atmosphere had been very strained whenever we met up. As me and Stanley didn't have any more information about the recruitment we went off as soon as we could to find out what it was all about and, by lunchtime on 5th November, we found ourselves enlisted into the army. Anyway, it was a Lancashire regiment. I don't know why they'd come to Yorkshire to recruit. Maybe there wasn't anyone left in Lancashire. I was a bit disappointed it was a Lancashire regiment as I'm a Yorkshireman but there was a lot more to think about than being disloyal to my home county. My

Grandad Lawton had been a sergeant in the Yorkshire Light Infantry and now I was in the King's Own Light Infantry, often called the caulies. That's by using the initials KOLI with an s.

Father didn't seem too bothered that I was leaving home to go to war. I arranged for him to keep my savings plan with the Prudential. I told him that I'd send money to put in it whenever I could. I was pleased with my savings which had now grown to nearly thirteen pounds. Jack was a bit upset that I was going and Helen had a good cry, especially as Phil had already gone too. I said my goodbyes to Elsie and we promised to write to each other every week. I felt sad at the thought of not being able to see her, even if it was only now and then. But, once me and Stanley were on our way to Preston Barracks the following week to be fitted up with our uniforms, which we'd been measured up for when we enlisted, all that was forgotten. Pollards and Eccleshill would have to do without us.

At Preston the paperwork seemed to go on forever. I got my army number which had to be memorised and I can still remember it after all this time. I was number 1433624. I hoped it was a lucky number. We'd full medicals, of course, and as they didn't check my legs, I came out A1, as they say. I'd been worried about my left leg which had never been the same since the motor cycle accident and still bothered me from time to time. The uniform fitting must have been a bit haphazard, though, to say the least 'cos my army trousers turned out to be a bit on the short side. As well as that, the hem of the tunic didn't quite meet the top of the trousers so there was a gap there unless I held myself in all the time and the thick woolly socks turned out to be too small, as well. It was the Home Guard all over again. When I pointed this out, as politely as I could, I was told in no uncertain terms that was all there was and to stop whingeing. We were given basic black boots which had a hard steel plate on the toe and 13 studs underneath. I counted that as an unlucky number. The boots were quite heavy and, as it turned out, not only slippery in the wet but very noisy when on parade, which is where we seemed to be most of the time.

However, as we stood there together in our new uniforms, me and Stanley couldn't help but smile. It didn't last long, though. Before we knew it, we were on our way north to Catterick to join the Primary Training Corps where we discovered that we were marked out to join the coastal defence force. After the carry-on of Dunkirk, army training had taken on a new urgency, so to speak, and the focus was on making our soldiers what they called offensively minded. When I heard that I thought it was an excuse for learning how to swear properly.

The commander in chief of the home forces in 1940 was General Ironside and after Dunkirk he made sure we were all going to be safe. The coast around the UK was made into a no-go area with concrete walls, tank traps, barbed wire, gun emplacements and search lights. All this was meant to slow down any invaders who came at us from the sea. The Home Guard were part of this defence too, watching out for paratroopers and boats bringing the enemy to us. This had been a great disappointment for loads of people, 'cos it was a glorious summer and they couldn't get onto the beaches. Places like Blackpool, though, were still open but you had to remember to take your own sheets, soap and ration book if you were lucky enough to be staying for more than one day. Anyway, there we were at Catterick learning how to march in straight lines and polish our boots properly. We slept on three big square cushions called biscuits. We also had proper rifles, not broom handles, and we often went training on the North Yorkshire Moors where it was cold and wet.

Me and Stanley were only there are few weeks, though, when we suddenly found ourselves in the Royal Artillery and posted off to Portsmouth to the Coast Battery to do coastal defence duties. It seemed we were only there two minutes before we were on the move again and sent to Bexhill to join the 90th anti-tank regiment. By this time me and Stanley had both been trained to operate anti-tank guns as well as all sorts of other guns, and my service record of the time shows that I was a Gunner. I think this is why I support Arsenal. Anyway, although we were kept busy cleaning this and that, it was quite a dull time. The only bright spark was that at Bexhill we'd our billets. The local town had been told of our arrival so there were quite a few ladies waiting for us as we got there. I don't mean they were offering their bodies to us, as most of them would have been married, but they all had a spare room. Stanley was taken by a rather grim looking lady with a black hat. I was chosen by someone who reminded me of my mother. She was tall with dark hair and had such a lovely smile.

I was quite heartbroken when we'd to leave but not in the same way as Stanley was. His grim looking landlady turned out to have a very nice daughter called Evelyn and Stanley fell in love. After that we were moved all over the place but at every opportunity Stanley was off to Bexhill. I don't know how he managed it but he did. I'd a couple of home leaves during this time and made the most of them. I'd written to Elsie to tell her when I would be back and we managed to meet up and go for a short walk round Peel Park but otherwise she was always driving her trolley bus. We again promised each other that we would keep in touch and write every week. She was a lovely girl and I hoped things would go further when the war was over.

Anyway, on what turned out to be my last home leave, I stayed at Mount Street with Jack and Helen. Father was never there and before I went back, I went to find father to give him some money for my savings plan. I eventually found him at Vera's house, down Charnwood Road. Jack had been as curious as me about Vera and had followed father one Saturday afternoon when he'd left the house sooner than usual. He followed him to Charnwood Road, so that was how we knew where Vera lived. Jack had said it reminded him of when we pretended to be detectives trying to solve the Piggery Murders. Anyway, I was surprised at how neat and tidy the house looked. Every house we'd lived in since mother died had been scruffy and neglected. I pushed open the little green painted gate, walked up the path and knocked on the door. It was like meeting a stranger. He didn't even ask me in for a cup of tea, just took the money. I was relieved when I went back to my regiment. This was in June 1943, just before we were taken off our coastal duties and sent on active service on the Empress of Australia. Of course, we didn't know where we were going. I suppose it was the army's way of giving us a chance to see our relatives maybe for the last time. I met up with Jack at Mount Street. Father had told Jack and Helen that he was going to find a smaller house now most of us had gone. So, Jack was looking for another job away from Eccleshill and Helen was going to live with Grannie Annie and Auntie Lucy.

After going to Bexhill, Stanley had made a dash up to Yorkshire to say goodbye to his family, so we met at the end of Norman Lane and got the bus together into Bradford. He couldn't wait to tell me that he and Evelyn had got engaged and were to be married as soon as he could get some more leave. I was so happy for both of them. I posted a letter to Elsie telling her I was going away but that I'd write every week, like we'd promised. I gave her the army postal number again in case she'd lost the other one. It was something to look forward to. I'd had to leave my bookcase and The Boys Book of Astronomy behind as I couldn't fit them in my kit-bag.

So, we went from Bradford to Liverpool on the train and at Liverpool docks we found the Empress of Australia which looked like the Queen Mary with three great big funnels. She was painted grey and had been converted to have enough room for 5,000 troops. There were dozens of us queueing up to get on board and it was a relief when my paperwork had been checked and I was given my hammock. When I say there was room for 5,000 this is a bit of an exaggeration as we didn't have much room at all. Our sleeping quarters were on the mess deck which meant that every night we'd to hook our hammocks on to the ceiling and climb in by standing on the tables and then take them down again in the morning. I'd never slept in a hammock before but I managed without falling out, which was more than some of the others did. I slept on my back and never once dared turn over. It was comfy but once in you couldn't move until you got out. My duvet thing reminds me of sleeping in a hammock especially when the sheet gets wrapped round my legs.

Anyway, what was difficult was going to the doings if the water was choppy. You never knew when you were going to fall off if the ship did a sudden lurch. The smell in there was awful too. There was always a queue somewhere especially for the showers which were salt water. This made my hair go as stiff as a board. But, I found out that I'm quite a good sailor and I wasn't sea sick at all, as a lot of the others were. The days were long, though, and we were just sat around for most of the time. It wasn't a holiday cruise with an entertainment staff. We'd to make our own entertainment so it was an endless round of cards, chess and draughts, or so it seemed to me. Others found somewhere to lie down and have a sleep. Me and Stanley and someone called Peter, spent a lot of time trying to learn bridge. Another soldier, called Gordon, from some posh part of Liverpool, had a go at teaching us but, try as we could, we just didn't get the hang of it. I don't think our Yorkshire accents and his Liverpudlian accent helped matters, either. Sometimes we couldn't understand him and at other times he couldn't understand us. I felt really sorry for Gordon as he tried so hard but we were a lost cause, unfortunately. Sometimes we played poker but as I never managed to win, I kept away from these card games.

We'd sailed out of Liverpool in a convoy. There were loads of other ships and they followed each other into the Irish Sea and then the Atlantic. The speed of the convoy was that of the slowest ship so we could all keep together. At night time we all closed up and sometimes we seemed to be almost touching the ship in front. We were often kept awake at night 'cos the destroyers sailing with us sent out depth charges to keep submarines away. These boomed out at regular intervals all through the night. At other times, we'd to keep really quiet 'cos they were using sonar to detect submarines. We'd been told it would take about two weeks to reach our destination which was a secret. Eventually we got there and it turned out to be Alexandria. It had taken nearly four weeks 'cos we'd to keep making diversions to avoid u-boats. We probably travelled the equivalent of going to Australia.

We re-fuelled at Alexandria and had to stay on board watching dozens of Arab labourers carry big baskets of coal on their heads up the gangplank. Someone said they looked like ants on an anthill there were so many of them. Then we moved on to Haifa where we were taken by army lorries on a very bumpy ride to our destination which turned out to be tent city on the banks of the Suez Canal. There were ten of us in each tent and we'd to dig a big hole for the tent so that just the top of it would be showing. This was so the tent could be covered in sand and hidden from above. There was quite a steep ramp down into each tent. Again, we slept on three biscuits, like we'd at Catterick, but this time we'd mosquito nets as well. We didn't need those in Yorkshire. It wasn't a bad place to have ended up. There was a camp cinema and at night we could visit the Arab places where they smoked hash in those hubba pipes which were passed from person to person. There were also ladies of the night available but me and Stanley didn't bother with that. We'd our own young ladies at home. I hoped Elsie had got my letter. Anyway, it was army life and I just accepted what came. I couldn't change anything, after all.

Anyway, I can't say that camping on the banks of the Suez Canal was very exciting 'cos we were kept awake most nights by huge ships using the canal as a shortcut, which is of course, why it had been built in the first place. It connects the Mediterranean Sea to the Red Sea. It opened in about 1869 and saved ships 4,500 miles as they hadn't to go all the way round Africa to get to Egypt. Anyway, the first meal I'd out there was served in a big marquee which was our dining room. As usual, we'd all to queue up to get our food and then we sat down on wooden forms at the tables. The fellow next to me picked at his food with his fork and didn't eat much at all so I asked him why. He said he was looking for mites. I didn't believe him so he took me to a corner of the marquee, near the kitchen area, where there was a big metal container. He took the lid off and it was half full of flour. Then he told me to watch and he tapped the side of the bin. The flour started to heave up and down. It was actually moving 'cos it was full of mites. He said these things got into most of our supplies. It put me off my food to begin with but then I decided that they'd be cooked to death anyway and stopped thinking about them. I didn't want to be permanently hungry. There were no fish and chip shops out there. At other times our food would be very gritty so we all found out the proper meaning of sandwiches even if the bread did contain a free helping of flour mites.

One day we were told we were going on training manoeuvres that night. Everything was done at short notice. We got used to it. The company was split into three platoons and I was chosen to be the batman for the officer in charge of number two platoon. Before we set off, I'd to serve him his dinner but I couldn't find any hot water to wash the plates with, so I used what I thought looked like a clean cloth and gave them a good wipe. They were sparkling when I'd finished. I felt really pleased with myself. When we got back from our nocturnal activities, it was breakfast time, so I served him his breakfast on one of my sparkling plates. Unfortunately, unknown to me, I'd used a cloth which had been impregnated with a special kind of oil used for cleaning guns. It was no wonder the plates, which were metal, gleamed so much. As a result, the breakfast tasted just awful, just as his dinner the night before must have done. But the officer never said a word and ate the lot. I was never asked to be a batman again, though.

A few weeks later we were moved again. A lot of us spent our travelling time mostly lying on the roof of a railway carriage. This was where the breeze was and places up there were sought after. I wasn't too keen, though, as there was always the danger you could roll off. But for some, it was better than being sat on the floor in an overcrowded carriage with loads of other sweaty blokes. The seats had all been taken out to make as much room as possible. Riding on the roof turned out, in the end, not to be a good idea at all 'cos the sun was very hot and we didn't have any suntan lotion. So, loads of men who'd been up there, ended up with sunburn. This was in addition to the dysentery some had suffered in the previous camp. It was a single track and trains had to wait to pass each other at special places. It was very, very hot, even though we'd been issued with special shirts made from something called aertex, which were supposed to keep us cool. I began wishing we could have gone by camel. Again, when we eventually got there, it was another training camp and we were all in big tents with our biscuits. Our backpacks were getting bigger and bigger as we accumulated more and more equipment. Me and Stanley went to see the pyramids and the sphinx. I still have the photograph of me near the sphinx.

But, before all this, I got a letter from father. Now the one thing I couldn't change was his attitude towards me. I know I'd been my mother's favourite child but that was no reason to treat me the way he had since I'd grown up. Now, sitting in a tent in Egypt, I couldn't believe what he'd said in his letter. I'd written to all of them as often as I could, as sometimes there was nothing else to do. Each letter took me ages as I was still slow with my writing. Everyone wrote back except Elsie. I hadn't heard from her at all. Sometimes I got as many as five letters all at once. But that day, I only got one.

Father had written to tell me that he'd married Vera, left Mount Street to go and live in her house and that I wasn't wanted there anymore. It was short and to the point and upset me more than I'd admit at the time. He never even mentioned my Prudential savings plan. I showed the letter to Stanley and he said that when the war ended and we went home, that I could stay with him and Evelyn until I'd sorted something out. That was very nice of him but it still left me without a proper home. Soon after that, I got a letter from Jack letting me know that he'd found another job at Pool Paper Mills, near Otley and was living in lodgings near the town centre. Helen had gone to live with Grannie Annie and Auntie Lucy.

After we'd been sat waiting for what seemed like months, the war seemed to shift to Italy. The Afrika Korps, part of the German army, had been defeated months before and the word was that we were now ready to take Italy from the Germans. The best way into Italy was seen as through Sicily so we all got on another ship expecting to go there. But this was abandoned and we went to Naples instead. Well, I don't know if you've ever been to Naples but when we landed there most of the men on board couldn't get off fast enough to go in search of brothels. Apparently, Naples was renowned for them and the queues were longer than outside the best fish and chip shops on Friday nights. You could tell by the hats – flat army caps, turbans, side caps – that almost every regiment of the British army was represented there. Again, me and Stanley reminded each other of our young ladies waiting back at home so we just went in search of a good cup of coffee, which we didn't find.

The war was moving up Italy and I was now allocated to the bazooka team. It was a shared responsibility. One man would carry it like a big drain pipe whilst another carried the bombs and ammunition. I was usually given the job of number two which was to carry the case of bombs and I must have run miles with them over ground which was stony and very hilly. As well as a case of bombs or the bazooka, we also had to carry our water bottle, back pack and our rifle. I'd a Royal Enfield 303 with a bayonet. As we moved on we slept in our tents or, whenever we could, in abandoned houses. I liked these 'cos the weather was very bad with lots of rain and these houses were better than tents. In particular, I didn't like doing night patrols, 'cos the next day we would be on the move again and there was no opportunity to get any sleep. It was even worse if it had been a wet and cold night. I'd always thought Italy was a warm country and I was very disappointed. We needed warm clothing and our aertex shirts weren't good enough even with an army greatcoat over the top. But, it wasn't long before we got the right trousers and jackets courtesy, I think, of the Americans.

By the time we arrived, the Germans had more or less abandoned southern Italy but had put down defensive lines which stopped us moving north. The most famous of these was called the Gustav Line which proved a major obstacle. It stopped the Allies in their tracks 'cos of the mountain snowstorms. It looked as though we couldn't break through but a multi- national force of British, American, French and Polish troops managed it between January and May 1944. All this was called Operation Diadem. One particular position, though, was more difficult than the others and in the end became famous. This was the mountain monastery of Monte Cassino and our regiment was to be part of the attack which was organised by General Alexander and General Montgomery. Their idea was to attack from the south and then send in an invasion force lower down and attack Cassino from the other side. By this time, I felt as though I'd been in Italy for years.

I met up briefly with Stanley who had been promoted to sergeant and moved to another unit. We both admitted that we were very scared now that the real fighting was about to start for us. So far, we'd had a relatively easy life on ships and in tent cities. Stanley, however, loved being in the army and told me he was thinking about staying in after the war and making a career of it. He said that it was better than working in a mill and he was going to write to Evelyn to see what she thought about it. We said our goodbyes and went our separate ways, wishing each other good luck but that was to be the last I ever saw of him. I found out a few weeks later that he'd been killed by a mortar bomb whilst out on reconnaissance. I was upset for ages.

We weren't that close to Monte Cassino and found ourselves in the middle of nowhere. However, we were spotted and the Jerries attacked us. We all dived for cover and scattered all over the place. I was carrying the bombs and it's a wonder they didn't all go up as I fell into a hole to protect myself. Training was such that the bombs were the most important thing. Anyway, the line we now had was now all higgledy-piggledy but we managed to get back into formation somehow and I found myself looking after another two cases of bombs, the owners of which had run off. I now had 9 bombs to take care of. I carried them as best as I could and then came to some open ground and had to stop. Shells were coming out of nowhere and dropping all around us. We were all covered in dirt. I wondered how I would ever get my uniform clean again.

Then, someone shouted for me to run and it's wonderful what you can do when your life is at stake. There were troops everywhere and although it seemed chaotic to me, I expect there was a plan somewhere. I eventually found my bazooka team and we were given a position to hold as best as we could. We were there for two days and could hear the distant noise of the battle at Monte Cassino. We were all cramped up together in a hole which we'd dug out ourselves and covered with a piece of tarpaulin which one bright spark had carried with him. None of us got any sleep but we did have one good meal when Bert came back with a dead lamb after a trip to the doings. I don't know if he'd killed it or just found it, none of us asked, but it was very tasty. We made a small fire and roasted bits of it on sticks.

On the night of 11th May we heard lots of planes going over and later we found out that the Allies had bombed the monastery and the Polish troops had launched a second attack. There had been very fierce hand to hand fighting but this victory gave the British, French and American troops the chance to enter the Liri valley. The Germans went back to what was called the Hitler Line and the Poles took the monastery. By 18th May the local town of Cassino had been cleared of Germans and, as soon as they could, the Poles raised the Polish flag above the ruins of the monastery. The Poles eventually made a cemetery at Monte Cassino on the slopes of the mountain. I've a particular interest in what the Poles did, 'cos my niece's father came from Poland and fought with us at Monte Cassino. Of course, I didn't know him back then. The Battle for Monte Cassino and the fighting for the so called Gustav Line caused high losses of men. Over 60,000 Germans died and 115,000 Allied troops, including Stanley. After all these years, I can still get upset at the thought of him and what was not to be.

So, after all this we moved towards Rome which was still under German command and on 23rd May the Allies attacked the Hitler Line. They attacked at dawn and, after a lot of heavy fighting the Germans ran away just after 4 o'clock in the afternoon. There were a lot of casualties but we just got on with it and moved on towards Rome which was liberated on 4th June 1944. There were celebrations for a couple of days but then the Allies landed at Normandy and the focus of the war moved somewhere else. My birthday on 7th June was just another day.

Then we were all sent back to where it all started for us. I found myself stationed in Naples after which we were all shipped out to sit in the desert with the Mediterranean Expeditionary Force until we got back home to England on 6th May 1945. As we travelled back my thoughts turned to Elsie and, even though I hadn't got any letters from her, I was looking forward to seeing her again. I told myself that her letters had just gone astray.

On our return we were all given what it called a Testimonial. These days it would just be called a reference. I thought mine was really good, even though I say it myself. Here it is:

'Harry is a first-class soldier in every way who has done excellent work during the two years he has been with this battalion. Of average intelligence he is exceptionally willing and hard- working and always cheerful and co-operative. He has a quiet and steady nature and can be trusted absolutely. Loyal, reliable, smart and sober, I recommend him with confidence to any civilian employer.'

18:36:58 – 18:39:22

It seemed such a long time since he'd set off. Once he'd been able to walk up and down quite easily. When he had the budgies he was always going down to the village for bird seed and millet stalks. They ate everything so quickly he reckoned he kept the pet shop going single-handedly. But the pet shop was now gone replaced by a pizza take-away. He'd never bothered trying anything from there, preferring his fish and chips. He did miss the little Italian restaurant which had now become a curry house. Marco, who had owned the restaurant, had often given him a meal after he'd cleaned the windows, as well as many boxes of something called panettone, which were now stored in the pantry along with the dozens of tins he'd accumulated. But, Marco had gone back to Italy three years ago. There were now four curry places in the village. One had even opened up in what used to be the launderette. It was a shame he didn't like curry. He'd been put off ever since he'd been out in Egypt. Maybe he should give it another chance. He could start with curry sauce on his fish and chips.

He now had to cross Laburnum Grove again. He didn't know how these streets got their names. There wasn't any heather on Heather Road and certainly no laburnum trees on Laburnum Grove. On the main road near to where he used to live a new development had been called Venice Mews. It completely baffled him. This was Yorkshire, not Italy.

So, he carefully put his right foot down onto the road, holding the zimmer frame in front of him. Then the left foot, and a quick shuffle across the road in case a car came along. On reaching the other side, he lifted himself onto the pavement once more. The odd feeling he'd had in the fish and chip shop had not really gone away, so he stopped and waited until he could breathe more easily and then continued on his way.

Home Sweet Home

Our regiment came home to Liverpool on 6th May 1945 on the same ship which took me and Stanley out to war, The Empress of Australia. The difference was that instead of it getting hotter and hotter, it became colder and colder. Not that it was cold when I got back but I'd been used to a lot of high temperatures and it felt cool here. I was hoping for a hot summer. Of course, there were hundreds of us getting off the ship at that time and it took hours and hours. After the paperwork I eventually got clearance and went on shore to make my way to Liverpool Lime Street and onto home in Yorkshire with some back pay in my pocket, too. Everywhere I went there were soldiers, sailors or airmen on the streets. It felt strange to be back. After pushing my way through crowds, I felt pleased with myself for finding a seat by the window, on the next train to Leeds as there wasn't a direct service to Bradford. The train was full of ex-servicemen all going home as fast as they could 'cos the day after next, 8th May 1945, had been declared as Victory in Europe Day, or as it is usually known, VE Day. The whole country was set to celebrate the end of the war.

As I sat there, I let my thoughts wander as we crossed the Pennines back to Yorkshire. I'd a lump in my throat when I saw the moors again and all the lovely English countryside. I thought about all the wives and girlfriends and wondered how they'd get on with their men when they'd been away for so long. I didn't have a wife or mother to go home to, only a girlfriend, Elsie, who'd never written to me. I thought about Evelyn as well who would never see her Stanley again. I made a mental note to go and see her as soon as I could. I also wondered about where I'd go when I got back to Bradford as father had told me he didn't want me back and with Stanley dead I couldn't go and stay with him, either. I decided to go to father's first, though, just to see how the land lay and then, if things didn't work out, I'd go to Annie's.

I was stunned by the number of people packed into Leeds station and only just managed to push my way onto the train to Bradford. Me and my army bag squeezed into the last space. I'd grown quite a bit since joining the army and I was now 6ft 4 ins with hands and feet to match. My niece says we could cross the Atlantic in one of my shoes. In fact, the army had quite a bit of trouble finding boots to fit me as I'm a size 14. I spent weeks and weeks wearing boots which were a size too small and got a lot of blisters. I was always rubbing my feet with vinegar but it didn't do much good.

It was nearly 7 o'clock by the time I got to Bradford. I found a bus going to Eccleshill and went straight round to Charnwood Road. Once again, I pushed open the little green painted gate, walked up the path and knocked on the door. It seemed ages before anyone came but, suddenly, there stood father. I hardly recognised him. He was now 52 years old, his hair had gone grey and he'd also put on a lot of weight. His face was quite lined, too. I think he was as surprised at seeing me and the way I'd filled out. The tall, skinny lad was now a fully grown man, taller and broader than he was. We just stared at each other until I said 'Hello' and asked if he was going to invite me in. He waved his hand for me to go in, very reluctantly I thought, and left me to shut the door, before walking ahead of me in his carpet slippers. I followed him into the front room where he sat down in an armchair and flapped his hand at me again to sit on the settee. The room was very well furnished with green wallpaper and a red carpet. The three-piece suite was brown moquette and I spotted a gramophone on a well-polished little table in the corner. I remembered the other one being taken by the bailiffs. It was very cosy. I couldn't get over father wearing carpet slippers and smoking a pipe. I though Vera must be able to work miracles.

Anyway, there was another awkward silence and then father said he was glad I was home safely but wanted to know why I was there. He asked if I'd received his letter and then when I said I had, he asked again why I'd gone there. It seemed a strange question to ask a son who's just returned from fighting a war so I just blurted out that I'd nowhere else to go. He replied that he was now married to Vera and they didn't want any lodgers. But I think he must have been feeling guilty 'cos he offered me a bed for the night, making it clear it was only for one night. There was no mention of food or drink and I began wishing that I'd called in at a fish and chip shop on the way there. But, I was so tired by then that all I wanted to do was to lay down and fall asleep. So, after our brief conversation, I wished father goodnight and made my way up the stairs to the front little bedroom, which was the one he said I could have. The bed was damp but it was better than some of the places where I'd had to spend the night during the last few years, so I didn't mind too much.

As Vera wasn't there, I assumed she was still working at the pub and I heard father going out just as I was drifting off. I didn't seem to have been asleep for more than five minutes when I was woken up by the front door banging and a lot of shouting going on. It was father and Vera and they were having a right set-to. There was some more door slamming before I heard Vera shouting down at father from the landing that if I was still there in the morning then she'd be the one leaving.

Father came in to wake me about six o'clock but he needn't have bothered 'cos I don't think I went back to sleep after hearing what Vera had said. I got dressed quickly and went down to the kitchen as quietly as I could, to find father had made some tea and doorsteps with dripping. It was just like old times for a moment, just me and father there before we went off to work. I gulped down my tea and devoured the doorsteps and then asked him to give me my Prudential Savings book. I didn't know where I was going to stay but having some money to fall back on was a nice thought. He leaned over the table towards me and told me that the money I'd been sending back had been used up in other ways and that it had made up for all the cost of bringing me up. When he married Vera, he'd given the book to Norma for safe keeping. So, nothing had gone into it since I'd left. No mention was made of the money I'd given him when I'd been home on my last leave.

I just sat there stunned and suddenly knew that once I walked out of the door, I never wanted to see him again. In that moment, I realized that my father had never really loved anyone except my mother and himself. He'd now found a cosy way of living which didn't include helping me, even if it was only for a week or two. I stood up, went round the table and told him to stand up as well. I was a good few inches taller than him now and for the first time in my life I could look down on him. I grabbed hold of the lapels of his jacket and lifted him up so he was just balancing on his toes. I told him what I thought of him, using choice swear words I'd learnt in the army and then pushed him back onto his chair. I put my great-coat on, picked up my kit bag and let myself out. There was no point saying goodbye. Goodbye is a shortened form of God Bless You and I was in no mood to feel like that towards my father.

I was in turmoil as I walked back down Charnwood Road in the cool morning air. Father had followed me to the door and shouted my name out but it was far too late and I walked away without looking back. The army had taught me how to have a rod of steel inside you and they had taught me well. I wondered about going over Annie's but just then, I remembered I still had the keys for the house on Mount Steet. I'd kept them safe in my kit-bag thinking that I'd be going back there. Maybe if it wasn't occupied, I could camp there for a while until someone found me and moved me on. I found the key ring. There were two very large keys and one small key on it. I knew the large keys were for the front and back doors at Mount Street but couldn't remember what the small one was for. So, I walked all the way to Mount Street only to find that someone was cleaning the windows and the house looked lived in. So, that idea was out of the window, so to speak. Then it came to me. The small key was for the padlock on the allotment hut so off I went there. I was expecting it to have been taken over by someone else, but the plot looked neglected although the hut was still there. The key worked so I opened up and put my kit-bag inside.

I was still very hungry and wondered if the Sunshine Cafe where Helen had worked, was still going. It was and I bought myself the biggest fry-up breakfast I'd ever had. I think they call it a full Monty and it was very good. I asked where they'd got all the bacon and eggs from but all the woman behind the counter did was tap her nose. In other words, I'd to mind my own business. I noticed that there wasn't much butter, though. Then I remembered that the lady was called Mrs Shuttleworth but as she looked very busy, I didn't say anything about Helen and went on my way.

Everyone was busy putting up flags and decorations for the VE Day celebrations. I looked in my pocket book and found a slip of paper with Norma's address. Whilst Laurence was away, Norma had moved to Dundas Street to be nearer to where she worked at Whitehead's mill. So, I changed my mind again and, instead of going to Annie's I went to find Norma in Dundas Street. It was also nearer for me than walking all the way to Annie's at Tyersal. So, I went back to the hut, collected my kit-bag and great coat and walked over to Laisterdyke hoping I would find a bed for the night. It was a fair walk with a heavy kit-bag on my shoulder and it was over an hour before I got to

Dundas Street. I don't know why I didn't get a bus.

When I got there, I rattled the door knocker and the door flew open almost at once. Norma had obviously been expecting Laurence and her face fell when she saw me. Anyway, she asked me in before giving me a big welcome hug. We both had tears in our eyes. I told her all about my visit to father and she offered me the spare room until such time as I'd sorted myself out. Norma made me a cup of tea before going upstairs to find some sheets for my bed which she kindly aired in front of the kitchen range before making the bed up. Hurrah! No damp bed this time. When she came back, I asked if I could go and have a lie down. When I woke up it was the next day and I still had my uniform and boots on. I was covered up by my army greatcoat. Norma must have put it over me. I'd been asleep for nearly 24 hours and very thankful I hadn't had to sleep in my allotment hut.

Norma had been working at Whitehead's in the burling and mending department which is where the cloth is checked for faults such as the slubs, which I've mentioned before. The burler and mender's job is to repair these and make the cloth look perfect. It was a highly skilled job which Norma had been doing for several years but she was worried she might lose her job 'cos the demand for cloth would go down now the war was over. Anyway, by the time I got up, she'd gone off to work. There was a note on the kitchen table telling me she'd be back at dinner time and to help myself to what I wanted, so I made a cup of tea and some toast. As there was only a little pat of butter I hadn't the heart to use it so I had my toast dry. It didn't matter. I just dipped it in my tea. I was looking forward to going down to Bradford with her later to join in the celebrations at the town hall. I wondered if I should go to see if I could find Elsie. Anyway, just as I was just finishing off the last bit of toast when there was a knock on the door. I went to open it and there was Laurence. He got the surprise of his life when he saw me. He'd had a difficult time getting back 'cos everyone was rushing round getting ready for the VE Day celebrations. I gave him the last of the tea and, after he'd taken his kit-bag upstairs, he sat in the kitchen with me and we exchanged stories. I told him Norma had offered me a room until I could find something else and he didn't seem to mind.

Then, we heard a key in the lock. It was Norma coming home for her dinner. Laurence quickly hid behind the kitchen door. As she came in Norma was saying she wished Laurence could be home to celebrate with her. Norma's face was a picture as he jumped out from behind the door. I decided to leave them alone for the rest of the afternoon and went for a long walk over to the trolley bus sheds. With Laurence coming home I'd begun to think about Elsie and wanted to see if I could find out what happened to her. I'd written loads of letters but she'd never replied. At the trolley bus sheds no one knew anything about her.

So, after we'd had our tea, the three of us went to Bradford to join the crowds in front of the town hall. There was a brass band and everyone was singing and dancing, doing the hokey-cokey and just having a good time. We'd heard there were going to be big bonfires in the parks and plenty of fireworks. I think there were lots of street parties, as well. Just like we'd done on coronation day in 1937 down Norman Lane. Except this time, we were celebrating the end of a war. It was a good job it was a nice day. It was also wonderful as the evening wore on, to see all the lights come on again after the blackout when showing even the tiniest of lights was a criminal offence. At one point, everyone was singing 'When the Lights Go On Again'. And then I saw someone I recognised. It was Elsie and she was arm in arm with a soldier in uniform. They were laughing and kissing and I now knew why she'd never replied to my letters. She didn't see me. It was time to go home. I was heartbroken.

After the excitement of VE Day, everyone had to sort out what was going to happen next. As more and more men started going back to find their families and their old jobs, not everything was rosy. The woman who lived next door to Norma hadn't seen her husband for over three years and, when he eventually came home, they didn't recognise each other. She'd grown her hair long whilst he'd gone bald. There was a lot of trouble with children who'd grown up without a father. The problem, unlike the one I had, was that their father had actually missed them and thought he could just carry on where he'd left off. But the children had got used to a way of living without a father and didn't take kindly to being told what to do by this new person in their lives who they hardly knew.

It was the same for the wives, too. Sometimes the husband would come back deeply affected by what he'd done in the war, preferring to meet his friends in the pub and treating his home like a lodging house. Sometimes they were affected mentally with mood swings and bad tempers. Today we call this PTSD which means Post Traumatic Stress

Disorder and is taken very seriously. A lot of the country's housing stock had also been destroyed and this meant that hundreds of families found themselves living in temporary lodgings, often in poor conditions, or having to stay with relatives. A lot of adjusting had to be done. Many marriages didn't survive and the result of all this was that the divorce rate rocketed and, just at the time when it would seem that the country's families were being reunited, they appeared to be falling apart.

But, fortunately for us, we all came back in one piece except cousin Alfred, who had been killed in action in Sicily in 1943. His twin brother, Maurice, became a bomber pilot and was awarded the DFM in 1944. This is the Distinguished Flying Medal. If he'd been an officer he would have got the DSM which is the Distinguished Service Medal. I called in to see Auntie Lily and Uncle Frank as soon as I could and I thought they would never get over the loss of one of their sons. I left their house wondering why we'd done so much celebrating on VE Day. For some reason, Jack never got called up.

I'd another shock later that first week back. 'Cos Norma had moved back to Dundas Street, I thought it would be nice to catch up with people I used to know. I wasn't a drinker like my father but one night, I went to the Lord Napier with Laurence, I ran into John, the one whose bed bugs got me the night I stayed at his house. Like me, he'd grown up and was tall and good looking with a mop of fair hair which kept falling into his eyes. He'd a very pretty girl with him who turned out to be Winnie Fieldhouse. We'd all been in the same class at school and she hadn't been so pretty then. As we all sat talking over old times, John spotted someone else we all knew. It was Joe Pearson. He'd been a couple of years ahead of us in school and had enjoyed being the chief bully. He'd made my life a misery many a time. But now, standing at the bar waiting for his pint to arrive, we could see that as well as losing his right arm, his face had been badly disfigured, too. He made a point of standing close up to the wall without talking to anyone. I couldn't help but feel sorry for him, even though he'd treated me so badly all those years ago. At least I'd come home in one piece.

So, the first few weeks after coming home were very busy and on 7th June 1945, I celebrated my 21st birthday. I was still staying with Norma and Laurence and I wasn't expecting much at all but Sam had come home and had hired a room at the Quarry Gap Hotel. All the family turned up. The only one missing besides my father and Alfred, was Grannie Annie, who'd died a couple of months before I got home, aged 78. That was one funeral I would definitely have gone to. Anyway, food was still being rationed and so we made do with potted meat sandwiches and boiled eggs followed by lovely fresh raspberries which Annie had grown in their back garden. I got some silly presents including a red, white and blue hat knitted for me by Auntie Shackleton. I still have it to this day somewhere in a drawer. I used to wear it when I did the window cleaning. It was very warm but looked a bit like a tea cosy. Thinking about it now, I think it was a tea cosy!

At my 21st party I talked to Helen, who was still living with Auntie Lucy. She was nearly twenty and had put on a bit of weight which suited her. When she'd come home from the sanatorium in Ilkley she'd looked like a bag of bones. Now she looked well and was working as a typist in the offices at Whitehead's. Auntie Lucy looked just the same. Anyway, after Grannie Annie had died, she and Helen had moved to a little house on Mortimer Row. I asked about Auntie Edna and Uncle George but, apparently, they'd moved away and no one knew where they'd gone. Helen told me that she'd saved some of my belongings which Vera was going to throw out when she married father and they invited me back to Mortimer Row to have a look. The little ramshackle bookcase was in the front room now, along with some of my books and, most importantly, The Boys Book of Astronomy. They'd put all my clothes into a better cardboard box too and we all roared with laughter as I pulled them out. I'd grown so much that nothing would have fitted me in a month of Sundays. Auntie Lucy said she would take them all round to the next church jumble sale.

This jumble sale turned out to be so popular that people were queueing round the block so they could be first in and get the best things. This was mainly 'cos during the war there'd been such shortages and lots of people had simply worn out their clothes. It was a chance to find something new, or at least new to them. It was all very well making do and mending everything in sight but having to wear jumpers made out of other old jumpers became very boring. So, even though a lot of the clothes were made out of old jumpers, people jumped at the chance, so to speak, at the thought of getting something new to wear. A lot of the clothes were from people like me, coming back from the war and finding they didn't fit any more.

I'd already checked with Norma that she had my Prudential savings book put safely away. Even though nothing had gone in it for a long time, at least there were the savings I'd put in before I went away, to fall back on. My back pay from the army wasn't going to last very long. The other thing I did during these first few weeks was to get myself a job at Whitehead's. It seemed that the whole family was working there but as Whitehead's was the major employer in the area, it was simpler to go there than travel to somewhere else. Sam had managed to get his old job back almost at once, so he put in a good word for me and before I knew it, I was a working man again. 'Cos a lot of the men who'd come back had gone back to the jobs they had before the war, like Sam had done, I became a doffer again. The work was hard and boring but at least I'd a job and was able to give Norma something for my keep, plus a couple of shillings every week towards my savings. Norma said that the man from the Pru still came every Friday to collect the weekly payment and I trusted Norma to do this for me.

I also made time, before I started at Whitehead's, to make a journey down to Sussex to find Evelyn. I didn't know the exact address but Stanley had told me she'd moved from Bexhill to Cranshurst which was a little village about five miles away. It was on the railway line from London, so when I got off at Cranshurst, I went to the Post Office in the village to see if I could find their address. Post offices are a good source of information, at least they were back then. It was a long way and it was quite late in the afternoon by the time I got there. I walked up the garden path to Orchard Cottage, Plum Lane not knowing what I was going to say to Evelyn. An older lady came to the door who turned out to be Evelyn's mother and, after I'd told her who I was, she took me round to the back garden where Evelyn was sat reading a book. She gave me a big hug and we walked up to a little café in the village for a cup of tea, to find it had already closed.

So, we sat on a bench in the graveyard of the little village church. It seemed an appropriate place. When Stanley had stopped replying to her letters, she'd written to his mother, so she already knew he'd been killed in action. We both shed a few tears and I wished I'd had something to give her other than memories. It was a very sad visit but I was glad Evelyn was beginning to see a future for herself without Stanley as she was talking about becoming a school teacher. She was a grand girl and they would have made a lovely couple. As it was too late for me to get home again that day, I stayed with them for that night and caught the first train back in the morning, promising to keep in touch with Evelyn. If I'd been a girl, I would've cried all the way home.

So, the weeks flew by. Laurence didn't go back to the Post Office but got a job on the railways as an assistant signalman at Tyersal junction. He seemed to enjoy what he did and Norma didn't lose her job, either. I was still at Norma's when Annie announced that she and Sam were expecting their first baby. There was great excitement at this news 'cos it would be the first baby to be born into our family in what was called The New Era. Little Sam-Annie, as they nicknamed the baby, was due to be born in March, 1946.

Another Christmas came and went, this time with bright lights and plenty of Christmas trees for the first time in six years. This cheered everyone up no end, although rationing was still in force and this meant that the sort of Christmas we now take for granted with mince pies, turkey and everything else wasn't possible for most families. Tea, sugar, butter, eggs, cheese and jam were all still in short supply so having coupons to buy things was one thing but it also depended on what the shopkeeper had in stock. Laurence managed to get a chicken from one of his railway pals who had a hen-run, so we feasted on that with five sprouts each, a couple of potatoes and spam fritters. Although I still had the allotment, I hadn't got round to doing much with it apart from going over occasionally to tidy up, just in case. We finished off with rice pudding which has always been a favourite of mine.

In March 1946 Annie gave birth to her first son, Colin. This is who my 'niece' married in 1970. I can't remember much else happening that year but 1947 marked a turning point in a lot of our lives. The year seemed to be full of births, marriages and deaths. At my 21st birthday party Jack had told me he was seeing a girl called Shirley and so Jack and Shirley were the first to be married in April, just after little Colin's first birthday and the arrival of Annie's second son, Roger. Sam and Annie didn't come to Otley Parish church but the rest of us had a nice meal in the Blue Pig which was a pub just round the corner from the church. I think they went to Blackpool for their honeymoon. Jack also told me that he was still thinking about joining the police. I hoped they'd let him in.

The next time we were all together was in September for the second wedding when Helen eventually married Phil. They'd first met when Helen was in Ilkley recovering from TB and Phil was working at the sanatorium as part of his training to be a doctor. Once again, it was a sad time for me, 'cos they were going to live in Ilkley which meant a longish journey if I wanted to see Helen again. I think Auntie Lucy was a bit sad, too, as Helen had been a good companion for her. They were married at Bradford Register Office and, as we all came out into the sunshine, I noticed a man standing in a doorway on the other side of the road. It was father watching us, just like he'd done before. I didn't say anything.

So, Jack and Helen started new lives. Annie was busy with her family and Alice was also looking forward to her first baby in the new year. However, things never stay the same and in October, not long after Helen and Phil had got married, Laurence was killed at work. He was still a signalman but had been helping to move coal wagons. As he passed between two wagons one moved back and he was crushed. He was taken to Bradford Royal Infirmary but died three days later. I helped Norma as much as I could and thought all was well between us but in November I was in for a shock.

It was actually 20th November and the day Princess Elizabeth married Lieutenant Philip Mountbatten but I hadn't taken much notice of all that. The weather had been awful for the last few days with fog and rain and that night was particularly cold and miserable with what seemed like snowflakes drifting down. When my shift ended, I walked back to Dundas Street, which only took ten minutes if I went across the waste land at the back of the mill. I was looking forward to getting some fish and chips on the way home. Norma wasn't a very good cook so I went in for fish and chips whenever they were available at the fish and chip shop. I was hoping it would be open but I was disappointed. A notice on the door said that the fish supplies hadn't arrived so they were closed until they did. I trudged back to Dundas Street wondering what to have for my tea. I was very hungry, as usual.

Anyway, when I got there, I was surprised to see my kit-bag standing on the door step. I tried the door handle to get in but it was locked. I got my key out but it wouldn't go into the keyhole, so I knocked on the door. I could hear someone inside and then the door opened but only a little way. The door chain was on. Norma was on the other side and so I asked her what was going on. She told me she'd decided to move to Bridlington. I wasn't invited to go with her and I should go away and find somewhere else. I was stunned at this news. It was a dark November night with snow beginning to fall and I was told I couldn't even stay there one more night.

Then, suddenly, I remembered my savings policy which Norma had been looking after. As well as money for my board, I'd given her extra money every week to pay into the policy. There was a pause, then, she calmly told me, through the gap in the doorway, that there was no savings book. She said she'd been short of money during the war so she'd cashed it in on my behalf and, since I'd been living with her, she'd taken the extra money I'd given her for the policy to use for my board as I was expensive to feed. After admitting she'd forged my signature, she wished me good luck, shut the door and locked it. I was left standing on the pavement penniless, homeless and hungry. Thankful that I was wearing my army great coat, I reached into my kitbag, found the red, white and blue hat from Auntie Shackleton and wondered for a moment about throwing a brick through Norma's bedroom window. She'd been using me all along. Somehow, though, I managed to control myself and walked away without looking back, just like I had at Charnwood Road.

Then, I thought of Auntie Lucy who was on her own now that Helen had gone. The snow had really started to come down by the time I got to Mortimer Row. It was a two up and two down cottage and the area was very run down and shabby. Nowadays it's a conservation area and everyone wants to go and live there. Anyway, a light was on downstairs, so I knocked on the door and, as soon as she saw me, she asked me in and listened to my tale of woe over a cup of tea. I think she was missing Helen 'cos she invited me to stay as long as I wanted. I was now re-united with my bookcase and The Boys Book of Astronomy.

That winter of 1947 into 1948 was not as bad as the previous year when it had seemed to snow for weeks and reports on the radio said there were drifts of more than 20 feet. The country more or less ground to a halt. Roads were impassable, the fishing fleet had been frozen in and eventually food shortages began to happen, which made things even worse as rationing was still going on. I'd managed to get extra coal for the fire at Norma's by going onto the railway line at the back of Whitehead's and picking up the coal which had fallen off the wagons as they wobbled over the points and I now did this for Auntie

Lucy and me.

I lived with Auntie Lucy for five very happy years. We didn't have much money between us but she enjoyed cooking and I enjoyed eating whatever she made. I still had the allotment and became good at growing beans and cabbages. We spent many an evening quietly reading and she helped me out when there were words I didn't know. It took me into another world, well away from the noise and dirt of the mill. I don't think she'd ever thrown a book away and, being a librarian, she knew a lot about books. When I say a librarian, I don't think she was qualified with a degree, which they all have these days, but she worked in Bradford Moor Library for years, alongside Auntie Mary. Auntie Lucy never married so had no children. Sometimes we got round to talking about my mother. She told me all about their childhood and their growing up years. This always made me feel sad 'cos mother hadn't been able to tell me all these things herself.

I stayed on at Whitehead's as a doffer and went over to the allotment most Sunday mornings. It was nice to be able to return with something fresh for us to eat. On Sunday afternoon, I often went fishing with Jack. We'd decided it was a good way to keep in touch. Jack had found a spot on the River Wharfe at Cranny Nook and I got some old fishing rods from the shop where I'd bought my bookcase. So, whenever the weather was decent, I'd get on the bus and make my way over to Pool Bank. It was a sort of unwritten agreement between us. We were what is known as fair-weather fishermen. Proper fishermen go out in all weathers, but not us and definitely not if it was raining. It was nice sitting there in the peace and quiet just chatting about this and that and talking over old times. It was on one of those afternoons that Jack told me he was giving up his job at the paper mill and joining the police force. He'd applied some time before and had been accepted. In the long run it turned out to be a good decision 'cos he ended up as a Chief Constable but that was in the far distant future.

Then, in May 1952, something else happened to turn my life upside down. Rationing had been over now for a long time, although it still applied to some foodstuffs, and 'cos it no longer applied to petrol, a sort of motoring boom had happened. I'm not saying that the roads became as busy as they are today with traffic jams every two minutes but there were definitely more cars and lorries on the roads than before the war. I always seem to remember what the weather was like when these things happen and that day had been very hot. It was a Monday and I decided to call in at The Lord Napier and have a pint of beer before going home to Mortimer Row. When I got to the other end of Napier Street and turned into Leeds Road, I saw a crowd of people gathered in the road. It looked as though someone had been knocked down. An ambulance was just arriving so, as there seemed to be plenty of people helping, I carried on and went to pub for my pint.

I stayed longer than I intended as I got talking to some lads from work who were in and I didn't get back to Mortimer Row until well after seven o'clock. There was a note pinned on the door telling me to go to the nearby police station as soon as possible. This, of course, was well before the days of mobile phones or even the days when most houses had telephones. So, I made my way to the police station as fast as I could. I'd to sit and wait whilst the sergeant dealt with a couple who'd lost their dog but, as soon as I explained why I was there, he lifted the counter top and came round to show me into a side office, saying he'd be back in a moment or two. He came back with another police officer who asked me a few questions, making sure that I was the Harry who lived with Miss Calvert. Then he carefully explained that Miss Calvert had been in a road accident that afternoon and had died before the ambulance had got there. They had found my details in a diary in her handbag. Auntie Lucy had been knocked down on almost the same spot that the motor cycle had hit me all those years before. The driver didn't bother stopping.

18:39:22 – 18:42:27

When he'd got his breath back, he started up again. But, after just a few steps, he'd to sit down on the low wall again. He wondered why he felt so tired. He couldn't stop himself from closing his eyes and nodding off, waking up just as he was about to fall forward onto the zimmer frame. Everything was hurting. His legs and feet were hurting and now he'd a pain in his chest. The thought that he would be home in a few minutes encouraged him to stand up and continue.

He still felt very cold. The pavements were beginning to shine with frost. He knew he'd have to be extra careful. If he fell it might be hours before anyone found him. His fish and chips would have gone cold by then, too.

The low wall seemed to go on for ever before he finally came to Heather Road, so he sat down yet again wishing he'd not bothered with the fish and chips. Rice pudding would have been just fine. Then he remembered that the rice pudding had gone.

Out and Often Down

I walked back to Mortimer Row with a very heavy heart. Once again, the future looked bleak for me. The policeman had given me a large paper bag containing her possessions. When I got back, I sat in my chair opposite her now empty one and looked in the bag. There was a pair of black gloves, a green and pink scarf, one shoe. I never found out where the other one had gone. And a dark blue handbag. I'd always been told never to go into anyone else's handbag or purse and even now, it was a difficult thing for me to do. It was quite a while before I could bring myself to look inside. I'd never looked inside a lady's handbag before and I was amazed at what was in there. Handkerchiefs, tissues, her reading glasses plus a spare pair I'd never seen before. Small nail scissors, bus tickets, a hand mirror, her comb, the keys to the house, three pens, a leaflet advertising a film at the Lyceum, hair clips and a light bulb. The bulb would have been for her reading lamp. It had popped last night. In a pocket inside the handbag was a diary and a brown leather purse.

I looked in the diary first. The police had found me 'cos there, at the front, she'd carefully filled in my details in case of an emergency. On the other pages she'd written all sorts of other bits of information including what we'd for tea and books we'd read together. I'd a good old sob when I read some of this. Then, I pulled myself together and looked in the purse. It contained fourteen shillings and ninepence. This is about seventy pence in today's money but, of course, things didn't cost what they do now. I was very tempted to take it as it would have paid the rent and, with some money I had, I thought I'd manage to stay there for another two weeks if the landlord would let me. But, I'd had to sign a form at the police station which listed all her possessions they were giving me and this included the fourteen shillings and ninepence. Reluctantly, I put it back in the handbag, along with everything else.

With Auntie Lucy gone paying the rent by myself was going to be a big problem and that was dependent on the landlord letting me keep the tenancy on. There was just over seven shillings in what we called the slush fund which we kept in an old tea caddy in the kitchen. This would help with the rent. Today was Monday and the rent man came round on a Friday. We'd never had to hide from him but I thought I might have to this time. If I was very careful for the rest of the week I could probably manage but after that I wouldn't have much left from my wages. I didn't feel hungry at all but as I didn't want to wake in the early hours wanting a sandwich, I went round to the fish and chip shop and got a special. Then I went to bed feeling very depressed.

I was just about to get up the next day and go to work when there was a loud knocking on the door. It was the same policeman I'd talked to before. He'd come to tell me that I could make arrangements for Auntie Lucy's funeral as all procedures had been done. It all seemed a bit quick to me. I hadn't even got round to thinking about her funeral and I'd to confess that I didn't have any money for one. In the end she was buried on the Friday in the pauper's section of Undercliffe cemetery. It wasn't very far away from mother's grave. No one had headstones in this part of the cemetery. The family had had a whip round and raised enough for a decent, if cheap, funeral. We all said goodbye to each other at the graveside. We didn't even go and have a sandwich afterwards. Then the rent man came, as usual, on the Friday evening. Aunt Lucy had always dealt with him and so I explained what had happened and asked if I could keep the tenancy. I'd no idea how I'd manage but just then it was better than nothing. He said he'd let me know when he came the following Friday.

It had been such a sad day so, after the rent man had gone, I went upstairs and sat on her bed. All her things were still here and the room was filled with her scent. I expected her to come through the door at any moment but of course, she wasn't going to do that. As I sat there, I wondered what I was going to do with all her things. Not that she'd a lot. So, I decided to investigate. I'd nothing else to do. There was a small chest of five drawers. These seemed to be all filled with underwear, gloves, scarves, knitted hats and lots of other little things which women have. She kept her spare bed linen in the bottom drawer. I did the same in my bedroom. She also had a nice mahogany wardrobe so I slowly opened the door and looked inside. As with the chest of drawers, it was all very neat and tidy. The top shelf seemed to be filled with jumpers and the rail held all her jackets, skirts and dresses. I'd never seen Auntie Lucy in trousers. Then I'd a sudden urge to see what was stored at the bottom of the wardrobe.

So, I knelt down and, moving the dresses to one side, found three brown paper parcels tied up with faded pink ribbon and various cardboard boxes, as well as her shoes and a black metal box. There were a lot of old paper-back books too. I took everything out and put it on her bed. I didn't find a key though, for the black box. I began by opening the brown paper parcels. Inside the first one there was a set of pink baby clothes. The other two contained the same, except in the third one there was also an envelope addressed to Auntie Lucy. Inside was a birth certificate. It was for a baby girl born on 12th February 1918. Someone had put two red lines across it and written 'dec'd 14th February 10.30 am'. She'd been called Amelia Caroline Calvert. I sat and stared at this for ages. I wondered if Auntie Lucy had been in love with the father and if he'd been killed in the First World War. She would only have been 18 years old back then. She'd never mentioned this and now I would never know. I felt such a sadness for her and I started crying again. There was no-one there to see me. I couldn't find a death certificate.

After the shock of the brown paper parcels, the cardboard boxes were quite boring, being filled up with lots of our old bills. I don't think she threw anything like that away. They were all in date order. I suppose it's all part of being a librarian keeping things in their proper place. So, then I picked up the metal box. There was something in it but no key. I thought I'd have another look inside the wardrobe and, there, right at the back of the shelf at the top, stuck down with tape, was a key. It opened the black box. Inside was another long brown envelope which turned out to be Auntie Lucy's will. It was very simple and left everything she owned to me. There was also another old brown envelope and in this, to my astonishment, was nearly seventy-five pounds. My tears for Auntie Lucy turned to tears of joy and I found myself laughing out loud at this turn of good luck. On the Friday, when the rent man came back to say I could have the tenancy, I was able to pay him without worrying. He kept the key money Auntie Lucy had paid him, though, and I'd to pay that again.

So, for the first time in my life I'd enough money to see me through and a roof over my head which was, in theory, mine. I didn't change anything in the house but when I'd managed to clear Auntie Lucy's things from her bedroom, I moved into it myself. It seemed strange sleeping in her bed at first but it was very comfortable and it was a sunny room on an evening. I was still working at Whitehead's and it was so nice to come home and have a rest for a while on the big bed in the sunshine. I missed our chats about the books we were reading. In fact, I missed her a lot. I kept the allotment, though, and went over nearly every Sunday morning like I'd always done. Mrs Shuttleworth was still running the Sunshine Café and I often called in there for a bacon butty. I don't think there are many cafes which open seven days a week now. I walked over to see Sam and Annie every now and then. They seemed so happy and their sons, Colin and Roger, who were now six and five, were two of the nicest lads you could wish for. Alice and Frank had moved to Redcar where Frank came from and, of course, Norma had already gone to Bridlington. Jack was now a fully-fledged policeman and he and Shirley were living in Cleckheaton, a suburb of Bradford. Helen and Phil had moved to Horsforth which is near Leeds. I found all this out when we all met up for Auntie Cragg's funeral. She was only fifty-seven and it was another very sad day for us all. Looking back, I'm glad everyone made the effort to get there although I still couldn't bring myself to talk to Norma.

Christmas came and went. I'd gone over to see Sam and Annie and had a very happy day, especially with the two lads laughing and joking all the time. It was in the new year that I started thinking about getting a lodger. Although I didn't really need the money, it would be a bit of company and a bit of extra cash could be put back into Auntie Lucy's envelope. I didn't like using what she'd left me. So, I mentioned it to a couple of lads at work and at the end of the week a young man from the warehouse came to see if he could have the room. His name was Michael but for some reason everyone called him Mickerick. He came round to Mortimer Row that evening and moved into the back bedroom on the Saturday. It seemed like a good arrangement. He turned out to be a pretty good cook and sometimes when I was on late shift and he was home first there would be a slap-up meal waiting for me. We carried on in this way right through 1953, joining in the coronation celebrations in the June when we hung Union Jacks out of our windows and went to the Lyceum for a Coronation Dance. It all took me back to VE Day which wasn't a very good memory for me. I still wondered from time to time what had happened to Elsie and if she'd married her soldier.

Then 1954 arrived. Me and Mickerick just carried on our arrangement until one Friday in September, when I went off to work leaving Mickerick in bed with a bad cold. I went down to the warehouse to tell them he wouldn't be in that day and I got the surprise of my life when Mr Brayshaw, the warehouse manager, said he knew he wasn't going in 'cos he'd handed his notice in the week before. I went numb. I ran back to my shed, found the overlooker, Mr West, and blurted out that I'd to go back home urgently. I ran like the wind across the waste ground, up the back alley and all the way to Mortimer Row. The door was wide open so I went straight in and raced up the stairs to Mickerick's bedroom. He wasn't there. Neither were his clothes, nor some of mine, including my best jacket although my army great coat was still there. I was thankful my boots were size 14 or they would probably have gone, too. Then I looked in the bottom of my wardrobe. I'd kept to Auntie Lucy's system and put spare money into the brown envelope inside the cash box. I'd taped the key to back of the wardrobe but the box had gone. It wouldn't have been difficult to smash it open. How trusting I'd been. I went downstairs to see if anything else had gone and found that even the slush fund in the tea caddy had been taken. He'd left a note on the kitchen table saying he was sorry and had enjoyed being there.

That was no comfort to me, though, as I was back to square one with no money again. I only had my wages for the week and they'd be less 'cos now I'd missed most of the morning shift. Then, I remembered that I'd lent Earnest at work £3.00 to help him put a deposit down on a car. It doesn't seem a lot now but it was to me back then. I'd wondered at the time how he knew I'd have enough to lend him and now I realised that Mickerick must have told him about my black box. That had been a couple of weeks ago, so I went in search of Ernest. At least I would have enough to pay the rent and buy some time to think about what I was going to do. I thought about going to the police but I'd no proof. I'd trusted Mickerick too much.

I found Earnest having his dinner in the canteen. I knew that the wages lady had been round 'cos Mr West had taken mine and kept it safe in his locked desk. When I asked for my money, Earnest just looked at me and handed me £1 out of his wage packet. He leaned back in his chair smiling and said that we were all square now. For the second time that day I'd been made a fool of. Again, I'd no proof that I'd lent Earnest anything, just as I'd no proof there was any money in the box Mickerick had stolen. As he leaned back, I thought of the time my father had told me there was no money even though I'd been sending it to him whilst I was in the army.

So, I went up to Earnest, still in his chair smiling at me, and picked him up by the lapels of his jacket, as I'd done with my father. He was quite a thin man, about my age, so I'd no difficulty throwing him across the floor. He knocked over tables and chairs on his way to the opposite wall and the canteen went to a stony silence except for Earnest's cries. The outcome of this was that half an hour later I was summoned to the mill manager's office and given what is known as my cards. In other words, I was sacked. If it had happened on a night shift it would have been Sam who sacked me. I walked back to Mortimer Row with just the £1.00 in my pocket and a week's pay. As it was well into the afternoon there was no point in going to the Employment Exchange or Job Centre as it is now called, so I'd a rest on my bed and then went and got some fish and chips for my supper. What a day it had been. I hardly slept that night.

First thing the following Monday, I went to the Employment Exchange which was down Leeds Road. I was there ages giving details of me and my work record. I was worried that the incident with Earnest would be a big black mark against me but Mr West had given me a letter just from him saying that I was a good, hardworking, honest person. As he gave it to me, he whispered that it should have been Earnest going. So, there I was being told that I was suitable for a job at the trolley bus sheds at Thornbury. I was to go there straightaway and the man gave me a slip of paper to take with me. The job turned out to be everything no one else wanted to do such as sweeping up, making tea and cleaning the trolley buses when they came back. But, it was better than nothing and even though the pay was less than at Whitehead's I was glad to take it. I got to wear blue overalls which meant that my clothes didn't get as dirty as they had at Whitehead's but, best of all, I got a free pass for the trolley buses. These trolley buses didn't run on rails but were electric, fastened to overhead wires. They went into Bradford all the way down Leeds Road and all the way to Saltaire as well, where they turned round and came back. Elsie had been a trolley bus driver.

It was good to still have a job and I didn't miss the grime and noise of the mill. In fact, I enjoyed working at the trolley bus sheds even though money was always a worry for me. Then, one day just before Easter, as I turned out of the trolley bus shed yard to walk home, three men suddenly appeared out of nowhere and pushed me down a back street. I didn't recognise any of them but they knew who I was and told me they were getting me back for assaulting Earnest. I tried to defend myself but it was useless. One against three is too much. When they were done, they walked away laughing. I don't know how long I was there but the next thing I knew was that someone was talking to me and trying to get me onto my feet. It was one of the trolley bus drivers who'd found me and he managed to help me walk back to the trolley bus shed where the manager took one look at me and called an ambulance. I was in hospital for two days. By some miracle nothing was broken but I'd bruises everywhere and moving was painful. Altogether, I was off work for over a week so didn't get paid. But, the other workers were really kind to me and had a whip round which provided just enough to cover the rent.

I stayed working at the trolley sheds for another four years. Although money was tight with very little left over at the end of each week, I didn't take in any more lodgers. Instead, I made ends meet by going and searching for coal near the railway lines like I'd done when Auntie Lucy was still alive. I ate a lot of doorsteps filled with lard. I also helped out sometimes at Mrs Shuttleworth's café on a Sunday morning. This wasn't far from the allotment and I always went home with a large bag of bread and buns and a few extra shillings in my pocket. Fish and chips were a rare treat. My free trolley bus pass was also very useful, though, 'cos sometimes on a Saturday I'd go to Saltaire and then walk up to Shipley Glen. It's quiet up there and I could sit on a rock and watch all the other day trippers. If I took a sandwich it was a free day out. One of the ladies at work had a sister who was an usherette at what was the Odeon cinema in Bradford and sometimes she'd give me a free ticket to see the latest film. It was a time when musicals were getting very popular and I remember going to see Oklahoma. I didn't have a television so I listened to the radio a lot. I liked Billy Cotton's Band Show, Family Favourites and on Sunday nights there was the Max Jaffa show. All these were music shows. Rock and Roll was just starting up and there was a programme from Luxembourg which played pop music. It was a time of Teddy Boys who wore long jackets with velvet collars and tight trousers and shoes with thick rubber soles just like I worn in the army. To save fuel and keep warm I often went to bed early with a hot water bottle and a book.

By this time, I'd lost all contact with Jack and the incident at Whitehead's had made things difficult between Sam and me so I didn't go over to see them at all. That first Christmas, when I was on my own, I just went to the Lord Napier, had half pint of beer and then went back home and made myself cheese on toast. It was a couple of years after that, maybe in 1956, when I bumped into Annie in the centre of Bradford. I'd gone for some new boots. I'd been saving up for ages. We travelled back to Laisterdyke together and she said how sad she'd been to hear what had happened to me. She asked me to go over to their house the following day, Sunday, so I left Mrs Shuttleworth's early and went to Tyersal. I didn't know what I was going to say to Sam but I'd no need to worry 'cos he made me very welcome and told me that Earnest had also been given the sack because he'd been caught going in people's pockets and stealing cash from jackets and coats that were on hooks on the wall in the warehouse. My encounter with him in the canteen was still talked about and I'd become a sort of hero. It still didn't make me want to go back there, though.

After that I kept in touch with Sam and Annie and they were good enough to give me a meal whenever I went over to see them. Their lads, Colin and Roger, were growing up fast and I wanted to give them something nice for Christmas 1958. I told John at work about this and he invited me to go for a drink with him one evening. He said he knew someone who could get hold of good quality jumpers for young lads and if I went to the pub and met his mate, I could tell him exactly what I wanted for Colin and Roger. So, I went to the Coach and Horses to meet John and his friend. Then another two blokes turned up. Nobody said anything about lad's jumpers. I sat with my half pint and was wondering about going back home when someone suggested that we all went to John's house for a game of cards. I didn't want to look stupid, so I went along with them. It turned out they were going to play poker. I'd played a bit in the army when there wasn't anything else to do but I wasn't very good. Anyway, I went and was soon sat down at John's kitchen table. The stakes were only pennies which didn't seem too bad and I won the first three hands. Then the stakes started going up and before I knew it, I was nearly £10 in debt, so I sat the rest of the game out. John had lent me my stake money and when they were finished, he asked me when I'd be paying him back. There was a silence when I told him I didn't have that sort of money until one of the others, Arthur, spoke up and said that maybe I could repay the debt by helping them out the following Sunday night. They were planning to rob a local newsagent and needed a lookout in case the police came by. If I agreed to do that then the debt would be cancelled. It seemed that I'd no choice in the matter.

I didn't want to be part of this at all, as I knew the newsagent, Mr Shah. He sold all sorts of things besides newspapers and in the past, when I'd been short of money, he'd let me have milk or bread and said I could settle up later. I knew he worked long hours, as well, opening up early and closing very late. He lived with his wife and three children in a flat above the shop. His only time off was on a Sunday afternoon when he went out with his wife and children and then he went up to the attic and did his accounts. So, I felt very guilty at having to agree to help someone rob him.

I didn't sleep very well that week but the following Sunday night found me in the Coach and Horses with John and Arthur and another man I didn't know called Mike. It was just the three of them. We all left about 10.00 pm. It was a cold, wet night in November. Mr Shah's shop wasn't very far away and I was told to stand in the doorway as if I was waiting for someone. If a police car came into view I was to bang on the door as loudly as I could. They all disappeared down the alley at the side of the shop and then I heard the sound of breaking glass. I just hated being there, knowing that Mr Shah and his wife and children were upstairs in the flat. Suddenly, a police car came round the corner. I just panicked and forgot all about banging on the door to warn them. I just turned and ran as fast as I could back to Mortimer Row. I locked the door behind me and hid under the kitchen table. Eventually I came out and went to bed but it was another sleepless night for fear of them coming to get me. I went to work the next day and the talk was all about how John had been caught robbing Mr Shah.

Seemingly, they hadn't been able to find any money in the shop 'cos Mr Shah had it all with him in the attic whilst he did his accounts. He took it to the bank every Monday morning. As there was nothing in the shop, they went up to the flat in search of the money. All would have been in darkness except for a light under the door to the attic. Mrs Shah was, apparently, woken up by strange noises and when she heard Mr Shah shouting, she crept out into the living room and dialled 999. The police car hadn't gone very far so turned round and all three of them were caught red-handed. John, Arthur and Mike had been arrested and were likely to go to prison. As it was all my fault they'd been caught, I was worried sick they'd come back one day, or send some of their friends, like Earnest had. So, I decided that I'd have to leave Laisterdyke. With a very heavy heart I handed in my notice. I did this 'cos it was the only way I'd get references. I spent that week living on my nerves, forever on edge that someone was out there waiting for me. So, I left the trolley bus sheds and Mortimer Row at the end of November 1958. I'd kept putting a few coins into the old tea caddy, like Auntie Lucy and me had done all those years before and now I was glad I had. I poured it all into my kitbag and packed as much stuff as I could into it, including The Boys Book of Astronomy. I put on my army greatcoat, which was still serviceable after all this time and headed for my allotment hut. It was the only place I could think of where I wouldn't be found.

As well as my kitbag I'd managed to carry a couple of blankets from Mortimer Row. I'd also got a deck-chair in my hut which someone on the allotment had given me. Sometimes I would sit in it and survey what I called my little piece of England. It had orange and black striped material and was one of those old wooden ones that you always start putting up the wrong way. So, I sat in my deck-chair and wrapped myself up in the blankets but I was still very cold. Next day I got some newspapers from a dustbin as a sort of insulation. I'd taken some bread and cheese and some apples as well as a couple of bottles of beer and a packet of digestive biscuits. I had these over the next two days as I didn't dare open the hut door. Well, I'd to open it a couple of times to answer the call of nature. I went at night in a corner under some bushes, after digging a hole for the doings! The newspapers came in handy. On the third day I ventured out and went to Mrs Shuttleworth's café for a cup of tea. It was lovely after the stale beer. I'd kept on helping her out occasionally on a Sunday and even though she was such a friendly person, I couldn't bring myself to tell her the predicament I was in, but I think she guessed 'cos during our chatting she commented that Pollard's was doing well and they were advertising for workers.

So, I went straight there after finishing my cup of tea. There was a list of vacancies on the board outside the office and it said to ask for Mr Mitchell, who'd been the works manager when I'd worked there before. I went into the office and the following Monday I found myself back in shed number 6 as a doffer once more. Billy had been replaced with a lad who, for some reason I never found out, was called Stewpot. He ignored me so I ignored him and just got on with my work. I helped Mrs Shuttleworth out as much as I could for the rest of that week, so didn't go hungry and the money from the tea caddy slush fund saw me through my first week at Pollard's until I got paid on the Friday. With my first wage I went to the second-hand shop, which by some miracle was still there, and bought myself a little truckle bed, a primus stove, a small pan and a tin opener. I already had some paraffin in the hut. I didn't go over to Tyersal that Christmas and after going for a long walk through the woods I'd baked beans and sprouts for my Christmas Day dinner followed by four iced buns from Mrs Shuttleworth. The primus stove heated the hut up a bit, too. I was cold and lonely but at least I felt safe.

But by the end of January, with a lot of winter still to come, I thought I should try and find somewhere better to live. I'd done some improvements to make the hut as comfy as possible but the nights were long. I'd got an old transistor radio but didn't dare use it in case someone heard it. The rain often kept me awake spattering away on the roof. I'd put a thick layer of newspapers down on the floor and got some old rugs from the second-hand shop but it was still damp and cold. I was also getting fed up of cold baked beans. Eventually I found myself a room on Mount Avenue. This would be about the middle of February. It was just a back bedroom on the first floor of a terraced house and five of us shared the bathroom. My landlord was called Frank Nattrass and he looked after his tenants very well. The house was kept clean and there was a two-bar electric fire so I could heat my room up, although I'd to be careful as it was on a meter and didn't seem to last very long before I'd to put another coin in. We all shared the kitchen which was very useful and I warmed up tins of baked beans and rice pudding. I also went to the Sunshine Café, for bacon butties for my tea and still helped out on a Sunday. Fish and chips filled the gaps. Mount Avenue was just round the corner from where we'd all lived on Mount Street so, in a way, I'd come full circle.

I was still very careful about going out in case I was recognised and my little world shrank even more. I'd a sort of circuit, going from my room to Pollard's to the allotment and then the Sunshine Cafe and back to my room. There was a corner shop just near Pollard's so I bought what food I needed there. I didn't grow much on the allotment but kept it neat and tidy so no-one said anything. I was very grateful to all the other allotment holders 'cos they'd all chipped in to pay my rent over the years. I tried to repay their kindness by digging their plots for them whenever they needed a bit of help. As the weeks went by, I began to be a bit more confident but still didn't go anywhere near Laisterdyke in case I met someone who knew what I'd done. So, I lost contact with Sam and Annie and Alice, too. I sent a postcard saying I was ok but didn't say where I was. I asked them to tell Alice I was ok, too. It had been a long time since I'd met up with Jack or Helen. I wasn't too bothered about what Norma was doing or father, for that matter.

When 1960 arrived, I was still in my room on Mount Avenue and still working at Pollard's. I hadn't been anywhere near Leeds Road or Laisterdyke for a long time, enjoying long walks over the fields and through the woods at weekends. I liked going through the woods and sometimes I bought some fish and chips to eat just sitting on a log and watching the birds. There was an old hut down there, too which I'd used as a shelter a couple of times when it had rained. Once, late in the afternoon, when I'd been going back to my room with my fish and chips, I thought I'd sit down and eat them there and then before it got really dark. So, I sat down on what I thought was a large rock under the shelter of a tree. As I sat down the rock moved. I was scared out of my wits. I dropped the fish and chips and ran. As I looked back, I saw that I'd sat down on the back of a tramp who wasn't too pleased at getting squashed.

Anyway, one Saturday morning, it was about Easter time and I'd been to the cobblers to have my boots repaired. I was just walking back to Mount Avenue, when I saw this little old lady coming towards me with two very heavy shopping bags. One of the bags suddenly fell on the floor and what was in there rolled all over the pavement. I went to help her and got such a shock when I realised it was Vera. I put the things back in the bag and asked her if she would like me to carry them back to her house for her. I don't think she knew what to say to me so just nodded. I hadn't been anywhere near Charnwood Road for 15 years.

We walked back very slowly without saying anything. I felt my stomach going into a knot as we got to the house. I followed her into the kitchen and she offered to make me a cup of tea. It was my turn now not to know what to say. I was wondering if father would make an appearance when she told me that father was upstairs in bed. He'd developed ulcers on his legs which meant that he found it difficult to walk. This must run in our family 'cos I've got the same complaint now. So, she invited me to go up and see him. I wasn't at all keen on this idea but I did it. I climbed the stairs slowly, trying to keep my feelings under control. I pushed open the bedroom door and was met by the sight of a fat old man propped up on some pillows.

His hair was completely white and his face looked like an old crumpled piece of brown paper. Without opening his eyes, he said a few choice swear words about how long Vera had been out. I was about to turn and go when Vera came in. She went over to the bed, shook him by the shoulders and told him to open his eyes and look at who was here. Some more choice swear words came out when he saw it was me. Now it was his turn not to know what to say. As he leaned back, tears started to roll down his cheeks. It was all too much for me and I went back downstairs as fast as I could. Vera came after me, tugging at my sleeve to stop me from opening the front door and leaving. I was still shocked at the way a once tall good looking healthy man had turned into the person I'd just seen upstairs. I agreed to have another cup of tea.

As soon as we sat down with the teapot between us on the table, she began to tell me what had happened since I'd last seen father. He'd kept on working for Bradford Corporation but got fed up of repairing roads so got a job as a dustbin man. Vera couldn't talk him out of this even though she pointed out that it was heavy work in all weathers and he was not getting any younger. This, of course, was before the days of wheelie bins when you put your rubbish into a metal bin and the dustbin man carried it down to the wagon for you. Eventually, father's health began to fail. First of all, he got such a bad cold he was in bed for two weeks. This left him with a permanent cough and picking up the heavy bins had affected his back which ached all the time. He began having days off on a regular basis and was eventually offered early retirement. So, just after his 62nd birthday, father gave up work and Vera became the breadwinner.

Having no hobbies or interests other than going to work or the pub, father had become more and more distant, just like he'd done with us. Vera had thought of leaving more than once. Eventually, though, the ulcers on his legs became worse and soon he was staying in bed all day. It'd now been more than two years since he'd been downstairs 'cos he couldn't walk more than the few yards to the bathroom anymore. As she was telling me all this, I realised just why Vera was looking so old and worn out.

I stayed talking with her for a long time and by the end of it I'd agreed to move into their spare bedroom and help Vera look after father. To this day I can't understand what possessed me to do this except it suited me from a finance point of view. I'd be able to keep most of my wages from Pollard's and do some saving up at last. What Vera needed was help lifting father to the bathroom and then in and out of the bath, that was when he agreed to have one. She was still working as a barmaid now at lunch times as well as evenings. I'd to admit that since my last visit the house definitely looked the worse for wear. The garden was overgrown and the windows looked as though they hadn't been cleaned for years. Vera was simply not able to cope with everything plus father. But between us, we could. So, at the end of the following week I moved from my little room on Mount Avenue into the little bedroom I'd slept in all those years ago for just the one night. Father now had the front bedroom to himself and Vera slept in what was known as the back bedroom. This time the bed had been aired but I did wonder if I was being taken for a fool again, as I put The Boys Book of Astronomy on the bedside table.

I kept on with my doffer's job, seeing to father before I went to work, coming home again at lunch time to help him to the bathroom and then again, each night. By this time, I'd opened an account with the Leeds Permanent Building Society and was able to put most of my wages in. I kept enough back for my bacon butties and bus fares, otherwise all my expenses were met by Vera and father. The threat of being found by John, Arthur or Mike had long since been forgotten. Most nights found me in the kitchen reading a book, Vera in the front room watching television and father upstairs in bed. He kept saying he wanted to go down stairs now that I was there and one evening we gave in, got him out of bed and to the top of the stairs. He went down by sliding on his backside, bumping like a bouncing ball all the way, landing in a heap at the bottom. After a struggle, as he was very heavy, we managed to walk him into the front room where he sat down in what had been his armchair. He watched television for a couple of hours and then demanded to be taken back upstairs. It took us nearly two hours and involved a lot of shoving and swearing. He never went down again.

The doctor called in every now and then, gave us a prescription for some pills and then left. The district nurse called in every other week to dress father's leg ulcers. I did them in between her visits. Father just stayed in bed all the time. One day, it would be the middle of March 1962, when I'd been with them for a couple of years, just as I was leaving father's room to go to work, he called me back and asked me to sit on the bed as he'd something to say to me. I thought he was going to tell me to go away again. Instead, he got hold of my hand and told me he was so sorry for what he'd done to me all those years ago. He said he wished he'd kept in touch with all his children and been a better father, especially after mother had died. He was crying as he said how much he'd loved my mother and that he'd never really got over her death. He asked me to forgive him for all the things he'd done. Then he asked me to bring him some fish and chips for his dinner which made me wonder if he'd really meant what he'd just said.

Anyway, I did what he wanted and went back to Charnwood Road at dinner time with two portions of fish and chips. After making a pot of tea, I took his fish and chips upstairs. As I went through the bedroom door, I saw that father was sat up in a very awkward way and would need moving. I put the tray on the end of the bed. But, as I got hold of him to push him back up, I realised he was no longer with us. He was quite cold. I didn't know what to do. I only had an hour and I'd to get back to work. So, I took the tray back down to the kitchen, ate both portions of fish and chips and left Vera to find father when she came home after her stint in the pub.

Vera made all the arrangements and I made the effort to tell the family. I didn't know where any of them were except for Sam and Annie so the following Saturday I went over to Tyersal to see them. I reckoned I was safe from the gang by now. It had been such a long time. We'd a lovely afternoon catching up with all our news, not that I'd very much. Annie cooked a smashing dinner. Colin and Roger were now even more grown up. They were proper young men. I thought about the Christmas and birthday presents I should have got for them but it was too late now. Annie said she'd write to the others and tell them about father but in the end, no-one had wanted to come. There was only Vera and me at father's funeral. He was buried in the cemetery at the end of Mount Street.

Once father had gone, Vera's attitude to me started to change. For a start, she now wanted me to pay the household bills 'cos her wages as a part time barmaid didn't stretch that far. We'd, of course, lost father's pension. I often came home to find dirty dishes in the sink which she hadn't bothered doing. This situation lasted until the new year of 1963. Christmas was the end of it all. I'd brought home a little tree I'd bought from the local greengrocer and decorated it with some lights. I also bought Vera a nice warm woollen scarf as a Christmas present. It all came to nothing, though. She never once mentioned the tree and didn't bother giving me anything. Apart from Vera's shift at the pub at lunch time, neither of us had anywhere to go on Christmas Day. She'd cooked a chicken on Christmas Eve so on Christmas Day I sat in the kitchen eating cold chicken and baked beans whilst she sat in the front room watching the Queen's speech on television. Sam and Annie hadn't asked me round either. I think it was possibly the most miserable Christmas I'd ever known and that's saying something. I'd been happier sat on my own in the cold allotment hut.

They say that a new year brings new beginnings and 1963 certainly did that for me. It wasn't far into January when Vera told me she was moving to Bridlington. I don't know why she'd chosen Bridlington as she certainly hadn't been friendly with Norma. It seemed a funny place to be going to. Anyway, as she'd already given in her notice to the landlord it was too late for me to take over the tenancy and now, I'd one week to sort out where I was going. It wouldn't be Bridlington. The prospect of the allotment hut rose up again.

I was glad that I'd got some savings with the Leeds Perm. It wasn't as much as it could have been 'cos Vera was extravagant with the coal and was always buying expensive food such as smoked salmon. I paid up each week, often just thankful that I'd a proper bed to sleep in each night. So, I went in search of somewhere to go, calling in at Mrs Shuttleworth's for a cup of tea first. I told her I was having to move and straight away she suggested I could have the rooms above the café. She'd been trying to clear them so she could possibly rent them out for a bit more income. We agreed on a rent and I moved into what I called my Sunshine Apartment. It wasn't too far from Charnwood Road so, as there was no furniture in the rooms at all except an old armchair, after sweeping them out, I paid the carrier at work to take my bed and some other furniture from Charnwood Road to my new apartment. I did this on a Saturday morning when I knew Vera would be out. As well as the kitchen table and two chairs, I took pots and pans, knives and forks, plates and cups, the kettle and enough bedding to make sure I would never be cold again at night. I even took the curtains from my little bedroom. I didn't bother to leave a note. I got the rugs from the allotment hut and bought a chest of drawers from the second-hand shop which was still going after all these years. That night, as I lay in bed, I felt happier than I'd done in a long time. I'd some savings. I'd a job. I'd a place of my own again.

It was Mortimer Row all over again.

18:42:27 – 18:49:33

He suddenly had such a longing to get back home, he stood up, grabbed the zimmer frame and moved off. The precious brown bag was still hanging there. He could see the front door to the flats. His left leg was really painful now and he could feel something trickling down his leg. It would be blood from one of the ulcers. He vaguely hoped it wasn't going to stain his sock. That would mean more washing.

Leaning heavily on the zimmer frame he reached island in the middle of the road and again, slowly and painfully, lifted himself up. Step by step he made his way across. He seemed to be standing on stones all the way, too, causing his foot to turn. At the far side of the flower bed, he lowered his feet and the zimmer frame onto the road and shuffled over to the pavement. He was so concerned to get home as fast as possible, he never even noticed he'd walked through the big puddle which had been there when he'd come home from the Day Centre. This time, though, he'd got his Doc Martens on so his feet remained dry. Somehow, he'd managed to avoid the dog dirt.

The last hurdle was to lift his feet up onto the pavement. His goal was in sight. He summoned up all the strength he'd left and then found himself at the front door. Almost home.

A Strange Kind of Life

I never saw Vera again. I walked over to Charnwood Road a few weeks later just in time to see a couple coming out and locking the door behind them. I knew then that the house had been re-let and she'd gone.

I enjoyed living in my Sunshine Apartment and life fell into a daily routine which suited me very well. I started at the mill at seven in the morning and finished at four in the afternoon, unless they were very busy and we were offered overtime. I say 'offered' 'cos it was often the case of 'you will work overtime' rather than your own choice. Anyway, finishing at four, as I said, suited me very well. Mrs Shuttleworth, or Mrs S as I called her, closed the café at four and usually went straight home. This left me to clear the place, wash the floor and tables and prepare for the next morning. I also cleaned the front window and door as Mrs S liked to make sure that people knew her café was clean and the best way to do this was to keep the outside looking spic and span. After I'd been doing this for a while, Mrs S said that there was no need to pay rent anymore as I did enough to cover it. I think she was also pleased to know that someone was living over the shop, as it was more security. I wasn't too sure about this, though, as I remembered what had happened to Mr Shah down Leeds Road but I didn't say anything about that. After I'd moved in, I put an extra big bolt on the stairs door up to my Sunshine apartment, just in case.

I also helped out on Saturdays and Sundays with washing up and anything else needed in the kitchen. I got very good at making sausage sandwiches and cutting a loaf into thin slices. Mrs S didn't like sliced bread. She said it tasted like cotton wool. I've never eaten cotton wool so I wouldn't know but it was her café so I did what she said. During that first summer at the Sunshine apartment, which would have been 1963, I spent my two weeks holiday from Pollard's painting the inside and outside of the café. I got the paint from George, the maintenance man at Pollard's. It had been left over after the canteen had been redone. It was a strange shade of green and we always hoped anyone who came in from Fishers wouldn't notice the colour of the walls.

There was even some over to do my Sunshine apartment with, which took on a spooky greenish feel when the sun went down or it was a dull, cloudy day. I didn't mind, though. It was still home to me, especially when I saw The Boys Book of Astronomy on the little table at the side of my bed. Mrs S was very generous and when she got a new television, she gave me her old one. It was black and white and had tubes in it. Modern televisions don't have tubes anymore but in them days they did. I don't know what they were but if your tube went the television had had it. Everyone dreaded the tube going!

I was 40 years old on 24th June 1964 but didn't tell anyone. These days everyone makes a fuss over this birthday but I just let mine slide by. I enjoyed living above the café and the only fly in the ointment was Mrs S's nephew, Ian Londin. He was the son of Mrs S's sister who had gone to Australia. I've always tried to get on with everyone but he was determined right from the start that I was put in my place as the unwanted lodger. One afternoon when I came back from work, as I went in the back door, I heard raised voices. It was Mrs S and her nephew arguing and it was all about me. He was saying she was stupid to let me live there for nothing and that she should charge me rent or get someone else in. She was losing money. In answer to this, Mrs S said she liked having me around and wasn't going to change anything as it was her café and she'd do what she wanted. If he didn't like it then he knew what to do. There was a moments silence, a few swear words and then the front door opened and banged shut. He'd gone and I didn't see him again until circumstances changed quite dramatically a few years later. During this time Mrs S's sister died and I knew he went to Australia for the funeral. I hoped he'd never come back.

In the summer of 1966 when we all had to have our two weeks holidays, I went to Blackpool for the day. The café didn't need painting so I'd some time on my hands. It was nice and sunny when I set off from Bradford Exchange Station. Bradford has two stations. One on one side of the city and the other right across on the other side. It can be a right nuisance sometimes, 'cos only the trains from Exchange cross the Pennines so if you want to go over there you have to walk across the city. Anyway, Exchange station isn't there anymore. It's been modernised and is now called The Interchange. I don't know why it's called that 'cos you still can't get a train from Shipley to Blackpool without that walk across the city. Anyway, by the time I got to Blackpool it was raining and it rained all day. I'd gone to Blackpool hoping to see Sam and Annie who had started going to the Doric Hotel for a week now that Colin and Roger were grown up. I thought I'd surprise them. It took me ages to find the hotel and when I got there, I found out they were going the following week. So, I didn't see them. I bought some fish and chips, sat in a shelter on the promenade and got the next train home.

I was still a doffer at Pollard's and one day I was offered a change of job. I could become a weaver if I wanted. I was told this was because there was a shortage of labour in the country and a lot of immigrants coming in from Asia were only able to do low paid work. However, this wasn't quite true. A lot of the Asians had worked in the textile industry in Pakistan so knew how to operate a weaving loom but were offered the low paid jobs which many folk here didn't want to do. But, after operating a weaving loom for a couple of weeks, I gave it up. I just couldn't manage to keep everything going and was relieved when I was put back to my doffing job. The money wasn't as good but at least I knew what I was doing.

At the back end of 1968, Pollard's was taken over by another company. There'd been rumours of this for weeks so when redundancy notices were handed out, I wasn't surprised one of them was for me. As I'd been at Pollard's now for over two years I was entitled to some redundancy pay so left a few weeks later with more in my pocket than I'd expected. I walked over to see Sam to ask if Whitehead's had any jobs but the coming of the Asians had provided more than enough for the workforce so there was nothing there for me either. I did find out, though that Norma had been over from Bridlington to see Sam and Annie and that Vera had died the year before.

Mrs S by this time was beginning to get old. She'd put on a lot of weight and her legs often swelled up like an elephant. So, when I came back from Sam's to say there wasn't anything, she offered me a job in the café. So, as well as cleaning tables, floors and windows, I now served on behind the counter and became even better at making breakfast butties. There was a good number of regular customers and Mrs S was even able to give me a small wage each week. I didn't need to think about meals as all the food I needed was in the café and I didn't pay rent, either. My savings were growing.

I should have known this happy state of affairs wouldn't last, though. One day in September 1969, it was a Friday and everything seemed as usual, Mrs S went into the back for some bread rolls and didn't come back. When I went to see where she was, I found her on the floor. There was no way I could lift her up and all the customers in at that time were women so I gave them all a piece of greaseproof paper to wrap their food in and told them they would have to go. As I ran out to the telephone box on the corner, I called out to them to shut the door as they went. There were no mobile phones in them days and Mrs S said we didn't need a telephone in the café as the one on the corner would do. Anyway, the ambulance came and Mrs S was taken to Bradford Royal Infirmary. I went to see her the following day which was a Saturday, only to bump into her nephew just as I got there, who calmly told me that Mrs S had died in the night.

I hadn't opened the café that morning but put a notice on the door that we would open at lunch time. I thought I'd be back by then. It never occurred to me that Mrs S would die. However, as we stood in the hospital corridor, her nephew told me that the café was now his and he was going straight there to lock up and make everything secure. He'd got a car so got there well before I did as I'd had to wait ages for a bus. He hadn't wasted a minute. All the chairs and tables were stacked ready to be moved out, together with the contents of the kitchen which he'd thrown into some cardboard boxes we kept under the counter. The till drawer was open and the money box where Mrs S had kept her takings was also open on the counter top. He told me I'd to be out by the following Saturday, leaving with smile on his face without offering me any payment for the week's work. Anyway, what he didn't know was that I'd already got my pay. After the ambulance had taken Mrs S away, I'd taken what I was owed out of the cash box.

During the next week I went to the Labour Exchange a few times but there was nothing there for me. I was thankful for my savings in the Leeds Perm, as at least I'd got some money to rent a room somewhere. I found one on Pullan Avenue which wasn't very far from the Sunshine apartment and moved my few possessions there on the following Saturday morning. Ian Londin turned up early to make sure I was out, locking the door after me and fixing a big padlock on too. I was very sad to be leaving as I'd been happy there.

My new room was another little back bedroom in a semi-detached house. The bed was one of those with metal springs under the mattress. It creaked every time I moved. The wallpaper was covered with faded pink roses and the ceiling had brown rings all over it where water had come in. The carpet was threadbare and there was no heating. Three of us shared the bathroom and she charged us extra for changing the sheets. But, again, it was better than being outside. My new landlady was called Mona Busby. She was a tall thin woman and within minutes of meeting she'd given me a piece of paper on which were written the three rules of the house. No smoking. No drink. No women. Suited me, although that night I went for a pint in the local pub, The Victoria. It had been a difficult day but at least I'd been spared the allotment hut. I'd kept it on all these years just in case I needed somewhere to stay.

Anyway, that night after I'd put my few things in my new room, as I said I went to the Victoria. I'd only just sat down when someone said hello to me. When I looked up it was Chillo. I hadn't seen him for year. We swapped our news and I found out he was living a couple of miles away and had a window cleaning round there. His father had died two years earlier. He told me all about window cleaning and made out that I could do it. All I needed was a ladder, a bucket and some rags. He made it all sound so easy and the next week I went with him to see how to do it. I'd cleaned the café windows for years so had some limited experience. I enjoyed helping him that day so went in search of some equipment. The second-hand shop was still going but now run by a man called Ronnie. I told him what I wanted. He'd a bucket but no ladders. However, he said he knew where he could get some and told me to go back in a couple of days. When I went back, standing in one corner of his back yard was a set of ladders. They were heavy wooden ladders, covered in various splashes of paint but not in too bad a state of repair. Ronnie had also found some chamois leathers and I left there on the brink of my new career as a window cleaner. As I couldn't take them back to my room, although ladders weren't on the forbidden list, I took them to my allotment instead, ready to start work the next day. I celebrated with a fish and chip supper.

It was only a short walk from Pullan Avenue to Mount Street so I thought I'd start my window cleaning business where I'd lived all those years before. I just knocked on doors and was surprised how many housewives wanted their windows doing. I went back to my room with coins jingling in my pocket. Again, Mona Busby only provided a room and I'd to find my own meals. Her kitchen was out of bounds, so I was pleased when the café opened up again and I began calling in for my breakfast. The new owner was young and enthusiastic. I didn't tell him I'd worked there.

I was at Mona's for about a year when I found a note under the door telling me the rent was going up. She was going to double it. Although the window cleaning paid quite well, I was still using my savings as I'd to eat out all the time. I didn't know what to do so went to the Victoria to think about it. On my way there I'd to pass Ronnie's and, there in the window, was a little notice advertising a room to let. I couldn't believe my luck, so went round there before someone else did. It turned out to be the front room of a terrace house down Moorside Road, just round the corner from Mona's place. My new landlord was John Peasholm. The rent was the same as I'd been paying at Mona's but this time breakfast was included, which was a saving. I went back to Mona's and packed all my things into my old kit-bag, including The Boys Book of Astronomy. When I told her I was going and wanted my key money back she just told me I couldn't have it 'cos I'd done too much damage to the room which had to be paid for. When I asked her to show me the damage, she changed her tune and said I was always coming in drunk and that I was lucky she'd let me stay so long. So, I'd to leave without my money even though what she said was a lie.

My room on Moorside Road was a lot larger than the little back bedroom but, as there was only a 2-bar electric fire on a meter, just like I'd had at Mr Nattress's, it was as cold as it had been at Mona's. I moved in at the beginning of November which was a damp and dreary month. Mr Peasholm also rented out the back room to a young couple who stayed out late and made a lot of noise when they came home. But, worst of all, I found out that I was sharing the room with a family of mice. I was sat reading in bed one night, which was the best way to keep warm, when one appeared at the end of my bed. We stared at each other for a few moments before it disappeared under the bed. I tried putting down mousetraps but could still hear the pitter patter of tiny feet in the night. Sometimes they had a go at eating my fish and chip paper in the bin and a few times, when I'd just be getting off to sleep, I'd felt them running over me.

I managed to stay there for a couple of months despite the cold and mice, staying in bed on Christmas Day and had just decided to move on when I had an accident. This would have been January 1971. By now I'd built up a good round but one frosty morning as I went up my ladder one of the rungs gave way and I fell off. It wasn't far but I twisted my left knee and scraped my shin. I hobbled off as best I could to take the ladders back at the allotment and went to my room for a rest. I found that I'd injured my knee badly and after a few days when it wasn't getting any better, I went to see the doctor. Doctor Green told me that it would take a few weeks to repair itself and going up and down ladders wasn't a good idea. The scrape on my shin wasn't healing properly, either, so he told me to rest and gave me some cream to put on it. I did as he said and slowly my knee got better but the scrape on my leg didn't heal properly and was often bleeding a bit.

It was a good six weeks before I could walk any distance and I'd been using my cash to pay for rent and food. Luckily for me I got a lot of cash from the window cleaning and kept it in plastic bags under my bed. Some of these bags had got holes in them from the mice which seemed to like chewing plastic. I don't think they'd have been after the money as they wouldn't have been able to spend it anywhere. Mr Peasholm had been very good to me during this time bringing me my meals, that I never had the heart to tell him about the mice, although I'm sure he knew they were there. As I got better, I was able to go to the Leeds Perm branch nearby and take some money out as the cash had more or less been used up. As I didn't have an income, though, my savings were going down and I was pleased when I was able to go back to my window cleaning round. But, when I got there I found someone else had taken over whilst I'd been waiting for my leg to get better. I got two jobs, though, but was turned away everywhere else. With no income and my savings going down, I decided I'd go back to the allotment hut and stay there. My little truckle bed was still there and I'd taken some bedding from the Sunshine apartment. The blankets were still there, as well. I was no worse off than at Mona's and I didn't have to pay rent to anyone. There were no mice there, either, and summer was coming.

I hadn't paid any key money to Mr Peasholm and, as he wasn't about when I went to collect my things, I just packed up my kit bag and walked away back to the allotment. It was late afternoon. My little truckle bed was still there and as I was so tired, I just laid down and went to sleep. The next thing I knew, the noisy cockerels at the far end of the allotments had woken me up. As I'd fallen asleep in my clothes I didn't need to get dressed so went round to the café for a mug of tea and a bacon butty. I'd the cash from the two jobs. The weather was good and my allotment was now the best on site as I was able to spend a lot more time seeing to it. I'd taken a couple of pans from the Sunshine Apartment, too, and, as I still had the primus stove, I was able to boil up some cabbage or eggs or potatoes. I was trying to make my savings last as long as possible. I didn't cook too often in the hut as there wasn't a lot of room what with the truckle bed, my gardening tools and bucket. I kept my clothes in a cardboard box like I used to do. I made a curtain from some cloth and hung it over the window on a garden cane. Rugs on the floor added a bit more insulation. The ladders were chained up outside.

I went into Bradford once a week to the Windsor Baths up Morley Street, near Chester Street bus station which was handy 'cos I'd to get the bus into Bradford. The bus station isn't there anymore. It's gone to the Interchange I told you about earlier. Anyway, at that time you could rent a bathroom for an hour and get a good wash. It didn't cost very much. I always came out feeling a lot better than when I went in. Now and again, I took my dirty socks and underwear and sometimes a shirt, with me, as well. I just put me and the washing in the hot bath water and we all got nice and clean. I dried them as best as I could when I got back, sometimes outside, sometimes just hung across a line in the hut.

Then, one day, as my leg was nearly back to normal, I decided to go for a long walk. It was a lovely summer's day as I set off towards Baildon Moor through Buck Wood, only having to rest outside the little wooden hut I'd seen before. I eventually came out near the Leeds and Liverpool canal and followed a signpost to Baildon village. I was hoping to find a pint of beer and I wasn't disappointed. There were three pubs to choose from and I went in The Bull, which was up Westgate. I only had enough money for one pint. The beer tasted lovely and I got talking to the landlord. He asked what I did for a job and when I told him about the accident and the loss of the window cleaning round, he said that Baildon could do with a window cleaner as all the shops were fed up of having to clean their own windows. He even offered to let me keep my ladders and bucket in his stables at the back of the pub. I was glad to hear there weren't any horses there anymore.

It was another long walk back to my allotment hut and the next day I did it all again, this time back to Baildon with the ladders on my back. I called in at The Bull to tell the landlord I'd arrived and he gave me my first job which was the windows of the pub. On seeing me up the ladders two more shop keepers came out and asked me if I could do their windows as well. At the end of the afternoon, I'd cleaned most of the windows down Westgate. Everyone had paid me cash so I walked back to my hut feeling like a wealthy man. I didn't have to carry the ladders, either, as I'd left them in the stables. I'd also celebrated with a pint in The Bull and then fish and chips sat on the seat at the end of Jenny Lane.

What with my weekly visits to the slipper baths, seeing to my allotment and the window cleaning, the summer of 1971 flew by. I'd managed to save some money and now had an account with the Bradford and Bingley Building Society which had a branch in Baildon. My way of living in the allotment hut lasted another year until the following September when, one Saturday morning, Donald who was the chairman of the Allotment Society, came over and showed me a letter from Bradford Council. The road was being widened and the allotments were to be closed. Everyone had been given a month's notice and the opportunity to move to a new site, where they would have to start from scratch. This was a right shock for me as I was really comfy and well set up by now in my little hut. I'd even insulated it with some bubble wrap I'd found in the street. But, there was nothing I could do, so I'd to make other arrangements.

I began thinking I was going to have to rent another room when, walking back one evening, I passed the little hut in the woods and realised I could move there. It was dry and the door closed properly. I didn't know who owned it but no-one ever seemed to be there. Another advantage was that it was a lot nearer to Baildon than my allotment. I'd started getting a bus so I didn't have to walk as far and moving to Buck Wood would save me the bus fare. So, in the back end of August, I moved to the little hut in Buck Wood. I left my gardening tools behind, except the spade which I thought would be useful for digging holes for the doings. I made the place as cosy as I could with my little truckle bed, blankets and rugs and bubble wrap. I still had my army greatcoat although it was beginning to look worn and old. Considering it was about 25 years old it wasn't bad though. It must have been well made. It was also useful as an extra layer on cold nights. That always reminded me of the night I spent under coats at John's when I'd been a youngster. I also still had my kit-bag and, best of all, The Boys Book of Astronomy. I'd looked at it so often the pages were ragged but I'd managed to memorise a lot of it. If I'd nothing to do at night I used to sit and see if I could say a whole page to myself without looking before the candle ran out.

I liked Baildon and I think Baildon liked me. There was an Italian restaurant there called Da Michelle's and they were always giving me an evening meal as well as paying me. I was forever taking an Italian cake back with me. There was a gent's outfitters there, as well, called George Moore's. One day George gave me a green Harris tweed jacket saying it was old stock and would keep me warm. I got a yellow woollen scarf and a bright green pom-pom hat from there, too. George was very generous. I still had the red, white and blue tea cosy hat from Auntie Shackleton but it had gone into holes and I only kept it for sentimental reasons. I didn't have anything else from my past except my army great coat and The Boys Book of Astronomy.

There was an outhouse in the back yard of his shop and sometimes I slept in there when it was too snowy or too wet to go back to the woods. George used it as a store for cardboard boxes so I'd make a little house out of them. It wasn't too bad. After a meal from Da Michelle's and a couple of pints at The Bull I always seemed to sleep well. The stables at The Bull would have been a better place to stay but the door didn't shut properly and I didn't fancy it much. But other people liked going in there 'cos one night after I'd put my ladders in the stable and had my pint in the pub, I went back to get my coat only to find it had gone. As I looked around in the gloom a noise came from the far corner and to my surprise there was a couple using my coat as a bed, busy enjoying themselves. It seemed a shame to stop what they were doing so I went back into the pub, had another pint and when I went back to get my coat it was on the hook and they'd gone.

Again, life slipped into a routine with me spending my days cleaning windows and my nights in the woods or in George Moore's outhouse. I think he knew I slept in there because a couple of blankets and an old pillow suddenly appeared in a plastic bag stuffed into one of the cardboard boxes. Neither of us said anything about this but it certainly meant I was nice and snug in my cardboard house. Then, one afternoon, as I was taking my ladders back to the stables, a man stopped me and asked if I could clean the windows of his house. His name was Mr Rogers and he lived in a big old house up by the edge of the moors called Cherry Tree Cottage. I didn't normally do house windows but I agreed to go once and see how I got on. Somehow, he managed to persuade me to go again and before I knew it, I was doing other jobs around the garden such as digging the vegetable patch or mowing the grass. All this took me away from my window cleaning so I wasn't earning any money when I was there. Plus, Mr and Mrs Rogers didn't pay me in money, only in meals. I suppose that was fair enough as Mrs Rogers was a very good cook but there were times when I wanted fish and chips, not a meat pie.

Anyway, things carried on like this until the autumn of 1975 when, one day, I went back to my hut in the woods to find it gone. There was only a brown patch of earth where it had been and a few pieces of wood scattered about. I found my little truckle bed and blankets thrown under a bush. The little bed was broken and the blankets wet through. But most of all I wanted my kit-bag and The Boys Book of Astronomy. I looked around again and eventually found the bag at the bottom of a slope not far from the stream. It was a bit wet and muddy but inside was my precious book and a few pieces of clothing. The bags of small change from the window cleaning were all gone. Auntie Shackleton's red white and blue tea cosy hat was hanging from the branch of a tree. I knocked it down with another branch and stuffed it in my kit-bag. Once again, I was homeless but this time there wasn't the allotment hut to go to.

18:49:33 – 18.59.30

The door clicked shut. He was glad it had clicked because a few weeks ago, when it was windy, the door had banged all night because the catch had broken and kept him awake. He blamed the newspaper boys who always rushed in and out as though the place was on fire. They just pushed the door instead of turning the handle. Anyway, it was alright now.

He looked up the stairs, undid the leather belt, and put the shopping bag on his arm, leaving the zimmer frame just inside the door. Then he grabbed hold of the hand rail with his right hand and put his right foot on the first step. As he did this, the hand rail moved with him and he suddenly found that the rail was no longer attached to the wall. The bracket had come out. Something else to report.

But, just then, there was nothing he could do but carry on up the stairs. So, worried that more brackets would do the same, he put his hands on the walls at each side and steadied himself on each step, ascending like a huge penguin swaying from side to side with each upward movement. He was glad he'd long arms and could reach the walls.

It wasn't easy, especially with the bag on his arm. He took each step very slowly and carefully. Suddenly, the pain in his chest was there again, this time stronger than before and he lost his balance for a moment or two. His leg hit the front of the next step. The already damaged ulcer received another blow which took his breath away. The shopping bag was making his arm ache.

So, slowly, slowly he went up, reminding himself of the lovely supper he was going to have. With a mighty effort, at last he pulled himself onto the landing. He thought it would be easier to climb Everest.

He waited a couple of minutes to steady himself, before fumbling about in his pocket for the key. Then he unlocked the door and went into his little flat.

All he'd to do now was have his fish and chips and go to bed. Then he'd feel better.

The End of The Road

I walked all the way back to Baildon and spent the night in George Moore's outhouse. The early morning was chilly now and I was thankful I'd been wearing my army great coat that day, as I kept my savings book in the secret inside pocket. I was always amazed that the coat had lasted so long but I'd looked after it very carefully, keeping it clean and repairing bits that had started to wear out. It was the same with my kitbag. It must have been made of strong stuff. So, the next day I went up to Cherry Tree Cottage to dig the vegetable patch and realised that there was somewhere better than the outhouse. Mr Rogers had an outside toilet and next to it was the store for all the garden tools. Above these was a large hay loft about ten feet long and three feet high. It wasn't used any more but still had some hay in it from the days when Mr Rogers's daughters kept horses. I knew all about the hayloft 'cos one day when I was getting a spade out, I'd gone up the ladder to see what was there. So, I'd some fish and chips and then a pint in The Bull and when it got dark, I walked up the moor road to Cherry Tree Cottage and up into what I called The Hayloft apartment.

I found the hayloft was just big enough for me and my kitbag and after I'd got two more blankets from the charity shop in the village, I was cosy even on the coldest nights. I'd to be careful, though, as I didn't want Mr Rogers or his wife to know I was there so I always left before they got up on a morning and went back after they had gone to bed at night. I slept in my Hayloft Apartment for the rest of that winter. I was glad we didn't have much snow as my footprints would have given me away. I used The Bull for my doings whenever I could, otherwise I just found a quiet place on the moors. I still went to the Windsor Baths every week.

By now I knew a lot of people in Baildon although none of them knew where I lived. Word must have got around that I was good at digging 'cos I was always being asked to go and dig someone's garden. One of the houses I went to was a big house with a big garden down Field Lane. This was for Mr and Mrs Leeming. I didn't do very much for them but one year they generously invited me to share their

Christmas Day dinner with them. They put on a lovely meal but I didn't like to tell them that another family, the Fosters, had also asked me to join them for dinner that day. As I didn't want to hurt anybody's feelings, I went to both and walked back up the hill to the Hayloft apartment, feeling full to bursting. I went to both dinners for quite a few years during which time I moved to better accommodation on Bertha Street which was just round the corner from Field Lane.

I was still window cleaning whilst I was staying in the Hayloft apartment and keeping my things in the stable at The Bull. My savings began to grow again very slowly. Then, in July 1976, when I thought Mr and Mrs Rogers were coming back from holiday at lunch-time I had a lie in but they caught me outside their house with a lot of straw bits clinging to my jacket. I tried to make excuses but Mr Rogers went up the ladder, saw all my things and soon put two and two together. But, there's a silver lining in lots of things and Mr Rogers said that I should go and live in a little house he knew down Bertha Street, just off Otley Road in Charlestown. He also arranged for me to go to Shipley Town Hall and see about allowances which I'd never claimed. So, before I knew it, I was living in Bertha Street, in a proper house with an inside toilet. My life had changed dramatically again.

Well, I say a proper house as it did have walls and a roof. It was at the end of a short row of what would probably have been weaver's cottages a long time ago but the window frames were rotten and inside it was cold and damp. In fact, my hut in the woods and the hayloft had been drier. But Mr Rogers had taken a lot of trouble over me so I didn't like to say I didn't want to go there. He'd even gave me some furniture. I got a bed, settee and a table with two chairs. The sitting room and bedroom both had curtains. When I'd told Mrs Leeming about my new home, she'd given me enough crockery, pans and clean bedding to equip an army, as well as an old television set which I put on one of the chairs. The council paid all my bills except gas and electricity and, of course, food, but my window cleaning just about covered them. Up until then I'd relied on meat pies from John the butcher and sandwiches from the bakery across the street plus the plates of spaghetti Da Michelle's were always giving me. Otherwise, it was fish and chips. But, now I'd a gas cooker I was able to make myself a sausage or bacon buttie whenever I wanted, in my new frying pan.

It was nice having a bathroom inside with hot water and even nicer having an inside toilet. I'd managed that part of my life well enough over the last few years but I never really got used to going in the cold and rain, especially if I'd to go at night. There was a bath in the house, too, but I couldn't use it as I tried to keep the ulcers on my legs dry. I now had two on the leg I injured when I fell down the ladder. Sometimes they were really painful. The doctor up Newton Way kept giving me cream for them but they never got any better. I started having days off now to rest my legs.

There wasn't any central heating in the house, either, but there was a coal fire in the living room and I found that if I got the fire going and left the doors open everywhere got warmed up. I got my coal from Mr Whittaker who was the coal merchant in the village. He often gave it to me for nothing when I cleaned his windows. Sometimes, though, it was an effort to carry a sack of coal all the way from the village centre at the top of the hill to my little house at the bottom. I'd often got other stuff to carry too which I'd been given that day.

I'd been living in Bertha Street about three years and had called into The Bull for my tipple after a day's work, when a young man came up to me and asked if I was Harry Lawton. It turned out to be Colin, my sister Annie's boy. We'd a long chat and I got all the up-to-date news of the family. It had been a very long time since I had been in touch with any of them. Annie had died in 1972 from breast cancer but no-one had been able to tell me as they didn't know where I was. Sam was still in the same house in Tyersal. Roger, who was Colin's younger brother was now married to Lynn and they had two boys, Richard and Martin. Colin and his wife, Christina, had just had their first baby in April. It was another boy called David. He was only six months old. It was a nice meeting and Christina called in to see me a few days later. They'd no idea I'd been living so close to them. They'd got married in 1970 and had bought a house in Pasture Road which was only a few minutes away. I must have passed their house loads of times on my way down the hill to Bertha Street.

I carried on with my Christmas lunches at the Leemings and Fosters for a few more years and also called in at Christina and Colin's too, as her mother and father were usually there on Christmas Day. I liked having a family again and wished I'd kept in touch with my brothers and sisters. In 1981 Christina had another baby boy, Jonathan. As well as Christmas and other times when I called in to see them, I remember watching the children's faces on Bonfire Night when Colin set off the fireworks and we all sat round with Christina's mother and father, eating parkin and crackly toffee. I didn't see Sam again, though, 'cos he died in October 1985. Seemingly, he'd not been feeling well and asked his next-door neighbour to go to the chemist and get him some aspirin. When Winnie came back, she found him dead in bed.

The house on Bertha Street had never been looked after properly and things started to go wrong. I'd never bothered Mr Rogers with things like dripping taps but on Christmas Day 1986, I woke up to find that I'd no electricity. It was a very dark morning so I found some candles and a torch, made a bacon butty in candle-light, as the gas was still going, and went back to bed until it was time to go to the Leemings and Fosters for my Christmas lunches. I didn't call to see Christina and Colin as I was tired and kept wondering if the electricity had come back on. Anyway, it hadn't but the gas was still working so I made a cup of tea and banked the fire up as high as I could and, for some reason I couldn't work out, I found that the television was ok too. So, I sat there with the light of the fire and television until it was time to go to bed, using my torch to find my way. I lit a candle when I got upstairs to save the battery.

I knew Christina would be wondering where I'd got to and, sure enough, she came round the next day, which was Boxing Day, with little Jonathan to see why I hadn't called in. She couldn't believe I'd no electricity and asked me to go and have my meals with them until it was on again. But, I thought she'd enough to on with looking after Colin, the boys and her mum and dad. I was alright. I'd lived in worse conditions and there was always fish and chips. The electricity was put back on just before New Year.

It wasn't much longer after the black-out episode that another major problem rose its ugly head. Some of the floor boards upstairs on the landing had been rotten since I'd moved in, so I was careful not to tread on the ones I knew about. What I didn't realise was that they were going in the bathroom as well and, one Friday morning, as I was sat on the toilet, the floor suddenly gave way and the toilet descended into the hallway below. The toilet didn't go all the way down but caught in a joist and tilted over so I was nearly thrown off. Thankfully, I'd just finished my doings. I didn't know what to do as I was stuck there, when I heard the letter box go. The postman had arrived so I shouted out as loud as I could for help. I don't know how he got in and I didn't care but he came and pulled me out onto the landing.

I was quite shaken up. The postman made me a cup of tea and then went back on his round and I sat down for a while wondering what to do. I decided to go and see Mr Rogers to tell him what had happened. I didn't have a telephone at that time. When I got up there no-one was in so, as I didn't know where else to go, I went to the doctors. The receptionist knew me from my frequent visits and after I'd told her what had happened, she called one of the doctors who organised one of the backroom staff, as I called them, to take me down to Shipley Housing office in a car. The doctor wrote a quick letter for me to take and I was given emergency accommodation in Shipley. I stayed there for three days until a man came and told me they'd inspected Bertha Street and found it unfit for anyone to live in anymore. He'd found me an empty first floor flat in Baildon on Heather Road so I could go there straightaway. It was almost in the village and best of all only a stone's throw from the fish and chip shop. It was a sheltered flat with a warden to see that everyone was ok. I called it my Flower Apartment. All this had happened so fast that I didn't have any time to tell Christina and Colin where I'd gone. Somehow, I never got round to telling them so I lost touch with my family again. I found out later that they'd tried to find me but no-one seemed to know where I was. The house on Bertha Street was empty.

The Flower Apartment was an upstairs flat on the first floor. Sometimes I found it difficult to go up and down the stairs with my leg but it was nice and warm compared to Bertha Street. It had gas central heating, a little kitchen with a proper pantry, a bathroom and what they call a bed-sit living room. The only sad thing about leaving Bertha Street was that whilst I'd been in the emergency accommodation in Shipley, someone had broken into the house and used my Boys Own book of Astronomy to light a fire in the grate. Mr Rogers told me about this after he'd been back to the house to see what could be moved up to Heather Road. Whoever had broken in had also smashed up the furniture and there was nothing left worth having, except my kitbag which was just near the front door. Maybe my visitors were going to steal this but decided not to. It was very worn and scruffy. I'll never know but I was pleased to get it back and the red, white and blue hat which was inside it. Once again, I'd nothing else that I could call mine. I even lost my army great coat which had been on a hook at the back of the kitchen door. Anyway, the flat had a nice brown and yellow carpet but no furniture except a single bed. Mr Rogers gave me lots of bedding as well as some crockery and pots and pans, just like Mrs Leeming had done and helped me with all the paperwork needed when you move house. I got a blue formica table, a very large mahogany chest of drawers and a wardrobe from the second-hand shop in the village. George Moore gave me an old side table.

Then, in the summer of 1987 I think it was, I had a big surprise. A lovely lady called Carole had asked me to go and help her out at the Baildon Carnival. This was held in a field just along from Heather Road, so I could easily walk there. But, when I got there, I found out that I wasn't needed to help at all. Instead, I was going to be given a television set. Carole had organised a collection around the whole village and, as well as the television, there was enough money to pay for a licence and insurance. I was taken aback at this kindness and didn't know what to say. There was a picture of me in the Telegraph and Argus being presented with the television by Carole.

I liked being in my new flat and kept on with the window cleaning except for the days when I needed to rest my legs. There seemed to be more and more of these. But, the window cleaning got me out into fresh air and I got a bit of spending money. It also meant that I got to see people and could have a good chat, plus I was always being given food, so that was another saving. And I liked my pint in The Bull, too. I was glad I didn't have to carry a bag of coal down the hill to Bertha Street anymore. It was nice being able to light a match to put the gas fire on. As well as food, I found that people started giving me other things. I got two more wardrobes, an old 1950's blue kitchen cabinet and loads of clothes in black bin liners. It seemed to me that whenever someone died, I got a bag of the deceased's clothes. If I was out when they came, the bag was just left by my door. I always looked through them but there was often nothing I fancied. One bag even had women's clothes in it and I definitely didn't wear those. I suppose it was easier to give these to me than take them into Shipley to a charity shop. It was a good job I'd got the wardrobes to put all this stuff in.

I was 65 years old in 1989 and eligible for the state retirement pension. It wasn't much but I decided it was better than nothing and decided to stop cleaning windows. My legs weren't very good and the ulcers were often painful. On one of my regular visits to the doctors I told Doctor Grey that I was finding dressing the ulcers difficult and so he organised the District Nurse to come and do it for me. At the same time, he told Social Services about me and I got some more benefits which were very welcome. Even though walking wasn't always easy, I thought I was managing very well. I could go down to the Co-op for my groceries or the fish and chip shop, as they were both a short walk away in the village.

But, just after my birthday in 1990 I'd a major set-back. I'd been feeling tired all day and had spent the day on my bed resting. I remember getting up to turn the television on but the next thing I knew was that I woke up in a hospital bed. Luckily for me I'd started buying things from the Rington's man just after I moved in. He usually came on a Friday. He called in that morning and when he didn't get a reply, he looked round the door and saw me just sitting there on my little green armchair. I'd been there all night, unable to move. He dashed off to find the warden and that's how I came to be in hospital. I'd had a heart attack.

A few days later Christina came to see me in hospital after Mr Rogers had telephoned her to let them know what had happened to me. I don't know how Mr Rogers knew their telephone number. I hadn't been in touch with them since my move from Bertha Street. They didn't know where I'd gone. I was in hospital another three weeks but when I got back home my little flat had been transformed. Christina, Colin, David and Jonathan had decorated everywhere, put up new curtains and cleaned the carpet. I even had new sheets on the bed and that's when I got the duvet thing. The whole place shone like a new pin. After this episode Christina called in at least three times a week often on her way home from her teaching job in Keighley. She also did some shopping and cleaning but most of all I enjoyed chatting to her. David and Jonathan who were 13 and 11 by this time, also came up to see me. Roger and his wife Lynn called in occasionally, too.

My legs weren't very good now and it was enough for me to wake up alive on a morning never mind going out in all weathers climbing up ladders. Social Services got involved again and there seemed to be someone coming to see me every day. I got sent a big purple chair which was supposed to be easy to sit on and get out of. But it was very uncomfortable so I never used it. It was a good place for the newspapers. Then there was the District Nurse coming to see to my legs, the warden calling every morning and the Rington's man on a Friday, not to mention Christina on an evening. My flat was like Piccadilly circus.

Now, the outside door downstairs could be opened by anyone and I found that I started to get visits from what we used to call travelling salesmen. Sometimes it was just a leaflet about a new take-away pushed through the letter box but sometimes it was an actual person. On one occasion it was the Jehova's Witnesses. Unfortunately for me I asked them in. I've never been religious and after two hours they found out that I wasn't ever going to be. They never came again. Then, another of these callers was a young man trying to sell mobile phones. He'd knocked on the door and, again, I asked him in. He didn't stay very long, though, and I was glad when he'd gone 'cos the bag on my leg needed emptying. However, he came back a couple of weeks later and just came into my flat. I don't think he even knocked on the door. I was in the bathroom at the time and shouted out to him I wasn't interested. Then, later that day I couldn't find my wallet. I always kept it in the bowl on the blue formica table but it wasn't there. When Christina called in, she looked everywhere, too, but it had gone. We came to the conclusion that the mobile phone salesman had taken it. She wanted to call the police but I just couldn't do with the botheration. I hoped he enjoyed the £50 which had been in the wallet.

In 1991 both Christina's parents died. I benefitted from this as she was able to see me more often which I liked and the following year she arranged for me to go on holiday to Scarborough with other old folk. I think this was through Social Services as we all went in a mini bus. We stayed in a nice hotel near the beach. It was filled with old folk like me. I enjoyed the food but not the company. The only thing wrong with me were my legs which didn't work very well. I took loads of pills the doctor gave me and, otherwise, felt very healthy. I'd forgotten all about my heart attack. But all the others on the trip seemed to have major health problems and talked about nothing else. It made me feel ill. Most of them were asleep in their chairs as soon as we'd had our dinner. That left me by myself for most of the afternoon, so I sat by the window and watched folk walking up and down the promenade. I was glad when I was back home. I didn't say anything to Christina.

In 1995 she arranged another holiday for me. This time I was going to stay with my sister, Norma, in Bridlington. I didn't want to go at all but thought it would give Christina a break, so I went. Roger took me in his car and brought me home at the end of the week. It was nice enough I suppose but we didn't really hit it off. We no longer had anything in common. It brought back so many memories of life at home after my mother had died and, what's more, I'd never forgotten the time she shut the door in my face on that cold night. It was a week of eating out of tins and I was glad when I got home. Again, I didn't say anything to Christina.

So, life continued much as it had done. I got some budgies and the District Nurse still came to dress my ulcers which never seemed to get any better. Then in 1997, Christina thought it would be a good idea for me to go to a Day Centre a few miles away in Menston village. By this time, I wasn't really going out except for a trip now and then to the fish and chip shop. I was quite happy watching the television. Anyway, it was through Social Services and I agreed with Christina that if I didn't like it then I'd no need to ever go back. But, I did like it and ended up going every Tuesday and Friday which is where my story started.

18:59:30 – 19:00:00

He closed the door behind him but didn't lock it. It didn't matter. All he wanted to do was rest. He never used to lock the door but one day someone had come in whilst he was in the bathroom and taken his wallet.

But tonight, he didn't care. He suddenly began to feel very hot and a bit dizzy, too. The pain in his chest was really something now. He felt hotter than ever, now, and dropped the shopping bag on the floor. The heat in the flat was overwhelming him. The gas fire was still on at full. So, he bent down to turn it off.

But before he could do so, the pain in his chest nearly split him in two and all he could do was sink down onto the yellow rug. As he fell, he glimpsed the bag, containing the fish and chips, lying on the floor. Never mind, he thought, I'll have them tomorrow.

But tomorrow never came.

*Available worldwide from Amazon
and all good bookstores*

www.mtp.agency

www.facebook.com/mtp.agency

@mtp_agency

www.ingramcontent.com/pod-product-compliance
Lightning Source LLC
LaVergne TN
LVHW091544060526
838200LV00036B/696